A Word Geography

of the

Eastern United States

A Word Geography

of the

Eastern United States

by Hans Kurath

Ann Arbor

The University of Michigan Press

PREFACE

THE present investigation is concerned with the regional and local vocabulary of the Eastern States. This geographically restricted vocabulary is in daily use among millions of Americans in all walks of life and characterizes them as New Englanders, Pennsylvanians, West Virginians, Virginians, North Carolinians, or South Carolinians. Travelers and readers of regional novels have not been unaware of these differences in vocabulary, and amateurs and scholars have from time to time collected regional and local expressions. But until recently we have not known enough about any of these expressions to deal with them scientifically and to relate their dissemination to the history of the American people.

The collections of the *Linguistic Atlas* for the Eastern States, begun in 1931 under the auspices of the American Council of Learned Societies, now provide us with a systematic record of the currency of selected words and expressions in all the states on the Atlantic coast from Maine to Georgia, and in Pennsylvania, West Virginia, and eastern Ohio as well.

In the *Atlas* survey, nearly every county in the Eastern States is represented by two speakers, one old-fashioned and unschooled, the other a member of the middle class who has had the benefit of a grade-school or high-school education. In addition, most of the larger cities are represented by one or more cultured persons. This systematic record of the usage of more than 1,200 persons gives us full information on the geographic and the social dissemination of the words and phrases selected for this study.

All statements made in this book regarding the present dissemination of words in the Eastern States rest entirely on the materials in the collections of the *Atlas*. A rather full account of the spread of the various regional and local words for one and the same thing is given in Chapter III. In many cases a detailed record of usage in the Eastern States, or in a segment of this area, is offered on maps accompanying the description.

These maps also will help the reader to visualize the problems of drawing word boundaries (isoglosses) and enable him to gauge the validity of the isoglosses. The reader must constantly bear in mind that an isogloss is a simplified statement of the geographic dissemination of a word or expression, and, on the other hand, that dialect boundaries can be established only by means of isoglosses. There is no other scientific method of determining the boundaries of speech areas.

The precise localization of words and the determination of their dissemination in folk speech, common speech, and cultivated speech give us the necessary foundation for historical interpretations. The geographic and social distribution of words results from population movements, the development of trade areas and transportation systems, the growth of cultural centers and institutions, and the stratification of society. For this reason a realistic history of the vocabulary can be written only with reference to these phases of population history. This perspective is outlined in Chapter I.

Historical interpretations of the dissemination of individual words and of the development of the major speech areas and their subdivisions are offered in Chapter II. Boldness rather than caution has been the guiding spirit in these attempts. Many details will in time find a new interpretation, but the correlation of speech areas with settlement areas and trade areas is so striking that the major results of this pioneer investigation will probably stand the test of critical examination by future students of our language.

One fact of major importance seems to me to be fully established: *There is an extensive Midland speech area that lies between the traditionally recognized "Northern" and "Southern" areas.* This Midland area, which is linguistically distinct from the Northern and the Southern areas and is in part set off by sharp boundaries, corresponds to the Pennsylvania settlement area.

The common notion of a linguistic Mason and Dixon's Line separating "Northern" from "Southern" speech is simply due to an erroneous inference from an oversimplified version of the political history of the nineteenth century. The widely accepted assumption that there is a "General American" type of English proves to be equally unfounded in fact; no Southerner or New Englander would ever have made such a generalization.

The area treated in this book is a relatively small section of the United States. However, it includes all of the original thirteen states of the Union and, in addition, the areas settled after the Revolution prior to 1800, except Kentucky. Approximately fifty million, nearly two-fifths of the population of the United States, live in this area.

For the history of the American vocabulary—as well as for the history of American pronunciation—the Eastern States occupy a position of the greatest importance. It is here that the regional and local types of American English were developed during the Colonial Period. After the Revolution these types of English were carried westward and blended into new regional varieties when New Englanders and Pennsylvanians or Pennsylvanians and Virginians mingled with each other in the settlements beyond the Alleghenies and the Appalachians.

In the Middle West, the lower Mississippi Valley, and the farther West new words were coined, old words came to be used in new senses, and words were borrowed from the Indian languages, from the German and the Scandinavian languages spoken in the Middle West, and from the Spanish of the Southwest; but the main stock of the English vocabulary of these later settlement areas is nevertheless clearly derived from the speech of the earlier settlements on the Atlantic slope.

In his search for historical explanations for the speech areas of the Eastern States and their subdivisions, the author read rather widely in the general histories of the United States, in state histories, and in regional and period histories; he also consulted county and town histories on occasion. He has profited most from the writings of F. C. Turner, M. L. Hansen, A. M.

Schlesinger, D. R. Fox, T. J. Wertenbaker, G. G. Johnson, C. Bridenbaugh, and V. L. Parrington, and from the twelve volumes of *A History of American Life* (edited by Fox and Schlesinger) in which population history, social history, and cultural history are admirably treated. Paullin and Wright's *Atlas of the Historical Geography of the United States,* a great storehouse of ready information on population history, has been his constant companion.

The contributions of the American Council of Learned Societies, the Rockefeller Foundation, and the various universities and colleges in New England to the making of the *Linguistic Atlas of New England* are acknowledged in the Preface to the *Handbook of the Linguistic Geography of New England.* The field work in the Middle Atlantic States and the South Atlantic States was supported largely by the American Council of Learned Societies, but substantial contributions were made to the project by the American Philosophical Society, for the survey of Pennsylvania; by the Johns Hopkins University, through the efforts of Isaiah Bowman and Kemp Malone, for the field work in Maryland; by the University of Virginia, through the good office of Archibald A. Hill and Atcheson L. Hench; by the University of North Carolina, through the efforts of George R. Coffman and Howard W. Odum; and by Duke University, with the help of Paull F. Baum.

All of the materials from the Middle Atlantic and the South Atlantic States, which are as yet unpublished, were gathered for the *Atlas* by the late Dr. Guy S. Lowman, Jr., over a period of seven years, beginning in 1933. Without his skillful, painstaking, and self-sacrificing work, which took him to every county in this far-flung section of our country, this book could not have been written.

For my interpretation of the word geography of the Hudson Valley and of Virginia and North Carolina I have received many valuable leads from two unpublished doctoral dissertations written under my direction at Brown University: Jane Daddow (Hawkins), *The Speech of the Hudson River Valley* and Jeanette Dearden (Denning), *Dialect Areas of the South Atlantic States.*

For more than a decade Brown University housed the collections of the *Linguistic Atlas* and provided fellowships for graduate students who came to work with the author. He has profited greatly by these arrangements and gratefully acknowledges the help thus received.

A fellowship from the Guggenheim Foundation in 1944 provided the leisure for embarking on the historical interpretation of the speech areas of the Eastern States.

I am under obligation to Robert J. Menner and Edgar H. Sturtevant of Yale and to Margaret S. Ogden of the Middle English Dictionary at the University of Michigan for reading my manuscript, and to Phyllis Jones Nixon for the preparation of the glossary.

A grant from the Faculty Research Fund of the Horace H. Rackham School of Graduate Study of the University of Michigan has made it possible to include a large number of word maps, which should add greatly to the effectiveness of the volume.

To the Director of the Press, Dr. Frank E. Robbins, and to the Editor of Scholarly Publications, Dr. Eugene S. McCartney, I am deeply indebted for their helpfulness and for the many courtesies they have shown me.

CONTENTS

CONTENTS

NOTE

The groups of synonyms in Chapter III are presented in the order in which the items appear in the work sheets of the *Linguistic Atlas of New England* as published in the *Handbook of the Linguistic Geography of New England*, Chapter V. The arrangement is roughly topical. The heading of each item is followed by a number in parentheses which refers to the pages of the work sheets as printed in the *Handbook*.

Turning to the work sheets, the reader will get a reference to the map of the *Linguistic Atlas of New England*, where a full and detailed record of usage will be found. Moreover, when the collections from the Middle Atlantic and the South Atlantic States are published, he will have ready access to the record of word usage in these areas. Scholars in the American English field will want these reference numbers; the more casual reader may disregard them.

The numbers in parentheses after the words under discussion in Chapter II refer to the headings in Chapter III.

CHAPTER I

THE ENGLISH OF THE EASTERN STATES: A PERSPECTIVE

SETTLEMENT AREAS AND SPEECH AREAS

See Figure 1.

IN 1790, when the first Federal Census was taken, an unbroken area of English settlements extended along the Atlantic seaboard from the Penobscot in Maine to the Altamaha in Georgia,[1] a sweep of 1,200 miles as the crow flies.

In Maine the settlements still clung close to the shore, but the other New England states were completely taken up, except for the northernmost parts of New Hampshire and Vermont.

Long Island, East Jersey, the Hudson Valley, and the tributary Mohawk Valley were under cultivation, and a wedge of settlements was being pushed westward toward Lake Ontario and the Finger Lakes.

West Jersey, Delaware, and the Eastern Shore of Maryland had been fully occupied except for the marshy grounds in southeastern New Jersey.

In Pennsylvania the settlements extended westward to the Alleghenies and northward to the fork of the Susquehanna.

Beyond the Alleghenies, between the Monongahela and the Ohio, lay a rapidly growing center of population, dating back to the middle of the century, but as yet rather detached from the settlements of Eastern Pennsylvania, Maryland, and Virginia, whence most of its inhabitants had come.

Maryland, the present Virginia, and the Carolinas were almost entirely taken up, and settlements had already been established in the eastern fringe of the present West Virginia and, in a broad belt, between the Savannah and the Altamaha in Georgia.

Far to the west, beyond the Appalachians, a new center was rapidly growing in the Blue Grass country of Kentucky (Lexington), soon to expand southward into central Tennessee (Nashville) and northward into Ohio and Indiana.[2]

The unbroken belt of settlements on the Atlantic slope dates back to the middle of the eighteenth century. At an earlier date we find on the Atlantic seaboard a chain of geographically and politically separate colonies.[3] Some of these had been started during the first decades of the seventeenth century: on Massachusetts Bay, on Narragansett Bay, on the Connecticut, on the Hudson, and on Chesapeake Bay; others were planted half a century later: on the Delaware, on Albemarle Sound and on the Cooper River in the present South Carolina. Each of these colonies had a life of its own for several generations and had closer ties with the mother country across the sea than with its sister colonies on this side of the Atlantic. When the several colonies finally established physical contact with each other, each one of them must have possessed distinctive social and cultural characteristics, including a dialect of its own—a unique blend of British types of speech, supplemented in its vocabulary by borrowings from the Indians or from Dutch or German neighbors.

These regional types of American English spread inland as the settlements expanded up the rivers and across the mountains, and they were blended anew when settlers from different colonies mingled on the frontier. There can be no doubting the fact that the major speech areas of the Eastern States coincide in the main with settlement areas and that the most prominent speech boundaries run along the seams of these settlement areas.

Until the industrial development of the nineteenth and the twentieth centuries the Atlantic

---

[1]C. O. Paullin and John K. Wright, *Atlas of the Historical Geography of the United States* (Washington and New York, 1932), plate 76 B.

[2]All of these early settlements, except those in Kentucky, are included in the present investigation. They are the 'mother areas' for all varieties of American English.
[3]Paullin and Wright, *AHG*, plates 60 A, B, C.

slope had the relatively even population distribution of an agricultural country. But even in
Colonial times there were, on the coast and at
the head of navigation on the rivers, busy ports
from which the produce of the colonies was
shipped to England and through which manu-
factured goods and new settlers entered the
colonies—Boston, Newport, New York and
Albany, Philadelphia, Alexandria, Richmond,
Norfolk, Charleston, and, though not until
shortly before the Revolution, Baltimore.

These seaports were not only centers of trade
for their hinterland, into which they reached out
with waterways and roads, and not only gateways
through which a continuous stream of immigrants flowed, varying in volume with the religious, social, and economic conflicts of Europe.
They were also the centers of cultural life and
of high society which kept in close touch with
London and dominated the back country socially
and culturally.[4]

The influence of these centers upon the speech
of their hinterland, and thus upon the development of the speech areas, is second only to the
influence of the original settlement as a factor
in shaping the regional types of speech on the
Atlantic seaboard and in determining their geographic boundaries. Under the dominance of
these urban centers local expressions and pronunciations have been replaced in the countryside by new expressions and pronunciations
radiating from them. We can observe this trend
from local to regional usage most clearly in the
Boston area, the Philadelphia area, and the
Virginia Piedmont. The Charleston area of
South Carolina presumably shows a similar
development but the linguistic facts are not yet
sufficiently known.

After the Revolution a powerful westward
surge set in.[5] From Western New England the
sons and daughters of Yankee families made
their way into central and western New York
State, into the northern counties of Pennsylvania,
and to the Western Reserve of Connecticut on
Lake Erie. Not many Dutch families from the
Hudson Valley joined in this westward movement, nor were there among the New Englanders
very many who came from farther east than the
Connecticut Valley. In Eastern New England,
as on the Hudson, the increasing population
was largely drawn into the overseas trade, which
was greatly stimulated by the Napoleonic Wars,
and into the rising industries. The descendants
of the farmers of Western New England, on the
other hand, sought their fortune in the western
lands and carried the speech ways of Western
New England into the Great Lakes Basin. The
southern boundary of this New England settlement area is reflected in a well-defined speech
boundary which runs in a westerly direction
through northern Pennsylvania.

During the last decades before the Revolution
large numbers of Pennsylvanians and many
immigrants from abroad who landed on Delaware Bay had occupied the fertile farm lands
along the Shenandoah and pushed their way
across the Blue Ridge into the piedmont of the
Carolinas before the coastal settlements of
Virginia and the Carolinas had expanded into
these areas. The Scotch-Irish and the Palatine
Germans from Pennsylvania and from overseas
constituted the major elements in the population
of these southern uplands, but Virginians, Carolinians, and Englishmen mingled with them.[6]

This southwestward thrust from Pennsylvania
through western Maryland into the Valley of
Virginia and the Carolina piedmont (1725–75)
was met by a series of thrusts up the rivers from
the coastal settlements of the South. Southern
settlers mixed with the Pennsylvanians along
the periphery of the Southern settlement area,
especially south of the James River, but the
seam of these two major settlement areas is
clearly reflected in a well-defined speech boundary which runs along the Blue Ridge in Virginia
and then swerves out into the piedmont at
Lynchburg.

After the Revolution the descendants of these
southern uplanders crossed the Appalachians in
large numbers by way of the Holston River and
the Cumberland Gap. They occupied the fertile

---

[4]Carl Bridenbaugh, *Cities in the Wilderness* (New
York, 1938), part III.
[5]Paullin and Wright, *AHG*, plates 76 C, D, E.

[6]T. J. Wertenbaker, *The Old South* (New York, 1942),
Chapter V. F. J. Turner, *The Frontier in American
History* (New York, 1920), pp. 99–106.

lands of central Kentucky and Tennessee, and established themselves in southern Ohio, Indiana, and Illinois during the first decades of the nineteenth century. They also infiltrated into the narrow valleys of the Kanawha and its tributaries in West Virginia.

Farther north the settlements in the Pittsburgh-Wheeling area on the upper Ohio expanded rapidly up the Monongahela into West Virginia, up the Allegheny to Lake Erie, and down the Ohio Valley. The settlers came from Pennsylvania east of the Alleghenies, from West Jersey, and from abroad, but there were also New Englanders among them. By 1810 the downward thrust from the upper Ohio had met the northward thrust from Kentucky in the region of Cincinnati and Louisville.

This far-flung Midland area, settled largely by Pennsylvanians and by their descendants in the southern upland, constitutes a separate speech area which is distinct from the Northern area—the New England settlement area—and from the Southern area. Its northern boundary runs in a westerly direction through the northern counties of Pennsylvania, its southern boundary in a southwesterly direction along the Blue Ridge and through the Carolina piedmont. The South Midland, to be sure, exhibits a considerable infusion of Southern vocabulary and pronunciations.

Since the Valley of Virginia and the Carolina piedmont had already been taken up by Pennsylvanians at the time of the Revolution, expansion from the southern settlements was deflected, at the turn of the century, in a southwesterly direction into Georgia. This movement was greatly accelerated by the search for new cotton lands. By 1830 the best of these lands in the Gulf States had been taken up as far west as the Mississippi, largely by the sons of the cotton planters of Virginia and the Carolinas. As a result all the cotton lands are Southern in speech.

NATIONAL STOCKS AND SOCIAL CLASSES

Until the arrival of large numbers of Ulster Scots and Palatine Germans from 1720 onward, the population of the Atlantic seaboard was almost entirely of English stock, except for the

Dutch in the Hudson Valley. The Englishmen who peopled the colonies came largely from the southern and the midland counties of England, but there were among them some families from Yorkshire and Lancashire and even from farther north. New England seems to have received a rather large proportion of settlers from London and environs, from East Anglia and from Kent. In Virginia, London was also well represented, but the greater part of the early population came in rather even distribution from all the counties south of Yorkshire. West Countrymen were fairly numerous both in New England and in Virginia.[7] It is, therefore, quite obvious that at first many regional varieties of English were spoken in the American colonies, which were blended into distinctively American local and regional varieties in the course of several generations.

After 1720 large flocks of Ulster Scots and Palatine Germans arrived on Delaware Bay and spread out into the back country of Philadelphia, and then westward to the Alleghenies and the Ohio Valley, and southward through western Maryland and Virginia to the Carolinas. In lesser numbers these elements also established themselves in New England and in the South.

The geographic dissemination and the relative strength of the non-English stocks at the time of the Revolution are strikingly reflected in the dissemination of their religious denominations—the Dutch Reformed churches in the Hudson Valley and on the Delaware, the Scotch Presbyterian churches, and the German Reformed and Lutheran churches in Pennsylvania and the southern upland. The concentrations of the Protestant-Episcopal (Anglican) churches, of the meetinghouses of the Friends, and of the Congregational churches have a similar significance for identifying concentrations of the English stock.[8]

The influence of the English-speaking Ulster Scots upon the speech of certain sections of Pennsylvania and of the southern upland cannot be doubted, but it is surprisingly intangible. The Dutch and the Germans, who spoke their own language for many generations and passed through a stage of bilingualism before they gave

[7]Paullin and Wright, *AHG*, plates 70 C, D.
[8]*Ibid.*, plate 82.

up their native language, have left a much more tangible impress upon the English of their areas of concentration.

When the great migrations across the Atlantic from Ireland and Germany began in the 1830's and swelled to enormous proportions in the next decades,[9] the Eastern States already possessed a variety of rather set regional and social types of speech, which these immigrants acquired in due course. Most of the Irish and the Germans who made their homes in the Eastern States during the nineteenth century lived in the cities, and their children learned their English largely from native teachers in the city schools. Some of the cities had compact Irish and German sections that remained bilingual for a time, but in two or three generations these too were assimilated, linguistically and otherwise, to the established local pattern. The French Canadians, the Italians, the Greeks, the Russians, and other foreign elements who followed the Irish and the Germans into the eastern cities are now undergoing this same process of assimilation.

The great majority of the American colonists, whether they came from England, Northern Ireland, or Germany, belonged to the middle class of European society or to the poor. The former started life in the New World as farmers or tradesmen; the latter worked as indentured servants, hoping to achieve the rights of freemen in due time. Those who came from the English countryside spoke the local peasant dialects, those coming from provincial centers such as Bristol and Norwich talked provincial dialects, and the Londoners spoke the social dialect of their class and could perhaps muster an approximation to the upper-class speech of London. Some could read, but many could not. The Palatine Germans spoke the folk dialects of the Palatinate and Hesse, from which the 'Pennsylvania Dutch' of the present day is largely derived.

Each of the colonies also had a nucleus of well-educated men of affairs—officials, planters, and merchants; and some learned men—ministers, teachers, and scholars. This small but influential group knew the literary language of England, and those among them who had grown up in London or had been educated at Cambridge or Oxford spoke Standard English or something approximating it. We must of course not assume that the spoken standard of England was as uniform in the seventeenth and eighteenth centuries as it is now. The conflicting evidence offered by the orthoepists of the time makes that perfectly clear. Nor was this standard of spoken English as widely disseminated socially and regionally as at a later time.[10]

Owing to the presence in all the colonies of a great variety of English speech, the Standard English spoken and written by the leading personalities became the model for the middle class, whatever their English provenience. Features of provincial and of local pronunciation, vocabulary, and grammar survive in all parts of America, but the system of sounds, the grammar, and the major part of the vocabulary of all the speech areas of the United States are essentially those of Standard British English.

The colonists sought to pattern their society on that of Europe, but the conditions of life in the New World made for a leveling of social classes. The seaports, which harbored officials and merchants who maintained close contact with British society, preserved the European class distinctions to a marked degree; but the back-country, and especially the frontier, produced a democratic middle-class society. This difference in social structure as between the seaports and the farm country was inevitably reflected in the social stratification of speech. In the farming areas social differences in speech are slight; in the cities on the Atlantic seaboard, notably Boston, New York City, and Charleston, they are rather striking.

Marked regional differences in social structure, and hence in the social stratification of speech, developed during the latter part of the Colonial period and during the early years of the Republic.

---

[9]Markus L. Hansen, *The Atlantic Migration 1607–1860* (Cambridge, 1940), pp. 280–306.

[10]As late as 1797 John Walker said in his widely used *Critical Pronouncing Dictionary and Expositor of the English Language*, 2nd ed. (London, 1797), p. xiii: "Nay, harsh as the sentence may seem, those at a considerable distance from the capitol do not only mispronounce many words taken separately, but they scarcely pronounce with purity a single word, syllable, or letter."

In Colonial New England social lines were less sharply drawn than in the South. To be sure, each town had its prominent families and, at the other extreme, its indentured servants and their descendants. There were also the property-owning freemen who had a voice in town affairs and held a privileged position in the church; and, on the other hand, those who lacked these privileges. But servants became freemen by acquiring property with the earnings of their labor, either in the town of their birth or, more often, by removing to the frontier.

The freemen constituted a large middle class of farmers and craftsmen, many of them literate even in early days, whose language was neither that of the elite nor that of the humble folk. The sons and daughters of these families learned to read and write in a school supported by the town, and the son of a freeman might go to college to be trained for the ministry.

Every New England town had its church or meetinghouse, faithfully attended by freeman and yeoman to hear the Sunday sermon, if he was a Congregationalist or a Baptist, or to listen to his fellow townsmen, if he was a Quaker. Whatever his religious affiliation, the New Englander read the Bible or had it read to him in his own home or that of a neighbor until he knew much of it by heart. Thus the common speech of New England was continually exposed to the influence of the grammar and the vocabulary of literary English.

Compulsory education and relatively well trained teachers also came earlier in New England and the New England settlements than elsewhere. As a result, untutored folk speech is to be heard nowadays only from a small part of the population in southern New England. The largely rural northern New England states, however, have preserved folk speech to a marked degree despite almost universal literacy.

In the seaports of New England social caste was much more pronounced than in the rural areas. This was, and still is, especially true of Boston, which harbored during the Colonial period a colonial governor and his entourage, and a large number of merchants and intellectuals who were in constant touch with London and the leading social and intellectual circles of England. A merchant's son was apt to spend years in England, representing the business interests of his family.

This social elite survived the Revolution and developed a culture of its own during the nineteenth century. Pride in these achievements has engendered a conservatism that bids fair to preserve the cultivated speech of Boston for many years to come as a distinctive type of American English.

A well-bred, well-educated, self-conscious elite, proud of its cultivated speech and its tradition of culture, is to be found in all the older cities of New England from Portland, Portsmouth, and Salem to Newport and Providence, and from New London to New Haven, Hartford, and Springfield. But the speech of the great majority of New Englanders is neither the cultivated speech of this elite nor that of the simple folk. It is the common speech of an intelligent and active middle class.

In the New England settlements beyond the Hudson and in the Basin of the Great Lakes we find essentially the speech of the middle class of Western New England.

In the southern seaports the social grouping was similar to that in the New England ports, but as far as the social elite was concerned the connections with England were even closer. The Southern merchants and planters belonged to the Church of England, they were received as equals in London society, and their sons were admitted as students to the English universities, a privilege that was denied to the dissenters of New England and of Pennsylvania. The College of William and Mary was founded early in Williamsburg, the seat of the royal governor of Virginia, but the great majority of the sons of Southern gentlemen got their education in England or from imported English tutors. In this manner the speech ways of this social class conformed to those of London to a considerable extent.

The social organization of the Southern countryside, at first not unlike that of New England, came to be radically different from it and the Middle Colonies as the plantation system took more definite shape in the early decades of the eighteenth century and created a new type of society.[11]

The cultivation of indigo, rice, tobacco, and cotton called for a large investment to make it profitable, and indeed workable, and the plantation system was the answer to the problem. From Chesapeake Bay to the Savannah, first in the tidewater area, then in the piedmont, this system of agriculture for the production of staples for the English and the European markets established itself during the eighteenth century and enjoyed a phenomenal growth up to the Civil War.

The plantation system meant that the South had no villages and few market towns; it meant that each plantation was not only an economic unit but a neatly graded social unit consisting of the master and his family, the overseer, the Negro house servants, and the Negro field hands. The white craftsman became subservient to the planter. The small farmer became an overseer, removed to the frontier, or clung to submarginal lands. There was no place for him in the plantation system with its slave labor; and if he chose to stay, his life was apt to decline to that of a 'poor white.'

In the plantation country all elements of the population except the planters and the upper classes in the seaports lived in marked isolation. This fact is strikingly reflected to this day in great local differences in the speech of the simple folk, both white and Negro. The speech of the planter class, on the other hand, was regional rather than local and relatively close to Standard British English because of the continuous contacts with the upper classes of English society during the Colonial period.

Social differences in the plantation country of the South were leveled down to some extent after the Civil War, partly through the impoverishment of the planter class, partly—perhaps largely—through the schooling of the less privileged classes. But to this day social differences in speech are much more marked in this section of the Eastern States than elsewhere, although in Virginia and South Carolina regional standards, which doubtless originated with the planter class, are replacing local dialects apace.

By and large the Southern Negro speaks the language of the white man of his locality or area and of his level of education. But in some respects his speech is more archaic or old-fashioned; not un-English, but retarded because of less schooling.

As far as the speech of uneducated Negroes is concerned, it differs little from that of the illiterate white; that is, it exhibits the same regional and local variations as that of the simple white folk. Distinctive Negro speech, the so-called Gullah, is to be found only in those parts of the Low Country of South Carolina and Georgia in which the Negroes have greatly outnumbered the white for two centuries or more. In its simplified system of sounds, its simple grammar, and its vocabulary this Negro dialect of English—similar to that of the Bahamas—has many features that are derived from African languages.[12]

The educated Negroes of the South and the leaders of this race are mostly descended from the house servants of slavery days, of whom a considerable number were mulattoes. This class of Negroes learned their English in their master's household and kept aloof from the field hands, who lived in separate quarters under the watchful eye of the overseer of the plantation.

The Pennsylvania settlement area—the Midland—is landlocked. Philadelphia on the Delaware is its only outlet to the Atlantic.

Until 1720 Penn's colony on the Delaware, including West Jersey and Delaware, was peopled largely by English dissenters. Quaker merchants, an intelligent middle class, directed its fortunes unchallenged until the decades preceding the Revolution. Connections with the mother country were largely commercial. Even if the leading families had wanted their sons to go to English universities they would have found the doors closed to them.

By the middle of the eighteenth century Philadelphia had become the largest city in the American colonies, second only to London in

---

[11] James T. Adams, *Provincial Society 1690–1763* (New York, 1927), Chapter VIII. Guion Griffis Johnson, *Antebellum North Carolina* (Chapel Hill, 1937), Chapters III and XVI.

[12] Lorenzo D. Turner, *Africanisms in the Gullah Dialect*

the English-speaking world. It was the chief center of learning and culture on the American continent until the turn of the century. Its men of affairs and its scholars—founders of the Philosophical Society and the College of Philadelphia —were recognized not only in England but also on the European continent.

From the earliest time, Philadelphia must have displayed a greater social independence of England than the other seaports. It had no royal governor and fewer English officials to provide intimate contacts with fashionable London society. Although some prominent merchant families joined the Anglican church in the decades preceding the Revolution, the Quakers retained their dominance socially as well as politically. It is noteworthy that Loyalists were less numerous here than in the other seaports when the Colonies declared their independence.[13]

Since Philadelphia had less marked class distinctions in early times, it lacks at the present time the well-defined class differences in speech that we find in the other seaports. It is a significant fact that of all the seaports Philadelphia alone failed to adopt a striking feature of Standard British pronunciation—the loss of *r* after a vowel, as in *hard* and *corn*.

To the west of the English settlements on Delaware Bay, in the fertile lands of the Great Valley and the Lancaster Plain, the Palatine Germans had their farms and villages; and in with them, and beyond, the Ulster Scots established their homes.

This whole area and the Southern upland populated by these stocks was a land of independent farmers, wholly democratic in character. There was no leisure class, and there were few servants or paupers. On the frontier a poor man could become a man of substance within his lifetime if he used his hands and his head.

This leveling of social differences inevitably entailed a leveling of social dialects. In the course of time a new type of cultivated speech, based upon the common speech of an active middle class, came into being in this Midland area.

The Palatine Germans ultimately learned the English of their neighbors, but traces of German speech habits persist in areas where German is still spoken or was spoken until recently.

CULTIVATED SPEECH, COMMON SPEECH, AND FOLK SPEECH

Social classes are less clearly defined in America than in Europe. Even in the old seaports on the Atlantic and in the plantation country of the South we find no such sharp cleavages as in England or on the European continent, and hence no such clearly defined social dialects as English peasant speech on the one hand and Received Standard English on the other. What we do find is a gradation from *cultivated speech* through *common speech* to *folk speech*. The span of variations and the number of speakers of each social dialect differ with the social structure of the several sections. *Cultivated speech* is widespread in urbanized areas; *folk speech* in secluded areas such as northern New England, the South Atlantic coast, and the Appalachians; *common speech* in the greater part of the farm country of the Eastern States. These social levels in speech, ill defined as they are, have long been recognized by students of American English, and the *Linguistic Atlas of the United States* undertakes to sample each type systematically.[14]

What has not been clearly visualized hitherto is the supreme importance of knowing all the levels of speech in their local, regional, and national variations if we would understand the history of our language in all of its complexity. Our regional types of cultivated speech rest upon the regional types of common speech as much as upon literary English, and common speech in turn has its roots in folk speech. Conversely, the cultivated speech of a region reshapes the speech of the middle class, the common speech; and features of the common speech encroach upon folk speech. The unmistakable trend from local to regional usage and from regional to national usage that characterizes the National Period of our linguistic history is essentially a process of the dissemination of upper-class speech forms

---

[13] C. and J. Bridenbaugh, *Rebels and Gentlemen; Philadelphia in the Age of Franklin* (New York, 1942), pp. 13–28.

[14] H. Kurath, B. Bloch, and M. L. Hansen, *Handbook of the Linguistic Geography of New England* (Providence, 1939), pp. 41–44. C. C. Fries, *American English Grammar* (New York, 1940), esp. pp. 9–13.

to lower social levels and across earlier local or regional boundaries.

If we would know the regionalism of Colonial speech, we must study the folk speech of the present day, which has preserved local and regional features of speech to a much larger extent than the speech of the middle class and the cultured. And again, if we undertake to trace the history of words and pronunciations in which American English differs from Standard British English, we shall follow a trail that leads through American folk speech to British dialects and to provincial variants of the British Standard.

Why should folk speech tend to be local in character and why should cultivated speech be regional or supraregional, if not national? Let us briefly consider this question.

The small farmer, the farm tenant, the fisherman, the mountaineer learns his language by ear. A person of this class reads little, if at all. He does his shopping the year round in the same general store where he meets his like to talk to. His occasional visits to a larger shopping center, the village or the county seat, have no appreciable effect upon his habitual speech ways. He may hear and learn some new words, but his pronunciation and grammar are little affected by these contacts.

In the local school he gets to know the written language, but if he settles back into the simple life of his forbears he will continue to speak much like his family and his neighbors of an older generation, even if he reads the local newspaper and the *Saturday Evening Post* or listens to the radio.

Schooling, one must remember, is of rather recent date in many parts of our country. In large parts of the South and the South Midland many of the simple folk attended school only for short periods, or not at all, until quite recently. Even in the country districts of New England and the Middle Atlantic States compulsory attendance at school until age fourteen or sixteen is of relatively recent date.

The survival of local types of folk speech to our times varies in inverse proportion to the intensity of schooling and the date of the introduction of compulsory school attendance. Urban and industrialized areas, where the concentration of population made intensive schooling economically possible and popular, have largely lost their local folk speech. Agricultural areas, and especially the sparsely settled sections of marginal subsistence, have adhered to their folk ways and their folk speech in varying degrees, depending at least in part upon the date of the establishment of public schools.

In Colonial America a large proportion of the population were simple farm folk who talked a great variety of local dialects. Many sections of the Atlantic seaboard preserved this character well into the nineteenth century, and some have retained it to this day. In other parts, especially around the seaports and certain inland population centers, the speech of the upper classes of society spread to the countryside, submerging the local dialects, even before the large internal migrations entailed by the growth of industrial centers. In other parts, notably in New England and the Middle Atlantic States, the shift from agriculture to industry uprooted a large part of the agricultural population and with it the local dialects.

The cultured person may receive his first schooling in his native community, where he associates with the children from the neighborhood. But as soon as he enters college or business school, he meets people from other sections of his state and from neighboring states. Many of his teachers often come from different sections of the country, and they often 'talk like a book.' He may even attend college in a different section of our far-flung country. In Colonial times many a planter's or merchant's son studied in England or received his professional training there.

The educated man reads widely and is taught to write in the idiom of others.

All these contacts and experiences result in a deliberate or an involuntary abandonment of local and narrowly regional speech forms, or, at any rate, in the acquisition of an additional, less local, type of speech.

After the college years, the practice of a profession, wide business contacts, travel, reading, or the enjoyment of a life of leisure and of high society may further strengthen the inclination to avoid local and regional usage or to indulge in it only in dealing with the common people. Many a cultured American is master of two levels of speech and uses them at will.

For these reasons the speech of the cultured is less earth-bound than that of the folk. It is regional rather than local in character. In grammar and in vocabulary it is apt to strip off even some of the regional features, but in America the pronunciation remains largely regional since there is no national standard of pronunciation.

The speech of the common man occupies a position intermediate between that of the cultured and the humble folk, both socially and in its geographic spread.

The white-collar worker, the tradesman, the craftsman, and the well-to-do farmer each gets his schooling locally or in a nearby city. The grade school and even the high school which he attends are staffed very largely by teachers who grew up and were trained in the same section—at least until recently. During his formative years he associates almost exclusively with boys and girls from his immediate surroundings. When he takes his job, his contacts remain local. His day-by-day dealings are with the common man and the simple folk of the neighborhood rather than with the relatively small number of the cultured in his community.

The common man reads little besides the daily newspaper, a popular periodical or two, and perhaps a trade journal. He may read a novel now and then, but the smattering of the language of the great masters of the past that he gets in high school is soon forgotten. His language habits are hardly touched by the literary language.

In recent years he hears a Babel of dialects over the radio and in the movies. He understands them, may even mimic them, but he does not acquire them. He will of course adopt a fashionable word here and there or learn the pronunciation of an unfamiliar word from his favorite announcer.

It is rather strange that in our country with its ideals of democracy and its respect for the common man the scientific study of folk speech and of common speech should lag so far behind the work done in the European countries. But it is a fact. Students and teachers of English have focused their attention almost exclusively on the literary language and on cultivated speech—often enough without proper regard for the existing regional differences in the speech of the best educated. Folk speech has been dabbled in by scholars and by amateurs. But the speech of the large middle class has hardly been touched by trained linguists despite a lively popular interest in this subject.[15]

RANGES OF THE VOCABULARY

Our vocabulary of the arts and the terminology of the natural sciences and the social sciences are national in scope because the arts and the sciences are organized on a national basis, and a large part of the vocabulary of the arts and the sciences is shared by the entire English-speaking world. Indeed, a considerable part of it is common to the Western world.

Industries and commercial enterprises that are organized on a national scale, such as the automobile industry and the railroads, also have a nation-wide technical vocabulary which often differs radically from that of the British Empire.[16] The terminology of the printer, the newspaper, the stage and the pulpit, and of politics is also national rather than regional because the practitioners of these crafts and professions have nation-wide contacts and move about freely.

Enterprises and activities that are regionally restricted have, on the other hand, a considerable body of regional vocabulary, which, to be sure, may be known in other parts of the country even if it is not in active use. The cotton planter of the South, the tobacco grower, the dairy farmer, the wheat grower, the miner, the lumberman, and the rancher of the West have many words and expressions that are strictly regional and sometimes local in their currency.[17]

Regional and local expressions are most common in the vocabulary of the intimate everyday

---

[15] H. L. Mencken's *The American Language* has enjoyed an amazing popularity since its first appearance in 1919.

[16] *Ibid.* 4th ed. (New York, 1936), Chapter VI.

[17] Glossaries of the terminology of these enterprises are badly needed. The picturesque slang of the college campus and of the underworld has attracted the attention of scholars, but the vocabulary of these important elements in our population still awaits the hand of the lexicographer.

life of the home and the farm—not only among the simple folk and the middle class but also among the cultured. This segment of the American vocabulary has been systematically sampled in the Eastern States for the *Linguistic Atlas of the United States*.[18]

Food, clothing, shelter, health, the day's work, play, mating, social gatherings, the land, the farm buildings, implements, the farm stocks and crops, the weather, the fauna, and the flora— these are the intimate concern of the common folk in the countryside, and for these things expressions are handed down in the family and the neighborhood that schooling and reading and a familiarity with regional or national usage do not blot out.

It is the vocabulary in this range of life that gives us insight into the structure of the speech areas, large and small, their relation to settlement areas, trade areas, and culture areas, and the trend from local to regional and national usage. This is the important segment of the American vocabulary dealt with in this investigation.

---

[18]H. Kurath and others, *Handbook*, Chapter V: The Work Sheets. H. Kurath, M. L. Hanley, B. Bloch, G. S. Lowman, Jr., and M. L. Hansen, *Linguistic Atlas of New England* (Providence, Brown University, 1939–43), 734 maps, bound in six parts.
The field work in the Middle Atlantic States and the South Atlantic States has been nearly completed. A part of these materials has been edited. Similar sampling operations, though on a smaller scale, are in progress in the Great Lakes Basin and in the Ohio Valley under the direction of Albert Marckwardt of the University of Michigan.
The headquarters of the Linguistic Atlas of the United States were removed from Brown University to the University of Michigan in 1946.

EUROPEAN SOURCES AND AMERICAN INNOVATIONS

Our immediate problem is to determine the present geographic and social dissemination of individual expression in the Eastern States, to observe the coalescing of word boundaries with a view toward identifying speech areas, and to relate these speech areas and their boundaries to settlement areas, trade areas, and culture areas. This procedure gives us a realistic historical account of a selected body of vocabulary in the oldest part of English-speaking America.

American innovations and borrowings from Indian languages are fairly readily identified. The precise sources of words brought over from Europe, whether they be English, Dutch, or German, are not so easily recognized. Wright's *English Dialect Dictionary* provides a wealth of raw material for the latter part of the nineteenth century, but until the dialect geography of the British Isles has been worked out it will be hazardous to trace American words to any particular section of England or Northern Ireland because the geographic spread of many English dialect words has shrunk greatly since the seventeenth century. In the German, Dutch, and Flemish areas of Europe the geography of the dialects and the historical trends are much better known than those in the British Isles owing to the excellent work of linguistic geographers during the last decades, but the great regional dictionaries are still in the making. For these reasons no attempt is made at this time to trace the European sources of this large segment of our everyday vocabulary.

CHAPTER II

THE SPEECH AREAS OF THE EASTERN STATES

INTRODUCTION

EVERY word that is not in nation-wide use has its own spread geographically—as well as socially; yet the word boundaries tend to coalesce in some sectors and to be spaced more or less widely in others. Wherever they coalesce to form more or less close-knit strands or bundles, we have speech boundaries of varying importance. If we have at our disposal a sufficiently large number of regionally or locally restricted words, we are able to draw dialect boundaries.

In the Eastern States there are two boundaries of the first degree of importance, one running in a westerly direction through northern Pennsylvania, the other_in a southwesterly direction along the Blue Ridge in Virginia.

Boundaries of the second degree run (1) in a northerly direction from the mouth of the Connecticut River to the Green Mountains of Vermont, (2) from the fork of the Susquehanna in Pennsylvania to Sandy Hook in New Jersey, (3) from Dover in Delaware in an arc through Baltimore to the Blue Ridge, (4) from the lower James in Virginia through the piedmont of North Carolina to Roanoke in the Blue Ridge, (5) between the Peedee and the Santee in South Carolina, (6) along the northern watershed of the Kanawha in West Virginia, and (7) from Roanoke in the Blue Ridge through the piedmont of North Carolina to the Blue Ridge in South Carolina.

Boundaries of less importance are dealt with in their proper places.

The boundary between two areas may be rather clear-cut, as in northern Pennsylvania and along the Blue Ridge in Virginia, or it may be in the nature of a transition belt characterized by spaced word lines (isoglosses). Such belts run in a northerly direction through central New England, through the 'waist' of New Jersey, along the Alleghenies in central Pennsylvania, along the northern watershed of the Kanawha in West Virginia, through the north-central piedmont of North Carolina, and, presumably, through the western piedmont in South Carolina.

Speech areas, large and small, can be 'spotted' by selecting representative isoglosses from the available examples. This convenient device is employed throughout this chapter to delineate in a simplified manner the dialectal structure of the Eastern States insofar as it is revealed in the everyday vocabulary. In most cases the word lines are chosen to exhibit the focus or 'core' of an area as well as its periphery or margin. One must, of course, keep in mind that this procedure does not tell the whole story. The full complexity of regional and local usage is displayed in the *Linguistic Atlas* itself.

In Figure 2 the focus of each of the more distinctive subareas of the Eastern States is set off by a single word line or isogloss.

Figure 3 presents a scheme of the major speech areas of the Eastern States and their subdivisions, which is based upon the isoglosses of more than 400 different words treated in this book.

The heavy solid lines in Pennsylvania and in Virginia mark the clearly defined sectors of the boundaries between the North, the Midland, and the South. At either end of these sectors the lines of demarcation between the three major areas—drawn as double lines—are less clear. Here the isoglosses are less numerous, more widely spaced, and often shifting.

The subareas are set off by single lines, whether the boundaries between them be of the second degree of importance or weaker. In general, the subareas are more distinctive on the coast than in the upland, notably Eastern New England, Greater New York City, the Virginia Piedmont, and the part of South Carolina south of the Peedee.

Since this scheme of the dialectal structure of the Eastern States rests upon the analysis of a rather generous sample of the everyday vocabulary, it may be assumed that it is essentially correct. Additional lexical material may change the relative strength of certain boundaries, but hardly enough to overthrow the lines of demarcation drawn between the major areas.

Features of pronunciation and of grammar seem to exhibit regional distributions that resemble the dissemination of words very closely.

TABLE I

THE NORTHERN AREA

× regular — fairly common rare	Ohio	New York State		New England	
		Upstate	Hudson Valley	Western	Eastern
(1) The North					
pail (17)	X	X	X	X	X
whiffletree (21)	X	X	X	X	X
boss! (37)	X	X	X	X	X
johnny cake (44)	X	X	X	X	X
darning needle (60)	X	X	X	X	X
angle worm (60)	X	X	—	X	X
stone wall (16)		—	X	X	X
nigh-horse (39)	—	—	—	—	X
(2) The North without Eastern New England					
stoop (10)	X	X	X	X	
stone boat (21)	X	X	X	X	
fried-cakes (45)	X	X	—	—	
lobbered milk, loppered milk (47)	X	X	X	X	
sugar bush (61)	X	X	X	—	
button ball (61)		X	X	X	
belly-gut(ter) (95)	X	X	—	—	
(3) The North without the Hudson Valley					
buttry (10)	—	—		—	—
spider (17)	X	X		X	X
fills, thills (20)	X	X		X	X
teeter board (22)	X	X		X	X
coal hod (23)	—	—		X	X
hasty-pudding, Indian pudding (50)	X	X		X	X
Dutch cheese (47)	X	X		X	—
horning (82)	X	X		—	

The analysis of regional pronunciations will probably raise the boundaries of Eastern New England and Greater New York City, and the line between the North Midland and the South Midland, into greater prominence.

THE NORTHERN AREA

The Northern speech area corresponds to the New England settlement area, together with the Dutch settlement area which lies embedded in it. The southern boundary of this area runs in a westerly direction through northern Pennsylvania. On the East Branch of the Susquehanna (near Scranton) the line turns off in a southeasterly direction and cuts through New Jersey to the Atlantic coast below Sandy Hook.

The subareas of the North are (1) Western New England and the New England settlement area west of the Hudson to the Great Lakes, (2) Eastern New England, including the upper Connecticut Valley, and (3) the Hudson Valley, including western Long Island and East Jersey.

Eastern New England and the Hudson Valley have many local expressions, which make them stand out as distinctive subareas in the broad expanse of the Northern Area.

We find a considerable number of regional expressions that are common to all of the North, others that are found in all of the North except Eastern New England, some that occur in all of the North except the Hudson Valley, and some that are lacking both in Eastern New England and in the Hudson Valley.

Table I presents examples to show these types of geographic distribution.

The inner dialectal structure of the Northern area is indicated in the accompanying maps by means of representative word boundaries (isoglosses).

THE NORTH

Characteristic Northern expressions that are current in all of New England and the New England settlement area in New York State and northern Pennsylvania, as well as in the Hudson Valley, on Long Island, and in East Jersey, are: *pail, swill, whiffletree* or *whippletree, comforter* or *comfortable, brook, co-boss!* or *come boss!, johnny cake, salt pork* and *darning needle.* See Figures 4, 5a, and 5b.

Pail (17) is the regular name throughout the North for the well-known container with flaring sides and a bail. The compounds *water pail, milk pail, swill pail* likewise are current in this entire area. This usage prevails in the Western Reserve of Ohio, in the northern counties of Pennsylvania, as far south as Wilkes-Barre on the Susquehanna and Easton on the Lehigh in northeastern Pennsylvania, and to the 'waist' of New Jersey (Trenton–Sandy Hook). All of the Midland and the South use *bucket* in this sense, but *pail* is not unknown in the cities of Philadelphia and Washington.

Containers of this type are now made of metal but were formerly of wood. Most New Englanders use *pail* indiscriminately for the metal and the wooden varieties, as such expressions as *cedar pail* and *wooden pail* show; but along the coast, from Narragansett Bay to New Brunswick, many apply *pail* only to the modern metal container and call the older wooden one a *bucket*. *Bucket* survives also in the compounds *well bucket*, *fire bucket* (on ship board), *sap bucket* (in maple orchards), and on the seaboard, in *swill bucket*.

It is fairly clear that early New England had both *pail* and *bucket* and that *pail* had largely replaced *bucket* at least in Western New England before the westward expansion into New York State, i.e. by the time of the Revolution.

The development in the Midland and the South is the precise opposite. Here *bucket* came to be the general term, and *pail* survives only in North Carolina and Tidewater Virginia as the name for an old-fashioned wooden water or milk pail with one long stave for a handle.

The liquid food given to pigs is called *swill* (17) in the North, *slop* elsewhere in the Eastern States. The southern boundary of *swill* runs through northern Pennsylvania, but in New Jersey we find *swill* all the way south to Delaware Bay and even in northern Delaware. Furthermore, *swill* occurs on the coast of North Carolina from Albemarle Sound to the Neuse. On the other hand, *slop*, which is in general use in the Midland and the South, survives to some extent in New England (including conservative Cape Cod and Nantucket) and on the Mohawk.

We must infer from this situation that both terms were current in the oldest parts of the North, the Midland, and the South; and that later one of the terms won out in the North, the other in the greater part of the Midland and the South. The end result of the process has been attained in the later settlements, while parts of the coastal area still have divided usage.

Whiffletree and/or *whippletree* (21) are in general use in all of the Northern area. The boundary over against the Midland *singletree, swingletree* is sharply defined all the way from New Jersey to Ohio, except that a *swiveltree* island appears in New Jersey along the *whiffletree/swingletree* line. *Swiveltree* does not turn up anywhere else in the Eastern States and may well be a local descriptive term (cf. *swivel chair*) —or does it have a Dutch background?

Whiffletree predominates over *whippletree* in New England and is universal in the Hudson Valley and in East Jersey. In central New York State and in the northwestern counties of Pennsylvania *whippletree* is more common.

Comforter and *comfortable* (29) are distinctive Northern words for a thick quilt. The boundary between these terms and the Midland *comfort* is well defined and runs the normal course from Sandy Hook in New Jersey through northern Pennsylvania to the Western Reserve of Ohio. However, the cities of Trenton, Philadelphia, and Wilmington on the lower Delaware have adopted the Northern terms, probably as New York City trade words.

Comforter predominates in Eastern New England, *comfortable* in southwestern New England and in the Hudson Valley (except for Manhattan, which has mostly *comforter*). It is of interest to note that Maine says almost exclusively *comforter*, New Brunswick with its New York and New Jersey Loyalist settlements predominantly *comfortable*.

Brook (30) is current in all of New England, New York State, the northern counties of Pennsylvania, and East Jersey and occurs in the names of small streams throughout this area. West of the Green Mountains and the Berkshires *creek* is used as a synonym of *brook* and appears in such names as *Otter Creek* in Vermont and *Catskill Creek, Schoharie Creek, Canada Creek* in New York State. The Dutch *kill* survives only in geographic terms within the Dutch settlement area on the Hudson and the Delaware, e.g. in *Batten Kill, Peekskill, Catskill Creek, Schuylkill River*.

The line between Northern *brook* and Midland *run*, reflecting a settlement boundary, is rather sharply defined, but the Midland *run* has acquired currency in the northern counties of Pennsylvania.

The Northern cow call is *boss!, co-boss!, kə-boss!,* or *come boss!* (37). This call has survived also in the New England settlements on the Ohio around Marietta. In Pennsylvania west of the Susquehanna and in Ohio the boundary between the Northern *boss!* and the Midland *sook!* is clearly defined. East of the Susquehanna, Pennsylvania German and Dutch calls and the simple *co!* still compete with the Northern *boss!*

On the coast of New England and on Long Island Sound the simple *co!* and an old-fashioned *coaf!* are heard. The *co!* of southern New Jersey probably comes from the New England shore.

Bossie! (37) is the corresponding call to calves in the North, but East Jersey has preserved the Dutch call *tye!*

Johnny cake (44) is the characteristic Northern term for corn bread, which is known as *corn pone* in the Midland and the South. We find it everywhere in this sense except in Rhode Island, where it denotes a small griddle cake. *Corn bread* competes with *johnny cake* throughout the North and has largely eliminated it in urbanized areas. On Narragansett Bay *corn bread* is old and universal.

Salt pork (46) is a Northern expression which we find in New England and the greater part of rural New York State. In northern Pennsylvania and seemingly also in the Buffalo sector *side pork,* a blend of Northern *salt pork* and the Pennsylvania term *side meat,* has become established, and this expression is not unknown in the Hudson Valley and in parts of New Jersey. Urban areas no longer have a fixed term.

Darning needle (60A) is the regular expression for the dragon fly in the North. The line of demarkation over against the Midland *snake feeder* is remarkably clear and sharp, except that the cities on the lower Delaware—Trenton, Philadelphia, and Wilmington—have adopted the Northern term. The literary *dragon fly* is, of course, known to the better educated.

New England has a number of local terms for the earthworm and, in addition, the regional expression *angle worm* (60). None of the old local terms has crossed the Hudson River, but *angle worm* has spread to the entire Northern area. Long Island and East Jersey have it, but in the greater part of the Dutch settlement area *fish worm* is far more common, in Greater New York City *earthworm*.

It is of some interest to observe that relics of *angle worm* survive on the Southern coast.

Sick to the stomach (80) is a phrase we find in common use throughout the North. The surroundings of Marietta on the Ohio still show traces of this New England expression. In southern New England and in Metropolitan New York *at* is replacing *to* in this phrase.

In coastal parts of other settlement areas, *to the stomach* has survived independently—thus on Delaware Bay, on Delamarvia, and in North Carolina. Here, too, *at* is taking the place of *to.*

In New England, the greater part of New York State, and in northeastern Pennsylvania *stone wall* (16) is the regular name for a fence built of loose stone. In the western part of New York State, in northern Pennsylvania, and in the Western Reserve of Ohio the Midland *stone fence* is now firmly established, and this expression has found its way also into East Jersey, where it now stands by the side of the New England *stone wall* and the local *stone row.*

Kerosene (24) is the only term for that product in the Northern area. The Pennsylvania expressions *coal oil, lamp oil,* and *carbon oil,* which have spread far into the Southern area, have not encroached upon the northern counties of Pennsylvania, except in the direction of Erie, and have not struck root in East Jersey or New York State.

What is known as a *snack* in the South and as a *piece* in the Midland is most commonly called a *bite* (48) in the North. We find this expression in common use in New England, New York State, and New Jersey, outside of New England often by the side of *snack* or *piece.* *Bite* is less common in the northern counties of Pennsylvania and the Western Reserve, where the Midland phrase *eat a piece* has struck root.

It should be noted that *bite* is also current in the Philadelphia area and on upper Chesapeake Bay.

The left-hand horse of a team is called the *nigh-horse* (39) in all of the Northern area. In Eastern New England this term is universal; in

Western New England, the Hudson Valley, and the New England settlements to the west it stands by the side of *near-horse,* which seems to be gaining ground. *Nigh-horse,* it should be noted, is found also on Delaware Bay and, in scattering fashion, on Chesapeake Bay, surely as an independent derivative of British usage.

THE NORTH AND ADJOINING PARTS OF THE MIDLAND

There is rather striking evidence that certain Northern words have spread into the Midland, partly along the important New York–Philadelphia route, partly through the medium of print.

Picket fence (16), for instance, is a true folk word in all of the North, whereas in the Midland and the South *paling fence* or *paled fence* is in regular use among all classes, *picket fence* only among younger people and especially among city dwellers. It is thus fairly clear that this Northern term has spread to Delaware Bay, Chesapeake Bay, and the Ohio Valley rather recently.

In similar fashion *faucet* (18), which is in regular use among all social groups in the North, is encroaching upon *spicket* or *spigot* in parts of the Midland and the South.

Skunk (59) and *chipmunk* (59), too, are clearly of Northern origin. They are in universal use from New England to Ohio and have been passed on to the Midland and parts of the South. On Delaware Bay and on Chesapeake Bay, however, *skunk* and *chipmunk* may well be old since in these areas, as in New England, Algonkian languages were spoken when the white man arrived.

Pole cat is the old folk term for the skunk in the Midland and the South, but *skunk* is now more common north of the Potomac and not unknown to the south of it.

Similarly, *ground squirrel* is shared by the Midland and the South as an old folk term, but *chipmunk* has largely replaced it in Eastern Pennsylvania and has spread to Maryland and the lower Shenandoah. Marietta on the Ohio has retained the New England term.

THE NORTH WITHOUT THE HUDSON VALLEY

The Dutch settlement area on the Hudson shares a fair number of Northern expressions with the New England settlement area, partly as a common inheritance from the British Isles, partly as importations from New England. But the Hudson Valley also has its local words of Dutch or English origin.

Among the Northern expressions that are current only in the New England settlement area we find such household words as *eaves troughs, curtain, spider, tunnel, coal hod, teeter board,* and farm words like *scaffold, bay, loo, bossie!, whoa!, kə-nan!,* and *rowen crop.* See figure 6.

Eaves troughs or *eaves troths* (11) for the gutters on the roof is in general use in most of New England, and in New York State from Albany westward. It occurs also in northern Pennsylvania beside *eaves spouts* (which seems to predominate in the Western Reserve of Ohio), and on both sides of the Ohio from Marietta down to the Kanawha beside *eaves spouts* and *spouting.*

In New England itself *eaves troughs* is rare along the coast from Cape Cod to Maine, where *gutters* is in general use, and not very common in New Hampshire and eastern Vermont, where *eaves spouts* predominates.

The Hudson Valley has only *gutters.* This expression is also used to some extent in Western New England and Upstate New York, especially in the cities—probably as a New York City trade word.

Curtains (9) is the old folk word for roller shades in New England and its offshoots. It is still common in New England and the northern counties of Pennsylvania but has only a precarious hold in New York State. Metropolitan New York and the Hudson Valley have only *shades.*

Curtains occurs in this sense also on Delaware Bay and along the Southern coast.

Scaffold or *skaffle* (14) and *bay* (14) are New England words that were carried westward into Upstate New York and northern Pennsylvania but did not get established in the Hudson Valley south of the environs of Albany, or in East Jersey. Both terms denote parts of the New England barn: *skaffle* a raised platform for storing hay or grain, *bay* a section for storing hay that runs from the barn floor to the loft or the roof. In New York State and northern Pennsylvania these terms are no longer common, and they do not seem to survive in the Western Reserve.

It should be noted that from Narragansett Bay to Cape Cod and in parts of Maine *ground mow* is more common than *bay*.

In all of the New England settlement area *spider* (17) is the word for the cast-iron frying pan. The dividing line between Northern *spider* and Midland *skillet* is sharply defined in Pennsylvania. *Spider* has established itself in the Albany area but not on the lower Hudson or in East Jersey; it is rare on Long Island. *Frying pan* has largely superseded *spider* in urban areas.

Spider occurs in this sense also on lower Chesapeake Bay and the Carolina shore, obviously as an independent derivative of British usage, since intervening Delaware Bay has *skillet*.

Tunnel (19), for the funnel, is another New England word that was carried westward into Upstate New York, but it is no longer common there. The Hudson Valley has only *funnel,* and this term now has wide currency in southern New England as well.

The *coal hod* (23) of the Northern area is also a New Englandism. The term is common in all of New England and not infrequent, though losing ground, on the East Branch of the Susquehanna, on the Finger Lakes, in the Western Reserve, and around Marietta. The Hudson Valley, Long Island, and New Jersey have almost exclusively *coal scuttle,* and this term has spread from the Hudson Valley westward through New York State and the northern counties of Pennsylvania along with the New England *coal hod.*

The seesaw is known as a *teeter,* a *teeter board,* or a *teetering board* (22) in all of New England except the southeastern sector from Narragansett Bay to Cape Cod and Nantucket. We find these expressions also in the entire New England settlement area, to the shores of Lake Erie in Ohio, and in the Ohio Valley from Marietta downstream.

The Hudson Valley south of the Highlands, southwestern Connecticut, and East Jersey have *teeter-totter,* and this Hudson Valley expression competes with the New England *teeter* (*board*)

in the Mohawk Valley, on the upper Susquehanna, along Lake Erie, and in the Ohio Valley.

In the North *seesaw* is distinctly a book word, which, however, has attained rather general currency in urban areas.

The two most common calls to sheep in New England are, or were, *kə-nan!, nannie!* and *kə-day!, kə-dack!, kə-dick!* (38). Both of these calls were carried westward in the New England migration to the Susquehanna and the Great Lakes. The boundary over against the Midland call *sheep(ie)!,* is clear and sharp in Pennsylvania and Ohio. Marietta has adopted the Midland call.

Whoa! (38), beginning with the *h*-sound, is a characteristic Northern variant of the call to stop a horse. The greater part of the South, all of the Midland, and the Hudson Valley have only *woa!,* which appears also in New England beside *whoa!*

By the side of the usual *moo* older New Englanders say *loo* (36) for the noise made by cows. This expression is rare in New York State but can still be heard in northern Pennsylvania and the Western Reserve. It is related to the Southern *low.*

The New England settlement area has a variety of terms for the second crop of hay that do not occur elsewhere in the Eastern States. Of these expressions *rowen* (riming with plowing) and *rowen crop* (41) are common in all of New England except Maine, and in New York State; and relics of it are found in the Western Reserve of Ohio. The other expressions appear in scattered fashion from New Brunswick to Lake Erie: *aftermath, aftergrass, aftergrowth, aftercrop,* and *lattercrop.*

Second crop is taking the place of these older terms, in New York State also *second cutting.*

New Englanders of the older generation still use *buttry* (10), pronounced in two syllables, for the pantry, and many of the younger generation remember it as an old family word. In the New England settlement area of New York State and Pennsylvania this expression now has the same standing as in New England.

Buttry is unknown in the Hudson Valley and in the entire Midland and South. Even in New England such conservative coastal sections as Narragansett Bay, Essex County, and the New

Hampshire coast show no trace of it. On Narragansett Bay *closet* is the old term, north of Boston *pantry*.

Buttry is a variant of *butlery* but is now popularly associated with *butter*.

From New England to Lake Erie *fills* or *thills* (20) is a common name in rural areas for the shafts of a buggy. *Fills* predominates over *thills* in the more conservative parts of New England and in the settlement area beyond the Hudson.

The Hudson Valley, the Midland, and the South have only *shafts* (pronounced *shavs* or *shaffs*, rarely *shafts*), and this term is also current throughout the *fills* area.

The phrase *to home* (32) is still widely used by the side of *at home* among the rural population of New England, the central part of New York State, and on the upper Susquehanna, less commonly along Lake Erie.

Hasty-pudding (50) is the well-known New England term for mush made of corn meal. West of the Hudson *hasty-pudding* is very rare. We find instead *Indian pudding, corn meal pudding*, or simply *pudding* (especially in the phrase *milk and pudding*), expressions that are fairly common in this sense also in parts of New England. Some New Englanders, however, apply *Indian pudding* only to a sweetened corn meal pudding.

The Midland and the South have *mush*, and this expression is also used to some extent in the New England settlement area beside the terms containing *pudding*, in the Hudson Valley beside the local *suppawn*.

Fire fly (60A) is a common rival of *lightning bug* in all of New England except western Vermont. On Massachusetts Bay there are many from all social levels who use only *fire fly*, but elsewhere the two terms stand side by side. In New York State, as in Vermont, *lightning bug*, our national term, has largely eliminated *fire fly*. It is of interest to observe that in Metropolitan New York and in Philadelphia *fire fly* has considerable currency among the better educated, since it is supported by literary usage. As far as Philadelphia is concerned, *fire fly* may be old in part, since the term appears on the conservative Jersey side of Delaware Bay.

THE NORTH WITHOUT EASTERN NEW ENGLAND

Some Northern expressions are current in Western New England, in the New England settlement area of New York State and Pennsylvania, and in the Hudson Valley but not in Eastern New England. Several of these expressions are of Dutch origin, like *stoop* and *sugar bush*; others are of English stock, e.g. *button ball, hard maple, lobbered* or *loppered milk, stone boat, drawing wood*. There are also some terms that are found neither in Eastern New England nor in the Hudson Valley, but throughout Western New England and the New England settlement area to the west, as *Dutch cheese* and *fried-cakes*. See Figures 7 and 8.

Button ball (61) for the sycamore or plane tree is a striking example of this type of dissemination. We find it in all of Connecticut, in Massachusetts west of the Connecticut River, in all of New York State and East Jersey, and around Erie in Pennsylvania. It does not seem to survive in the Western Reserve of Ohio, where the West Midland *sycamore* is in general use, or in northeastern Pennsylvania, where the *button wood* of Eastern Pennsylvania became established.

Lobbered milk and *loppered milk* (47) are in common use for soured curdled milk from the Connecticut River to the Western Reserve and also on Long Island, in Rhode Island west of the Bay, and in adjoining parts of eastern Connecticut. The variant *lobbered* is regular in Rhode Island, the northern Berkshires with their large Rhode Island settlements, and the northern counties of Pennsylvania, *loppered* in western Connecticut and the southern Berkshires; elsewhere the two variants stand side by side. In Pennsylvania the southern boundary of this term is sharp, in New Jersey badly frayed.

Drawing wood, hay, etc. (21) is a characteristic Northern expression that is current by the side of *hauling*, sometimes with a differentiation of meaning. *Drawing* is used everywhere in the Northern area except in coastal New England, on Long Island and in East Jersey, where *carting* prevails.

From Western New England to the Great Lakes, *stone boat* (21) is the regular term for the wheelless horse-drawn vehicle made of heavy planks, on which stones are dragged from the field. In the Connecticut Valley, on Long Island, and in East Jersey *stone boat* competes with the *drag* or *stone drag* of coastal New England. *Stone boat* is not entirely unknown in southeastern New England and has become established on the Allegheny and the upper Ohio by the side of the Midland term *stone sled* or *drag sled.*

Stoop (10) is in general use from Long Island and East Jersey to Albany for a small porch or platform at the front, side, or back entrance to a house. This Dutch term, a cognate of *steps,* was carried westward to the Great Lakes by New Englanders after it had been adopted in Western New England. At present *stoop* is in fairly common use in Western New England from Connecticut to Vermont. It is well known on Massachusetts Bay but little used in Rhode Island or Maine. In New England *stoop* always denotes a small porch or platform as distinct from the long, narrow *piazza.*

Sugar bush (61) did not spread beyond the Berkshires and the Green Mountains in New England and is not very common even there. On the other hand, *sugar bush* is now the regular expression for a sugar maple grove in Upstate New York and the adjoining counties of Pennsylvania as well as in the Western Reserve. The adoption of an expression containing the Dutch *busch, bosch* by the New Englanders who settled in Upstate New York was facilitated by the fact that New England had such a variety of local expressions—*sugar orchard, sugar place, sugar lot,* and *sap orchard.*

The *sap bush* of the Hudson Valley probably reflects the local Dutch expression.

For the unraised doughnut Upstate New York, northern Pennsylvania, and the Western Reserve have *fried-cake* (45) beside *doughnut.* In parts of Connecticut—Litchfield County and the New London area —*fried-cake* is still a fairly common folk term, but elsewhere in New England it is rare. Eastern New England says *doughnut* and southern New England has adopted the Dutch *cruller.* Since the Hudson Valley has *cruller,* the *fried-cake* of Upstate New York is obviously a New Englandism.

Dutch cheese (47) is the most widespread Northern term for cottage cheese. It was coined in Western New England with reference to the Dutch of the Hudson Valley and spread eastward in New England almost to the Atlantic coast. It is used on Narragansett Bay and on the Merrimack in New Hampshire but not on the Massachusetts coast or in Maine. From Western New England *Dutch cheese* was carried westward into Upstate New York, the Western Reserve of Ohio, and into northern Pennsylvania, where the boundary over against the Midland *smear case* is clear-cut.

The entire Dutch settlement area, however, has *pot cheese,* modeled on the Dutch *pot kees.*

From the Berkshires and the southern part of the Green Mountains to the Great Lakes *horning* (82) is the regional expression for a mock serenade. This term does not occur in the Connecticut Valley or farther east, except in Rhode Island. Since many Rhode Islanders settled in the northern Berkshires and adjoining parts of Vermont, *horning* may well be a Rhode Island contribution to the Northern vocabulary.

The Dutch settlement area has *skimerton.*

From the lower Connecticut River to Lake Erie *belly-gut,* or *belly-gutter* (95), is the usual expression for coasting 'face-down' on a sled. This New Englandism is common north of the Hudson Highlands, but the lower Hudson has *belly-wop, belly-wopper,* as do Long Island and East Jersey. Whether the expression *belly-gutting* of Western Pennsylvania is of New England origin is an open question. There is some evidence that New Englandisms like *stone boat* (21) have traveled down the Allegheny River from the northern counties, which were settled by New Englanders. Since *belly-gut* is quite rare in Eastern Pennsylvania it seems likely that the Pittsburgh area has adopted the Connecticut term.

Curiously enough, the island of Martha's Vineyard has *belly-gutter.*

NEW ENGLAND (AND LONG ISLAND SOUND)

Some words that are, or were, current in all of New England or in large sections of it did not strike root in the New England settlements of New York State and the Western Reserve.

A number of these expressions, like *emptins* (45) for a kind of leaven and the call *hoist!* (with the vowel sound of *high*) or *hie!* (37) to a cow that is being milked, which barely survive in New England today, may simply have been lost earlier in the New England settlements beyond the Hudson.

Such euphemisms for a bull as *gentleman cow, gentleman ox, top cow, sire, toro, critter,* and *animal* (33) were not to the taste of the plain-spoken frontiersman, if indeed they are not later creations of the Victorian era in New England. A New Englander of the old school may call the outdoor toilet the *necessary* (12), but there seems to be no trace of this veiled term west of the Hudson.

Other New England expressions that are widely used along the coast and on Long Island Sound but not in the upland also failed to get established west of the Hudson, e.g. *breeze up* (7), *norwester, northeaster* (and some other weather terms); *creek* (30) for a salt water inlet, *carting* (21), *rifle* (23), and *gutters* (11).

Winds and tides are preëminently things that concern the shore dweller and the seafarer, and he has distinctive terms for these natural phenomena that the upland settler hardly knows; hence the restriction of certain weather terms, and of *creek* for a salt water inlet, to the coastal area.

Carting (21) is a very common expression for 'hauling' in all of coastal New England—from Maine to Cape Cod and from Nantucket to the Connecticut shore; and yet we find no trace of it in New York State west of the Hudson, where *drawing,* the expression of the New England upland, is in general use.

The coastal term *carting* became established on Long Island and in East Jersey. The *carting* of southern New Jersey may also be of New England origin, but there are relics of *carting* on lower Chesapeake Bay and on Albemarle Sound which point to independent derivation from a British source.

Expressions that are peculiar to Eastern New England rarely, if ever, appear in Upstate New York or farther west. It is well known that these areas, which were taken up by the white man after the Revolution, received most of their settlers from Western New England. On the seaboard the growing population became ab-sorbed in trade, in seafaring, in the fisheries, and presently also in various industries that came into being at the turn of the century. Hence it happened that words of Western New England rather than those of Eastern New England got established in New York State and on the Great Lakes whenever these two sections of New England differed in vocabulary.

From Massachusetts Bay to Casco Bay in Maine, on Long Island, in East Jersey, and in the Hudson Valley, *gutters* (11) is the regular word among all social classes for what the greater part of New England calls *eaves troughs* or *eaves spouts. Gutters* is now heard by the side of these older terms on Cape Cod and Narragansett Bay and in the cities of the lower Connecticut Valley and the Connecticut shore; but it is clearly a recent trade word in these parts of New England. For this reason it does not appear as a folk word in the New England settlements beyond the Hudson.

Rifle (23), denoting an emery covered wooden whetter for the scythe, occupies the same general area as *carting,* i.e. the New England coast, Long Island Sound, and East Jersey. Like *carting* it did not become established in Upstate New York or farther west.

Expressions that occur in larger parts of Western as well as Eastern New England usually survive in the New England settlement area beyond the Hudson. On the whole, New England has been more conservative than the secondary settlements. The following examples illustrate this trend.

Lowery (5), riming with *flowery,* for 'gloomy,' is not an unusual weather term in New England, except for Cape Cod and the Merrimack Valley, but it does not seem to have survived west of the Hudson. The same is true of *beller, bellow* (36) and of *go 'long!* or *go on!* (38) for *get up!*

Corn house (14) is common enough in all of New England by the side of *corn crib,* except on Narragansett Bay, but exceedingly rare in Upstate New York and farther west.

Griddle cake (45) is doubtless an old word in eastern Massachusetts, Rhode Island, eastern Connecticut, and the Connecticut Valley from Middletown northward. In these parts of New England it is used in both rural and urban areas, and by the old and the young of all social groups. In Maine, New Hampshire, and Essex County, Massachusetts, *fritter* is still often used in this sense, but *griddle cake* is taking its place.

Griddle cake is not common in western Connecticut or the Hudson Valley and is about equally matched with *pancake* in western Vermont. It is fairly clear that *griddle cake* has been yielding ground to *pancake* in the western section of New England and that the latter is spreading into Eastern New England.

Griddle cake has not survived in Upstate New York. In Metropolitan New York both terms are current, often in different senses. In Manhattan *griddle cake* is a newcomer, probably also in other parts of the Metropolis and on the Jersey shore.

Selectman (69), *common* (85), *green* (85), and *shire town* (85) are New England expressions that have not become established in the New England settlements although they were doubtless used there in earlier days.

The *selectmen* are the chief town officers in all of the New England states except Rhode Island, where they are known as *councilmen*. In Maine, New Hampshire, and northeastern Massachusetts (from Concord northward) *selectmen* is stressed on the first syllable (which is usually pronounced as *seal,* less commonly as *sill* or *sell),* elsewhere on the second.

The village green, held in common, is known as the *common* (85) in most of Massachusetts, New Hampshire, eastern Vermont, and Maine, and as the *green* (85) in Connecticut. From Narragansett Bay to Cape Cod both *green* and *common* are found—Plymouth itself having *green.* Essex County, too, has both terms. Villages that became cities often turned the *green* or *common* into a park, e.g. the *Boston Common* and the *New Haven Green.*

Although the term *county seat* is current in all parts of New England at the present time, the older *shire town* (85) is still in common use in the northern New England states and not unknown in Massachusetts. Some pronounce *shire* to rime with *fire,* others with *fear.*

EASTERN NEW ENGLAND

Eastern New England is characterized by many local expressions that have to do with the farm,

the house, utensils, cooking, the fauna, and the flora. On the farm we find such local expressions as *lean-to, pig sty, drag, horse and team, ox goad, double runner, cosset, harslet, whicker, co!* and *coaf!, choke!* and *chook!* Distinctive food terms are *white-bread, yeast bread, riz-bread, riz doughnut* or *raised doughnut, bonny-clapper* or *bonny-clabber, sour-milk cheese* and *curds, apple dowdy* and *pan dowdy, hogshead cheese,* and *tonic. Pogy, mummichog, cohog* or *quahog, rock maple,* and *button wood* are some of the many local expressions for fish and trees. See Figures 9 and 10.

Some of these expressions are current in all of Eastern New England, including Rhode Island, eastern Connecticut, Worcester County in Massachusetts, and the upper Connecticut Valley (from Northampton or Deerfield northward). Others are restricted to the Atlantic coast from Narragansett Bay to New Brunswick; still others are found only north of Boston, or in one or several of the subareas such as Narragansett Bay, the Plymouth area and Cape Cod, Essex County, or the Merrimack Valley.

The following expressions occur in all of Eastern New England or large parts of it.

Drag (21) is the regular name for a wheelless vehicle on which stones are dragged from the fields. It is used also on eastern Long Island and on the Connecticut shore to the mouth of the Housatonic. Western New England has *stone boat* in this sense and this expression occurs by the side of *drag* in Worcester County, Massachusetts, the upper Connecticut Valley, and to some extent on Narragansett Bay.

Boys and girls of Eastern New England coast *belly-bump(er)* or *belly-bunt* (95) down the hill on their sleds. These adverbial expressions are almost universal east of the Connecticut River and in nearly all of Vermont and are not unknown on the eastern slope of the Berkshires. *Belly-bunt* predominates in Worcester County, the upper Connecticut Valley, and in parts of Maine, *belly-bump(er)* in coastal New England.

Double runner (22) is the name of a double sled from Narragansett Bay to New Brunswick, including Worcester County and the greater part of New Hampshire. *Double runner* competes with *traverse sled* in the upper Connecticut Valley, with *double ripper* in eastern Connecticut.

In Eastern New England as well as in the lower Connecticut Valley *team* (38) often means the draft animal(s) together with the vehicle, in the coastal area sometimes the vehicle alone, as in the phrase *a horse and team.*

Goad (19) is the usual expression for the ox goad from Narragansett Bay to New Brunswick. In Maine the word usually rimes with *board.*

Sty, pig sty, hog sty (15) are fairly common in coastal New England, less so in the Connecticut Valley. Western New England has only *hog house, hog pen,* and *pig pen,* which compete with *sty* in Eastern New England.

Lean-to (15) and *tie-up* (15) are common names in eastern Massachusetts, New Hampshire, and Maine for the shed-like addition to the barn in which the cows are housed. *Lean-to* predominates in Massachusetts, *tie-up* in New Hampshire and on the coast of Maine. Both expressions are infrequent on the upper Connecticut.

Whicker (36) for *whinny* is in common use in southeastern New England (eastern Connecticut, Rhode Island, the Plymouth–Cape Cod area, and the islands of Martha's Vineyard and Nantucket) and in the greater part of Maine. The intervening section of the coast has only *whinny, whinner,* like Western New England. Maine probably derives *whicker* from the settlers that came from the Plymouth area and *whinner,* which is equally common, from Massachusetts Bay.

The cow calls *co!* and *coaf!* (37) are heard only in the coastal section of Eastern New England and to some extent on Long Island Sound. Elsewhere in New England only calls containing *boss!* are heard.

The chicken call *biddie!* (38) is current with varying frequency in all of Eastern New England beside *chick!* It is not used in Western New England except along Lake Champlain.

Harslet (37) for the edible inner organs of a pig is largely confined to coastal New England—eastern Massachusetts, New Hampshire, and Maine. Other parts of New England have mostly *pluck,* which turns up also in the Hudson Valley and farther west.

For the homemade wheat bread baked in loaves Eastern New England has *white-bread, yeast bread,* and *raised-bread* or *riz-bread* (44).

In the same area doughnuts made of raised dough are called *raised doughnuts* or *riz doughnuts* (45), the sweetened unraised variety simply *doughnuts* (45), whereas in Western New England the former are known as *doughnuts,* the latter as *crullers* or *fried-cakes.* This difference in usage gives rise to many a lively discussion in New England.

In Eastern New England *bonny-clapper* (47) or *bonny-clabber* is the usual term for curdled sour milk; and *sour-milk cheese* (47) is the common term for cottage cheese. *Bonny-clapper* is current in this entire area, except Rhode Island; *sour-milk cheese,* on the other hand, is now largely confined to the coastal area since *Dutch cheese* has spread nearly to the coast of Massachusetts.

Dowdy, pan dowdy (47) is the name of a desert made of fruit and sweetened dough—a sort of cobbler—that has currency on Massachusetts Bay and in New Hampshire and Maine, and is not unknown on Cape Cod and Narragansett Bay.

Tonic (49) for soda water is a distinctive Boston trade word which in the last two or three generations has spread southward to Cape Cod and Nantucket, up the Merrimack Valley into New Hampshire, and along the coast of Maine to the Penobscot. It is of interest to note that *tonic* has not spread to the cities on the Connecticut River or gained a foothold in Rhode Island. The Boston trade area for this commodity obviously does not extend to the Connecticut Valley or to Narragansett Bay.

Along the coast from Block Island and Nantucket to eastern Maine, *pogy* (59) is the name of a herring that is known as a *menhaden* on Long Island Sound. *Pogy* rimes with *stogy* and is not to be confused with the Connecticut *poggy,* which rimes with *foggy,* and denotes an entirely different fish—the *scup* or *scupaug* of southeastern New England.

The large clam, known as the *round clam* in most of Connecticut, has generally retained its Indian name from New London to Nantucket and from Cape Cod to Maine. From eastern Connecticut to Nantucket, including Narragan-

sett Bay, *quahog* (60)—beginning like *quarter*—
is the usual form of this word; on Massachusetts
Bay and in Maine the form is *cohog,* beginning
like *coat.* Between these two sections, notably in
the Plymouth area, both these pronunciations
are current as well as *quohog,* starting like
quote, which looks like a blend of the two.

Breezing up and *breezing on* (7), referring to
the wind, are familiar expressions on the New
England coast from eastern Long Island and the
New London area to Nantucket, and from Cape
Cod to New Brunswick.

Rock maple (61) is the distinctive name given
to the sugar maple in Eastern New England,
including the upper Connecticut Valley. *Sugar
maple* is of course also used in this area.

The sycamore is generally known as a *button
wood (tree)* in all parts of Eastern New England
where it grows. The line between the eastern
button wood (61) and the western *button ball*
follows the western boundary of Rhode Island
but runs much farther west in Massachusetts,
where the Connecticut River seems to be the
dividing line.

Some of the old coastal expressions have been
eliminated in the urbanized area of Boston and
surroundings and reduced in currency in the
Plymouth–Cape Cod area. Other words that are
found only north of Boston—in Maine, New
Hampshire, and Essex County, Massachusetts—
were formerly doubtless current on Massachusetts
Bay and in the Plymouth area. Among the expressions that are now largely confined to this
conservative northeastern sector of New England
we may mention the following:

Spindle (56), for the top of the corn stalk,
and *to spindle (out),* meaning 'top out,' occur
from Narragansett Bay to Cape Cod, and again
from Essex County, Massachusetts, to eastern
Maine. See Figure 11.

Tilt, tilting board (22) is the regular term
for the seesaw in southeastern New England
(from the islands in Narragansett Bay eastward).
This term occurs also in Essex County. In the
coast towns of New Hampshire and Maine the
variant *tilter, tilter board* is current, which is
probably a blend of the Cape Cod term *tilt* and
the Massachusetts Bay term *teeter.*

Ground mow (14), for a stack of hay extend-

ing from the barn floor to the roof, is found only
from Cape Cod to Plymouth and along the coast
of Maine. In origin it is probably a Plymouth
Colony word.

Other "Down East" expressions are: *bannock,
Indian bannock* (44) for a thin corn cake (on
the Merrimack and in Maine, with relics on
Narragansett Bay and Nantucket); *fritter* (45)
for a griddle cake (on the Merrimack and in
Maine); *pancake* (45) for a fritter cooked in
deep fat; *curd, curd cheese* (47) for cottage
cheese (in Maine and on the New Hampshire
coast); *tumble* (14) for the hay cock (in parts
of upland New Hampshire and Maine, with
relics in Worcester County, Massachusetts, and
in the Berkshires); *high-beams, great-beams* (14)
for the loft of a barn (mostly in the upper Connecticut Valley and in Worcester County, Massachusetts); *chook!, choke!* (38), a call to pigs
(from Cape Ann in Massachusetts to eastern
Maine; also on Nantucket, Martha's Vineyard,
and Block Island); *webbins* (39), denoting the
lines for driving a horse (from the Merrimack
to the Penobscot); *culch, sculch* (10) for junk,
trash (from Massachusetts Bay to Maine and
northwestward to northeastern Vermont); *funnel*
(23) for the stove pipe (from Massachusetts Bay
to eastern Maine and northwestward to the
upper Connecticut Valley); *eaves spouts* (11) for
the eaves troughs or gutters (in the upland of
Maine and New Hampshire and most of Vermont, with relics on Cape Cod, Nantucket, and
Narragansett Bay); *intervale, interval* (29) for
a river bottom (from Massachusetts Bay to
Maine and westward to Lake Champlain and
the northern Berkshires, with relics on Cape Cod
and in eastern Connecticut); *sap orchard* (61)
for the sugar maple grove (in the upland of New
Hampshire and Maine); *grand-sir* (64) for
grandfather (from Cape Ann to the Penobscot
and westward to the Connecticut River); *to
moderate* (7), with reference to the wind (on
Nantucket, Cape Cod, Cape Ann, and in scattered points along the coast of Maine); *lulling,
lulling down* (7), of the wind (on the coast of
New Hampshire and Maine); *smurring up* (5),
meaning 'getting foggy,' and *smurry* (5), meaning 'foggy, drizzly' (mostly in eastern Maine;
rarely on Cape Cod and Martha's Vineyard);

porch (11) for the kitchen ell of a house (fairly common on Martha's Vineyard and Nantucket, on Buzzards Bay and Cape Cod, and again along the coast from the Merrimack to eastern Maine, with relics on eastern Long Island and in the New London area).

The Merrimack Valley, including the northern parts of the counties of Essex and Middlesex in Massachusetts and the southeastern counties of New Hampshire, has retained some striking localisms: *teaming* (21) for 'hauling'; *blare* (36) for the loud cry of a calf; *mud worm* (60) for the earthworm; *white-arsed hornet* (60) for the white-faced hornet; *orts* (17) for garbage, and *orts pail* for the garbage pail (only in Essex County, Massachusetts); *creeper* (17) for the cast-iron frying pan (only in Essex County, now rare); *neb* (20) for the hub of a cart wheel (only in Essex County); *teedle board* or *tiddle board* (22) for the seesaw (only in Essex County).

Since Massachusetts Bay passed its vocabulary on to large sections of Eastern New England in Colonial times and became urbanized in the course of the nineteenth century, it possesses only a small number of strictly local expressions at the present time. In the material now available only two such local terms have been noted: *minnims* (61) for *minnows,* in the counties of Middlesex, Suffolk and Norfolk (cf. *minnies,* in northern New England); and *spoon hunt, spoon haunch* (62) for the mountain laurel, in Middlesex County, Massachusetts, and adjoining parts of New Hampshire (cf. *spoon wood,* in Worcester County).

Southeastern New England has the character of a relic area. On Narragansett Bay and Buzzards Bay, on Cape Cod, and on the islands of Martha's Vineyard and Nantucket a considerable number of distinctive local expressions have survived in the countryside. See Figure 12.

Some of these expressions are current from Narragansett Bay to Cape Cod, an area comprising the original Providence and Rhode Island Plantations and the Plymouth Colony: *tempest* (6) for a storm (from New London and Block Island to Cape Cod and Nantucket, and northward almost to Boston); *quahog* (60) for the large round clam (from New London to Cape Cod and Nantucket, contrasting with the *cohog* of Massachusetts Bay, which has intruded itself into the Plymouth area and Martha's Vineyard); *scup* (59) for a small fish with a large head that is known as a *poggy* or *porgy* in Connecticut (from Narragansett Bay to Cape Cod and Nantucket); *mummichog* (61) for the salt-water minnow (from New London to Martha's Vineyard); *cade* (35) for a pet lamb, and the sheep call *cade!* (from Narragansett Bay to Cape Cod); *coop!* (38), a call to chickens (on lower Narragansett Bay and eastern Long Island). *Rare-ripe* (55) for the spring onion is common on Narragansett Bay, Martha's Vineyard, and Nantucket, but it occurs also in Essex County, Massachusetts, and in the Connecticut Valley towns from Middletown to Windsor.

Other expressions are found only on Narragansett Bay, which has had a commercial and cultural life of its own from the earliest Colonial days to the present: *closet* (10) for the pantry; *loft* (14) for the barn loft (a term that rarely has this meaning elsewhere in New England); *johnny cake* (44) for a corn griddle cake (known as a *Rhode Island johnny cake* in eastern Connecticut, to distinguish it from *johnny cake* in the sense of 'corn bread'); *apple slump* (47) for a deep-dish apple pie; *dandle* (22) for the seesaw (only west of the Bay); *eace worm* (60A) for the earthworm (only west of the Bay); *shacket* (60) for the yellow-jacket (only west of the Bay); *horning* (82) for the mock serenade (only west of the Bay); *pig's squin* (37) for the edible inner organs of a pig (only east of the Bay); *Dutch cap* or *hay cap* (14) for a hay stack with a sliding roof (only east of the Bay); *cob pie* (47) for a deep-dish apple pie (only on Aquidneck, including Newport).

In contrast to Narragansett Bay, the Plymouth–Cape Cod area has preserved rather few unique expressions, among them *apple grunt* (47) for a deep-dish apple pie, *cleave-stone* (54) for the freestone peach, and *hooked Jack* (83) for 'played hooky.'

The islands off-shore share the localisms of the mainland, but a few strictly local words have been noted: *tippity-bounce* (22) for the seesaw, on Block Island; *mummichims* or *chims* (61) for the salt-water minnows, on Martha's Vineyard; and *masculine* (33) for the bull, on Nantucket.

The upper Connecticut Valley derives its vocabulary largely from Eastern New England. Other expressions were introduced by Connecticut settlers from the lower part of the Valley, especially around Hanover.

Purely local expressions are rare. One of them is *chivaree* (82), for the mock serenade, which is current in the northern third of Vermont from Lake Champlain eastward, and north of the White Mountains in New Hampshire. Since *chivaree* is found also in New Brunswick and adjoining parts of northern Maine, it may be of Canadian origin. The New England coast from Cape Cod to Maine has only *serenade*.

Traverse sled (22), for the double sled, is another. It is in general use in Vermont and adjoining parts of New Hampshire and occurs also, by the side of the coastal term *double runner*, in the Merrimack Valley and on the Androscoggin in Maine. *Traverse* probably comes from French-speaking Canada.

In addition to *sugar orchard* and *sugar bush*, the northernmost part of the Connecticut Valley, where the making of maple syrup and maple sugar is an important industry, has the strictly local expression *sugar place* (61).

THE HUDSON VALLEY

Relics of Dutch vocabulary are a characteristic feature of the Hudson Valley, the Catskills, and the upper Delaware.

In East Jersey and on the upper Delaware, here and there also in the Hudson Valley, farmers still call their cows with a *kush!* (riming with *bush*) or *kushie!* (37) as well as with the New England *boss!* or *bossie!* In the Albany area *sto!* (37) is heard beside *so!* at milking time, in Bergen County, New Jersey, *tytie!*, riming with *mighty*, when a cow is restless. *Tye!* (37), riming with *high*, is still a common call to calves in East Jersey, and *kees!* or *kish!* ($\overline{37}$) is occasionally heard on the upper Delaware and in the Catskills. The chicken call *kip!* (38) has survived all the way from Bergen County, New Jersey, to the Mohawk Valley. None of these calls occurs outside the Dutch settlement area, and they are, therefore, presumably of Dutch or Flemish origin.

Some food terms of Dutch origin have spread beyond the Dutch area, notably *cruller* and *pot cheese,* but others, such as *olicook* (45) for a doughnut, *rollichies* for meat roulades (see *The Dictionary of American English*), and *thick-milk* (47) for curdled milk, have probably always been Dutch family words and are disappearing fast. See Figures 13 and 14.

Kill (30) for a brook is no longer used as a common noun but appears in the names of streams throughout the Dutch settlement area, as in *Batten Kill, Catskill Creek. Killie fish, killie* or *kellie* (61), which are used on both sides of Long Island Sound and in East Jersey for a small bait fish that abounds in brackish inlets (see *The Dictionary of American English* under *killifish*), come from this Dutch word for a stream.

The preservation of *right* (64) in such expressions as *right good, right smart* in the Hudson Valley is probably in part due to Dutch phraseology.

The present spread of the Hudson Valley words *barrack, pot cheese, suppawn,* and *skimerton* reflects rather clearly the limit of the Dutch settlement area and its strongholds.

Pot cheese (47) for cottage cheese is in regular use in East Jersey, all of Long Island, and the Hudson Valley, and has become fully established in the Housatonic Valley in Connecticut. In the Mohawk Valley it competes with *Dutch cheese. Pot cheese* renders the Dutch *pot kees.*

Skimerton or *skimilton* (82) for the mock serenade is current in a well-defined area extending from the Housatonic in Connecticut to the upper Delaware in northeastern Pennsylvania, including the lower Hudson Valley and the Catskills. The Albany area has the New England expression *horning. Skimerton* comes from the British Isles.

Barrack (14), an adaptation of Dutch *hooiberg* denoting a square hay stack with a sliding roof, is found in the valleys of the Hudson and the Mohawk and on Long Island.

Suppawn (50), accented on the second syllable and not infrequently reduced to *spawn*, especially in the phrase *spawn and milk,* is a common name for corn meal mush in the Hudson Valley. It is of Indian origin.

The adverbial expressions *belly-wop, belly-wopper(s), belly-wopping* (95), referring to coasting face-down on a sled, are in regular use from Long Island to East Jersey. In the Albany area the Connecticut expression *belly-gut, belly-gutter* is more common, but *belly-wop* and its variants are also heard here and are not unknown in western Connecticut.

Some Hudson Valley words have spread westward in New York State and eastward into New England, where they usually stand by the side of New England expressions.

Thus we find the Dutch term *stoop* (10) for a small porch in common use not only in the entire Dutch settlement area from East Jersey and Long Island to Albany, but also in the greater part of New England and the New England settlement area in western New York State and northern Pennsylvania.

Saw buck (22), patterned on the Dutch *zaagbock*, stands by the side of *saw horse* in the Dutch settlement area as well as in western New York State and the western fringe of New England. In northeastern Pennsylvania this Dutch *saw buck* area adjoins the Pennsylvania German *saw buck* area.

Teeter-totter (22) for the seesaw predominates in East Jersey, on Long Island, in the lower Hudson Valley, and in adjoining parts of Connecticut, and competes with the New England *teeter, teeter board* in the Albany area and westward to Lake Erie.

Teeter-totter even occurs in the New England settlements around Marietta beside the more common *teeter (board)*. Both expression are of English origin.

Coal scuttle (23) is doubtless an old Hudson Valley term, and as such it has spread westward to Lake Erie. From East Jersey and Long Island to Albany it is almost universal; even in western New York State it is more common than the New England term *coal hod*. It should be noted that this British term became established independently in the Hudson Valley, on Delaware Bay, and in large parts of the South. New York and New Jersey Loyalists carried it to New Brunswick during the Revolution.

Gutters (11) is used to the exclusion of other terms on the lower Hudson and on Long Island,

but in the Albany area the New England *eaves troughs* competes with it. Here as in Eastern New England and in the South *gutters* is old.

The Dutch word *cruller* (45) for a doughnut has spread far beyond the Dutch settlement area, but, significantly enough, not into Upstate New York, where the New England term *fried-cake* is fully established. Its center of dispersion is the lower Hudson Valley. From here it spread southward to Delaware Bay (Philadelphia) and to the head of Chesapeake Bay (Baltimore), and eastward on Long Island Sound to Narragansett Bay, and then northward into nearly all of southern New England. *Cruller* came into New England too late to be carried westward in the New England migration to New York State and beyond.

The Hudson Valley has two expressions for the sugar maple grove, *sugar bush* and *sap bush* (61). *Sugar bush* has spread into Western New England and has come to be fully established in western New York State and northern Pennsylvania; *sap bush*, on the other hand, occurs only in the valleys of the Hudson and the Mohawk. *Sap bush* is an Anglicized form of the Dutch term; *sugar bush* looks like a blend of *sap bush* and *sugar orchard*, a common term in Western New England.

Although it is clear indeed that Hudson Valley words like *stoop, cruller, pot cheese,* and *sugar bush* have spread into New England—along Long Island Sound and from there up the rivers—we must admit that regional terms of English origin could establish themselves independently on the Hudson and on the Connecticut. This seems to have occurred in the case of *button ball* and *loppered milk.*

Button ball (61) is the regular name for the sycamore from the lower Connecticut Valley to East Jersey and in the greater part of New York State. The *button wood* of Eastern New England is unknown both in the old Connecticut Valley settlements and on the Hudson south of Albany.

Loppered milk (47) for curdled milk, as distinct from *lobbered milk*, occurs in Western New England from Connecticut to Vermont, in the Hudson Valley, and on Long Island. Since Vermont derives this expression from Connecticut, it must be old there. The occurrence of

loppered milk west of the lower Hudson—in the
Catskills—favors the assumption that it is old
in the Hudson Valley as well, although *thick-
milk*, which is modeled on the Dutch term, has
been handed down in Dutch families.

In conclusion we may mention a number of
terms that may be rather recent innovations in
the Hudson Valley.

Fish worm (60) for the earthworm is common
in the valleys of the Hudson and the Mohawk
and on the upper Delaware, but instances of the
New England *angle worm* are scattered all the
way through this section.

Snack (48) for a bite to eat is in general use
in Greater New York City and has spread to the
cities on the Hudson and the Mohawk.

School gets out (83) for *school lets out* is a
localism that has not spread much beyond
Greater New York City.

In Greater New York City and in the urbanized area surrounding it the regional and local
expressions of the farming sections have largely
been abandoned.

This part of the Hudson Valley has, therefore,
the negative characteristic of lacking such expressions. Positive local features doubtless occur in
the urban vocabulary of Greater New York as
they clearly do in matters of pronunciation, but
the evidence is yet to be gathered.

East Jersey is a part of the Hudson Valley
area; West Jersey, on the other hand, belongs to
the Delaware Bay section of the Midland.

East Jersey is now dominated by Greater New
York City and has been within the New York
trade area since colonial times.

In the northern part of East Jersey, notably
in Bergen County, Dutch could be heard until
recently, and there are a few individuals even
now who still know Dutch. It is, therefore, not
surprising that unique relics of Dutch calls to
farm stock are current here such as *kush!* (37)
to cows and *tye!* (37) to calves.

New Englandisms are common in all of East
Jersey, but especially in the Newark-Elizabeth
section and on the Raritan with their early New
England settlements. Some New England expressions have spread southward along the Atlantic coast to Delaware Bay: *carting* (21) for
hauling and the cow call *co!* (37). The presence

of New England settlements on Cape May ac-
counts in part for this phenomenon. The rare
call *hoist!* (38) on Delaware Bay is matched only
by the equally rare *hoist!* and *hie!* of New England, which is probably its immediate source.

On the Jersey side of the Delaware River a
number of unique expressions have been noted:
the hog call *poo-ie!* (38), which became established around Wheeling on the upper Ohio;
crib house (14) for the corn crib (only on Delaware Bay); *stone row* (16) for the stone fence
(only on the upper Delaware); and *swivel tree*
(21) for the whiffletree (north of Trenton).

Spindle (60A) for the dragon fly is the only
unique New Jersey expression so far noted which
is used in the greater part of the state—beside
darning needle in East Jersey, beside *snake doctor* on Delaware Bay (but not on the upper
Delaware, where *snake feeder* prevails).

WESTERN NEW ENGLAND AND LONG ISLAND SOUND

So large a part of the regional vocabulary of
Western New England was carried westward to
the Great Lakes that this section of New England, in contrast to Eastern New England, possesses rather few unique vocabulary items. Most
of these survivals are local in character.

Thus *angle dog* (60) is a Windsor Colony word
for the earthworm; *calathump* (82) for the mock
serenade is peculiar to the New Haven Colony
(relics of this term on the Delaware are of independent British descent); *ivy* (62) for the mountain laurel, and the variants *tinter, teenter* (22)
of *teeter* for the seesaw, are confined to the New
Haven Colony, the Connecticut Valley towns,
and their daughter settlements in Litchfield
County and the southern Berkshires; *top gallant*
(56) for the top of a corn stalk is largely restricted to Fairfield County in southwestern
Connecticut (Danbury).

Expressions that are current in the greater
part of southwestern New England—Connecticut
and western Massachusetts—but did not strike
root in the New England settlements west of the
Hudson are few in number. Some of these are
terms for things that did not exist or persist in
the new environment, such as *round clam* (60)
for the large salt-water clam and *green* (85) for
the village green. But in other cases the failure

to preserve the term in the new settlements is not obvious. Whatever the reason, *double ripper* (22) for a double sled appears to be confined to Connecticut and western Massachusetts.

LONG ISLAND SOUND

On Long Island Sound coastwise shipping from the earliest days until recent times and the commercial relations of the New England fisheries with New York City have served to disseminate words along the deeply indented Connecticut shore to Narragansett Bay and sometimes even to Martha's Vineyard and Nantucket. On the other hand, this whole area has also preserved striking localisms.

Among the terms that are current over long stretches of the Sound we find such fish names as *menhaden* (60) for a herring (as far east as Narragansett Bay), *poggy* or *porgy* (59) for a large-headed fish that is known as a *scup* from Narragansett Bay eastward, *round clam* or *hard clam* (60) for the large sea clam which has retained its Indian name *quahog* or *cohog* from Narragansett Bay eastward.

Scattered relics on Long Island Sound are: *pightle* (15), for a cow pen, on eastern Long Island; *hog boist* (15), with the vowel of *bite*, for the hog house (near Guilford, Connecticut, and on Point Judith at the mouth of Narragansett Bay).

THE MIDLAND AREA

The northern boundary of the Midland area coincides with the southern boundary of the Northern area, which has been described above (p. 12). It is more sharply defined in Pennsylvania than in New Jersey, where a complicated settlement history and the old lines of communication between Philadelphia and New York City intersecting the settlement boundary have frayed the word lines. We shall also have occasion to note the spreading of some Northern expressions from the New York area to Philadelphia and environs.

The southern boundary of the Midland runs along the crest of the Blue Ridge in Virginia. North of the Potomac the line turns east and sweeps in an arc through Baltimore to the Atlantic below Dover in Delaware. In Maryland

west of Chesapeake Bay this line is clearly defined. On the Eastern Shore, where Delaware Bay expressions have often spread far southward under Philadelphia influence, the boundary is less sharp.

South of the James River the Midland boundary swerves out into the piedmont and embraces a large section of the North Carolina piedmont. This southern sector of the Midland boundary is less sharply defined than the middle sector in Virginia because Southern expressions have mingled with the old Midland terms in the Blue Ridge south of the James and in the Appalachians to a much greater extent than farther north. Moreover, some Midland features have been carried down the valleys of the Cape Fear and the Yadkin-Peedee to the Atlantic coast.

The Midland area extends westward to the Ozarks and beyond. West of Pennsylvania its northern boundary runs through the central part of Ohio, northern Indiana, and central Illinois. The systematic survey of the speech of the Great Lakes Basin and the Ohio Valley, which is being carried out under the direction of A. H. Marckwardt of the University of Michigan, provides the localized material for drawing this line.[1]

The southern boundary of the Midland in Georgia and farther west is as yet unknown. It probably runs somewhat to the north of the cotton lands.[2]

The boundaries of the Midland and the major features of its inner dialectal structure are set forth in the maps given below by means of representative word boundaries (isoglosses).

The Delaware Bay area and the Pennsylvania German area—the oldest parts of the Midland area in point of settlement—are the most distinctive subareas of the Midland.

The Midland is not a uniform speech area, but it has a considerable body of words that sets it off from the North and the South. Its chief subareas are (1) Eastern Pennsylvania and West Jersey, in which the Pennsylvania German area is embedded, (2) Western Pennsylvania and Northern West Virginia, and (3) the Southern

---

[1] H. Kurath, "Dialect Areas, Settlement Areas, and Culture Areas in the United States," p. 341 in *The Cultural Approach to History*, ed. Caroline R. Ware. New York, 1940.
[2] Paullin and Wright, *AHG*, plate 142.

Appalachians and the Blue Ridge south of the James River. The crest of the Alleghenies separates Eastern Pennsylvania from Western Pennsylvania; the northern watershed of the Kanawha forms the boundary of the Southern Appalachians. It will be convenient to refer to Eastern Pennsylvania and West Jersey as the Philadelphia area, to Western Pennsylvania as the Pittsburgh area, and to group them together as the North Midland. The Southern Appalachians and the Blue Ridge south of the James are conveniently called the South Midland. The Pittsburgh area and the South Midland together constitute the West Midland, i.e. the Midland exclusive of the Philadelphia area.

Table II presents expressions that illustrate various types of geographic distribution within the Midland area, and incidentally the not infrequent overlapping into the Chesapeake Bay area, which is a part of the Southern speech area.

Some expressions are used throughout the Midland, others in all of the Midland except the Delaware Bay area, some in all of the North Midland (including the Shenandoah Valley and northern West Virginia); others are largely confined to Pennsylvania, to Pennsylvania east of the Alleghenies (including the Shenandoah Valley), or to the Pennsylvania German area and south-central Pennsylvania, and still others to the South Midland.

THE MIDLAND

The expressions that characterize the Midland as a whole and set it off from the North and the South largely belong to the sphere of the house and the farm. See Figures 15 and 16.

The roller shades inside the windows are called the *blinds* (9). This term has general currency on the lower and the middle course of the Susquehanna, in western Maryland, in the Valley of Virginia, the Blue Ridge province of North Carolina, and the entire section lying to the west. It has been carried southward into nearly all of Delamarvia and has become established in Baltimore (but not in Annapolis). On the other hand, it is no longer common on the Delaware and in southern New Jersey. The modern expression *roller shades* has taken its place in Philadelphia and among the Pennsylvania

TABLE II
THE MIDLAND AREA

✕ regular — fairly common · rare	South Midland				North Midland					Maryland	
	Cape Fear Valley	Western North Carolina	West Virginia	Valley of Virginia	Ohio	Western Pennsylvania	Central Pennsylvania	Great Valley	Delaware Bay	Western Shore	Eastern Shore
(1) The Midland											
blinds (9)	·	—	✕	✕	✕	✕	✕	✕	—	·	✕
skillet (17)	·	—	✕	✕	✕	✕	✕	✕	✕	—	—
spouting, spouts (11)	·	—	✕	·	✕	✕	✕	✕	✕	—	—
(little) piece (39) ...	✕	✕	✕	·	—	✕	✕	✕	✕	·	✕
to hull (55)	—	✕	—	—	·	—	—	—	—	✕	—
(arm) load (19)	—	✕	—	·	·	✕	·	✕			✕
snake feeder (60) ...	—	—	·		✕	✕	✕	✕	·		
sook! (37)	✕	✕	✕	✕	✕	✕	✕	—	·		
bawl (36)	—	✕	✕	✕	✕	✕	✕	✕	—		
want off (85)	✕	✕	✕	✕	✕	✕	✕	✕	—		
quarter till (5)	✕	✕	✕	✕	—	✕	·				
(2) The Midland without Delaware Bay					·						
poke (19)	✕	✕	—	—	✕	✕	·				
green-beans (55)	✕	✕	—	✕	✕	—	·				
sugar tree (61)	—	✕	—	·	✕	✕	—				
lead horse (39)	·	—	✕	—	·	✕	✕	—			
lamp oil (24)	—	✕	—	—	✕	✕					
you'ns (43)	—	✕	·		✕	✕	·				
(3) The North Midland and Chesapeake Bay											
stone fence (16)	—	—	✕	✕	✕	✕	✕		✕	✕	
worm fence (16)	·	✕	·	—	—	✕	—	✕		✕	✕
jag (19)			✕	✕	✕	—	✕	—	✕	
run (30)	—	✕	✕	✕	✕	✕	✕	✕		
smear case (47)	—	✕	✕	✕	✕	✕	✕	✕	✕	✕
side meat (46)	·	—	✕	✕	✕	—	—	✕		
(eat a) piece (48)	✕	✕	—	·						
(4) Eastern Pennsylvania and Chesapeake Bay					·						
coal oil (24)	—	—	·		✕	✕	✕	✕	✕		
flannel cakes (45) ...	·	—	✕	✕	✕	✕	—				
pavement (31)			✕	✕	✕	✕	✕				
snake doctor (60) ...	—	✕	—	—	✕	—					
baby coach (64)			—	—	✕	✕					
rick (14)	·	·	✕	·	·	✕	✕	✕			
(5) Pennsylvania											
ponhaws (46)	—	✕	✕	✕							
clook (36)	✕	✕	✕	—							
school leaves out (83)	—	✕	✕	—							
flitch of bacon (46) ..	—	✕	—	—							
thick-milk (47)	—	✕	✕	—							
overhead (14)	—	—	✕	—							
button wood (61) ...	·	✕	—	✕							

TABLE II *(Continued)*

	South Midland				North Midland					Mary-land	
× regular — fairly common . rare	Cape Fear Valley	Western North Carolina	West Virginia	Valley of Virginia	Ohio	Western Pennsylvania	Central Pennsylvania	Great Valley	Delaware Bay	Western Shore	Eastern Shore
(6) Central Pennsylvania and the South Midland											
saw buck (22)		—	.	—		.	×	×	.		
vootsie! (38)		.	.	—		.	×	×			
hommie! (37)		.	.	—			—	×			
saddle horse (39) ...	.	—		—			—	×	×		
fossnocks (45)		.					—	×	×		
fat-cakes (45)		.					—	×	×		
till 'by the time' (89)		.					×	×			
(7) Western Pennsylvania and Northern West Virginia											
baby buggy (64)		—	.		×	×	—				
sugar camp (61)		—	.			—	.				
(8) The South Midland											
jacket (27)	—	×	—	—		.			.		
fire board (8)	—	×	—	.							
milk gap (15)		—	×	—							
sugar orchard (61) ..		—	×	—							
clabber milk (47) ...		×	—								

Germans, and the coastal *curtain,* supported by New England usage in New Jersey, is rather widely used in the Delaware Valley and on Delaware Bay. As a trade word *shades* is now making a place for itself in large parts of the Midland.

In all of the Midland the flat-bottomed cast-iron frying pan is called a *skillet* (17), elsewhere mostly a *spider. Skillet* has spread to northwestern New Jersey and well into Delamarvia, perhaps as a Philadelphia trade word, although the term is no longer current in the city of Philadelphia. It is possible, however, that Delamarvia has this expression of old, since it is also rather widely current in Maryland west of the Bay and in the northern piedmont of Virginia, and sporadic instances of it are found even south of the James. *Skillet* appears in this sense also from the eastern tip of Long Island to Nantucket, an area in which the New England *spider* pre-

dominates. If we must grant, then, that *skillet* is current in several different settlement areas, it is nevertheless true that it is now primarily a Midland word.

In Philadelphia this regional term has been replaced by *frying pan,* which has a wide currency in all urban areas.

The gutters on the roof are known as the *spouting* or the *spouts* (11) in the Midland, except for West Jersey and the Blue Ridge. *Spouting* predominates over *spouts* everywhere within this area except on the Delaware and in the southern part of West Virginia. In Philadelphia and vicinity *gutters* is the usual designation. The Valley of Virginia and the Blue Ridge in the Carolinas have adopted the Southern *gutters.*

Instead of *a little way* (e.g. *a little way down the road*), or by the side of it, the Midland has the expression *a little piece* (39). This use of *piece* has spread nearly all the way down through Delamarvia from the Philadelphia area and has pushed its way down to the sea between the Cape Fear and the Peedee from the North Carolina piedmont. On the other hand, Piedmont influence has eliminated it almost entirely in the Valley of Virginia. The Midland origin of this expression is beyond doubt since it is found only in those two sections outside the Midland to which Midland features have often spread.

To hull beans (55A) instead of *to shell beans* is a Midland expression that has lost much ground. It is still common on the lower Susquehanna and in the Ohio Valley, less so in the Alleghenies, in West Virginia, and in the Blue Ridge (as far south as North Carolina). It is rather well established in the greater part of Maryland, perhaps as an importation from the Susquehanna Valley.

Arm load and *load* (19) are distinctive Midland expressions for an armful of wood. *Arm load* predominates in the North Midland, *load* in the South Midland. The term *armful* stands by the side of *arm load* in the North Midland and has nearly eliminated it in the Great Valley of Pennsylvania and in the Pittsburgh area; on Delaware Bay, however, *arm load* is well established.

The Midland term for kindling wood is *pine, fat-pine, rich-pine, pitch pine* (8). Although the record of usage is not complete, it is clear that *pine* is current in this sense from Delaware Bay westward and as far south as the Blue Ridge in North Carolina. *Kindling* seems to compete with it only in the Philadelphia area.

The distinctive Midland term for the dragon fly is *snake feeder* (60), which is found in the Delaware Valley above Trenton and westward. It is in regular use in central and western Pennsylvania and in the Ohio Valley, as well as in the Blue Ridge province of North Carolina and the westernmost part of Virginia. In large parts of West Virginia the Virginia Piedmont term *snake doctor* is now more common than *snake feeder,* and in the Shenandoah Valley the Midland term has been almost entirely abandoned. The common occurrence of *snake doctor* on either side of Delaware Bay as well as on the lower Susquehanna makes it probable that both *snake feeder* and *snake doctor* have been current in the Philadelphia area since Colonial times.

The Midland call to cows and calves is *sook!* or *sookie!* (37), usually undifferentiated. East of the Susquehanna, however, this call is often used only to calves. As a calf call *sook(ie)* has spread up the Delaware into northwestern New Jersey and from the Carolina piedmont down into the Low Country of South Carolina, areas which have separate calls for cows. The Pennsylvania Germans have largely retained their German calls in Eastern Pennsylvania, the Shenandoah Valley, and northern West Virginia.

Sheep!, sheepie! (38) is the regular Midland call to sheep. In the Appalachians south of the Kanawha the Virginia Piedmont call *co-sheep!* now competes with the Midland call. On Delaware Bay and the lower Delaware only a few of the older people remember a call to sheep.

Cows whose calves are being weaned are said to *bawl* (36). This expression is current throughout the Midland, including West Jersey, except only the Pennsylvania German settlements of Eastern Pennsylvania. It occurs sporadically in New York State, but nowhere else.

Constructions like *I want in* and *I want off* for *I want to go in* and *I want to get off* are familiar to us from the language of Shakespeare and his contemporaries. We know them also vaguely as a feature of regional folk speech in America. The records of the *Linguistic Atlas* show that *I want off* (85) is in common use in nearly all of the Midland, except among the best educated, and that it is not current at all in the North and the South. In the Delaware Valley and on the Jersey side of Delaware Bay this construction is now very rare, but it is well preserved in northern Delaware and still used by some of the older folks in Philadelphia.

In the greater part of the Midland the phrase *quarter till eleven* (5) is current. In south-central Pennsylvania and the entire Midland area lying to the south of Pennsylvania *till* is the usual preposition in this phrase, which has also found acceptance in a wide corridor leading from the North Carolina piedmont down the Cape Fear River to the sea. *Till* is used also on the upper Susquehanna and on the Allegheny River, but in the greater part of the Philadelphia area *of* is regularly employed, and in the immediate vicinity of Pittsburgh we find *of* or *to*. This example illustrates the fact that expressions of Pennsylvania origin are sometimes more extensively preserved in the Pennsylvania settlements to the south than in Pennsylvania itself.

THE WEST MIDLAND

Some expressions that are now found in the broad expanse of the West Midland—from Western Pennsylvania to South Carolina—were formerly also current in Eastern Pennsylvania, others not. Whenever sporadic instances of such expressions exist east of the Susquehanna we may be sure that they are relics of older usage in an area that has introduced many innovations. When such relics are lacking we *may* have a truly "Western" expression, i.e. one that was not current in the early English settlements on the Delaware. See Figure 17.

Poke (19) as the name of a paper bag is in general use in the West Midland. The Shenandoah Valley and the ridge and valley section of Pennsylvania between the Alleghenies and the Susquehanna also have it, but not the Great Valley, where the Pennsylvania German *toot* (riming with *foot*) is current, nor the valley of the Delaware.

Green-beans (55A) for string beans is another West Midland term. It is in regular use in West

Virginia, in the Ohio Valley, and in North Carolina from the Yadkin westward, and fairly common in Western Pennsylvania. Between the crest of the Alleghenies and the Susquehanna and in the Valley of Virginia it is no longer widely used. East of the Susquehanna it has been almost entirely displaced by *string beans,* which predominates also in central Pennsylvania and is encroaching upon the Pittsburgh area from the east and the north. In Virginia and North Carolina the southern *snap beans* is spreading westward.

From Western Pennsylvania to the Blue Ridge in North Carolina the sugar maple is called a *sugar tree* (61). In West Virginia and the southwestern corner of Pennsylvania this is the regular term; elsewhere in the West Midland *sugar maple* is equally common now and is clearly gaining ground. *Sugar tree* is still heard here and there in the Valley of Virginia and in south-central Pennsylvania.

The Midland has four different words for the left-hand horse of a team, *lead horse, near-horse, nigh-horse,* and *saddle horse. Lead horse* (39) is the regular expression in two large sections: (1) Pennsylvania from the Susquehanna Valley westward, and (2) the Appalachians and the Blue Ridge south of the Kanawha-James River line. Between these two sections lies the *near-horse* area of northern West Virginia. South-central Pennsylvania is probably the original home of *lead horse,* as *nigh-horse* is almost certainly the old word for the *near-horse* on Delaware Bay (the English settlements around Philadelphia).

The West Midland word for kerosene is *lamp oil* (24). In Pennsylvania it occurs only west of the Alleghenies, in West Virginia it has full sway except for the upper reaches of the Potomac, in Western North Carolina and adjoining parts of Virginia it competes with *kerosene.* Since West Virginia was the source of this commodity for the Piedmont of Virginia, *lamp oil* has become established there, too. The Shenandoah Valley and the northern Piedmont have adopted *coal oil* from Eastern Pennsylvania.

The simple folk of the Midland employ *you'ns* (43) as the plural of *you.* This usage is common in Pennsylvania from the middle course of the Susquehanna westward to the Ohio State line, and in northern West Virginia. It is not found on the lower Susquehanna and does not seem to survive in Ohio. In the South Midland *you'ns* is being replaced by the Southern *you-all,* which has already eliminated this Midland form in the Valley of Virginia and on the upper reaches of the Potomac in West Virginia.

THE NORTH MIDLAND

The North Midland includes West Jersey, Pennsylvania and adjoining parts of Maryland, the Shenandoah Valley, northern West Virginia, and the parts of Ohio adjoining Pennsylvania and northern West Virginia.

West of the Blue Ridge the southern boundaries of North Midland words tend to follow the northern watershed of the Kanawha; i.e. the valleys of the Shenandoah, of the upper Potomac, and of the Monongahela are apt to have these Pennsylvania expressions. However, some of these expressions do not extend as far south as the watershed, whereas others are found also in the Kanawha Valley. All of northern West Virginia is really a transition belt between the North Midland and the South Midland. See Figure 18.

For a fence built of loose stone the North Midland uses *stone fence* (16) as against the Northern *stone wall* and the Southern *rock fence.* This Midland expression has become established in East Jersey, in all of Delaware and Maryland, and even between the Potomac and the Rappahannock in Virginia. In northern West Virginia *stone fence* is in competition with the Southern *rock fence,* which has general currency in the South Midland.

Worm fence (16) is a distinctive Midland term for a rail fence laid zigzag fashion, which is known simply as a *rail fence* in the North and the South. On the periphery of the Midland the simple *rail fence* is quite common; on the other hand, *worm fence* is current in East Jersey, on Delamarvia, and to some extent in the northern Piedmont of Virginia.

A part-load of corn, wood, etc., is called a *jag* (19) in Pennsylvania, West Jersey, Delaware, Maryland, and on the upper reaches of the Potomac in West Virginia. The expression does not occur on the Virginia side of the Potomac and is therefore clearly of Midland origin in Maryland.

In all of the North Midland a small fresh stream, tributary to a river or a creek, is called a *run* (30). This expression is found in all of Pennsylvania (except for the New England settlements in the northeastern part of the state), in northern West Virginia, and in the adjoining parts of Ohio; also on Delaware Bay (but not in the greater part of Delamarvia) and in Maryland west of the Bay. In southern Maryland (the counties of St. Mary's and Charles) *run* is clearly of Southern origin, since this term is also in common use in the Tidewater of Virginia, where *creek* refers to a tidal inlet.

Run appears in the names of many small streams throughout the North Midland, so that even those who no longer use *run* as a common noun have occasion to refer to a particular stream in the neighborhood as *the run*.

Smear case (47) is the common name for cottage cheese in the North Midland from West Jersey to Ohio as well as in the Valley of Virginia and all except the southernmost part of West Virginia. Moreover, as a Philadelphia trade word it has spread southward throughout Delamarvia and Maryland west of the Bay and has gained a foothold on the Northern Neck of Virginia. In Pennsylvania *smear case* (from Pennsylvania German *Schmierkäs*) is the only popular term for cottage cheese; elsewhere it competes with various regional folk words. It is the only Pennsylvania German term that has spread considerably beyond the area in which Palatine Germans settled in larger numbers. Under the circumstances it is rather surprising that the term has not survived in the large Palatine settlements on the Yadkin.

In contrast to Northern *salt pork* and Southern *middlin(s)* the North Midland has the expression *side meat* (46). In the Valley of Virginia and on the Kanawha *side meat* stands beside *middlin(s)*, and this Southern term has also gained a foothold in northern West Virginia. In the Ohio Valley below Wheeling *side of meat*, *side of pork* are commonly used as alternate expressions to *side meat*. (Note that *side meat* is also found on the Carolina coast.)

Eat a piece (48), as against the Northern *eat a bite* and the Southern *eat a snack*, is a characteristic expression of the Midland which is current as far south as the James-Kanawha line. Along the southern margin of this area *piece meal* stands beside *piece*, and there are relics of it in the Pennsylvania settlements of Western North Carolina. In Philadelphia and vicinity *bite* is now more common than *piece; snack*, too, has made a place for itself in this city in recent times.

Piece is also used in northwestern New Jersey and, beside *bite*, in New York State west of the Hudson. If this is an importation from the Midland it has few parallels.

PENNSYLVANIA

Not all expressions that Eastern and Western Pennsylvania have in common have been carried southward into the Blue Ridge and the Appalachians. Among the terms that have not crossed the Pennsylvania line, although they occur both east and west of the Alleghenies, we may mention *flitch*, and several expressions of Pennsylvania German origin or background: *overhead, ponhaws, clook*, and *school leaves out*. See Figure 19.

The expression *flitch of bacon, flitch of side meat* (46) for a side of bacon, smoked or cured in brine, is current from the lower Delaware to the Allegheny River. This term is in general use in the central part of the state; elsewhere it competes with the regional term *side meat*.

Overhead (14), denoting the loft or a raised platform over the barn floor, occurs all the way from the Delaware to the fork of the Ohio. Scattered through the southeastern half of this area we find *over-den*, a borrowing from Pennsylvania German (cf. German *Obertenne*), which may also have prompted the coining of *overhead*.

Ponhaws (46), a synonym of *(Philadelphia) scrapple*, is in use from the Pennsylvania German section westward to Ohio and has survived also on the upper reaches of the Potomac in Maryland and West Virginia. The Pennsylvania German *ponhaws* corresponds phonetically to a Standard German *Pfannhase*, which literally means 'pan rabbit.'

For a setting hen one commonly hears in Pennsylvania the term *clook* (36), riming with *cook,* sometimes *cluck* or *clucker.* The expression is borrowed from the Pennsylvania German *kluck,* which corresponds to German *Klucke.* It is not common on the Delaware or west of the Monongahela in the southwestern corner of the state. The derogatory phrase *dumb cluck* obviously contains this word.

School leaves out (83), instead of *lets out,* is the usual expression in common speech from the Delaware to the Allegheny River. The westernmost part of the state does not have it, and it is less general west of the Alleghenies than farther east. The expression is not used on Delaware Bay. The confusion in the application of *let* and *leave* to render German *lassen* suggests that *leaves* has a Pennsylvania German background in this expression. The geographic distribution confirms this suspicion.

From the Susquehanna to the Allegheny River *fire bug* (60) is a common expression for the lightning bug. *Fire bug* is probably a blend of *lightning bug* and *fire fly.* The former is current everywhere, the latter was brought by the New England settlers to the northern counties of the state and may have been more widely current in Eastern Pennsylvania in earlier days, as its occurrence on the conservative Jersey shore of Delaware Bay suggests. See Figure 142.

EASTERN PENNSYLVANIA AND CHESAPEAKE BAY

Pennsylvania east of the Alleghenies is rather highly diversified in speech, as one would expect in view of its complicated settlement history. The English Quakers on the lower Delaware River and on either side of Delaware Bay, the Palatine Germans to the west of them in the Great Valley and on the Susquehanna, and the Ulster Scots in the Valley and Ridge province beyond constituted three distinct ethnic and cultural groups that were numerically fairly equally matched by the time of the Revolution. Furthermore, the conflicting economic interests of the Quaker merchants, the German farmers and tradesmen, and the Ulster Scot farmers and frontiersmen served to keep these groups apart and lead at times to bitter political conflicts between them well into the National Period of our history. No wonder, then, that striking differences in vocabulary have persisted in Eastern Pennsylvania.

Nevertheless, there is a distinctive body of words that are common to all of Eastern Pennsylvania, or the greater part of it. Examples in the Atlas collections are: *pavement* (31) for the sidewalk, *baby coach* (64) for the baby carriage, *flannel cakes* (45) for griddle cakes, the expression *till the time* (89) for *by the time, button wood* (61) for the sycamore, *coal oil* (24) for kerosene, and *snake doctor* (60) for the dragon fly.

Some of these regional words have spread southward from Philadelphia, an old center of trade and culture, to Chesapeake Bay, especially on the Eastern Shore of Maryland; others were carried southwestward through Maryland to the Shenandoah in the course of the settlement. This type of dissemination of expressions from Philadelphia onto the Eastern Shore and from the lower Susquehanna into Western Maryland and the Shenandoah Valley has already been noted in connection with the Midland and the North Midland words.

Pavement (31) is specifically applied to the sidewalk in Eastern Pennsylvania as far west as the Alleghenies and northward to the fork of the Susquehanna. It is not unknown in Scranton, but is apparently not in common use. The term is also current on the Jersey shore of Delaware Bay and has spread southward from Philadalphia into all of Delamarvia, to Baltimore and beyond, and into western Maryland (but not to Washington, D.C.).

In standard British English, *pavement* also has this meaning at the present time, but in America this application of the term is probably a Philadelphia innovation.

Baby coach (64) for the baby carriage, another Philadelphia word, covers a noticeably smaller area. It has spread up the Susquehanna Valley to Harrisburg and from there up the Juniata to the crest of the Alleghenies, but not to the upper Susquehanna. All of West Jersey and Delaware have it, and it is not unknown on the Eastern Shore of Maryland. Maryland west of the Bay has not adopted it. The present spread of this term for the baby carriage, a contrivance that took the place of the cradle during the latter part of the nineteenth century, must be somehow related to the Philadelphia trade area. See Figure 20.

Flannel cake (45) for a griddle cake made of wheat flour is used in all of Pennsylvania east of the Alleghenies as well as in the greater part of Maryland, including Baltimore, and in the Shenandoah Valley. We find it also in common use beyond the Alleghenies on the Youghiogheny in southwestern Pennsylvania, and scattered instances of it have been noted even farther west. Moreover, it is not uncommon on the lower James in Virginia.

On the other hand, *flannel cake* is not current in West Jersey and rather uncommon in Delaware and in Philadelphia, where *hot-cake* is in common use. Since the area of concentration for this term lies in south-central Pennsylvania it may well be of Ulster Scot origin.

Another expression that has its focus in central Pennsylvania is *till the time* (89) for *by the time* (*I get there*). This use of *till* is found between the Alleghenies and the Great Valley, including part of the bilingual German area, and in scattering fashion on the upper reaches of the Potomac in West Virginia. It is not current in the English settlements on the Delaware.

In this phrase *till* is almost certainly of Ulster Scot origin. The Pennsylvania Germans adopted it as a convenient rendering of *bis* in such phrases as *bis er kommt* 'by the time he comes,' since in their German *bis* had the same range of meanings as the Northern English *till*, as exemplified in *till sundown* and in the phrase under discussion. See Figure 21.

In Eastern Pennsylvania the sycamore is generally called the *button wood* (61), although *sycamore* and *button ball* are also current—the latter in Philadelphia and the immediate neighborhood. *Button wood* is found also in the northern counties of the state, in which Pennsylvania words are rare. Here it is at least in part derived from New England, as in East Jersey.

The regular word for kerosene is *coal oil* (24) in all of Pennsylvania, except for the Pittsburgh area and the New England counties in the northern fringe of the state. This term has spread far to the south, doubtless as a trade word, beginning with the 1860's. We find it not only in West Jersey and in Delamarvia, but in all of Maryland west of the Bay, on the upper reaches of the Potomac in West Virginia, in the Shenandoah

Valley, and on the Rappahannock in Virginia; furthermore, in southern Ohio and adjoining parts of West Virginia, beside the more common *lamp oil* of the Pittsburgh area.

Eastern Pennsylvania has a great variety of expressions for the dragon fly. The literary term *dragon fly* is common in Philadelphia and vicinity; *snake feeder*, the regional Midland expression, is found from the Delaware westward, but not in the immediate neighborhood of Philadelphia or on Delaware Bay; *darning needle*, clearly of New England derivation, is common in Philadelphia; and the Pennsylvania German area has, in addition, *snake heeder, snake guarder,* and *snake servant,* which are dealt with below.

Over and above these literary, regional, and local terms we find *snake doctor* (60) in scattering fashion from the Delaware to the West Branch of the Susquehanna, commonly on Delaware Bay, and fairly generally in Maryland west of Chesapeake Bay—and in Virginia. Since West Jersey and northern Delaware certainly do not derive *snake doctor* from Virginia, we must assume that there were two independent centers from which it was disseminated—the Virginia piedmont and the settlements on Delaware Bay. In Virginia *snake doctor* became fully established; in Eastern Pennsylvania, on the other hand, it had a number of early rivals, and this diversity in usage has opened the door to the literary *dragon fly* and to the new England *darning needle,* which has general currency in East Jersey and Greater New York City.

Rick (14) for an oblong hay stack has a rather unique distribution. It is in common use on Delaware Bay, in all of Maryland, in the Valley of Virginia, and in the piedmont of Virginia from the valley of the James northward—an unbroken area extending from West Jersey to southwestern Virginia. This type of dissemination south of the Mason and Dixon's Line is characteristic of expressions of Pennsylvania origin. Hence it is possible that *rick,* which now occurs only in scattering fashion in southeastern Pennsylvania, may nevertheless have its starting point in the English settlements on the Delaware. West Jersey and Delaware, where *rick* is common, often preserve expressions that have been lost in the urban area of Philadelphia and surroundings and that failed to be adopted by the Pennsylvania Germans.

Two expressions, *hot-cakes* (45) for griddle cakes made of flour, and *bag school* (83) for *play hookey*, are characteristic of the Philadelphia area in the narrower sense.

Hot-cakes is current only on Delaware Bay, in Philadelphia and its suburbs, and on the Pennsylvania side of the Delaware Valley as far north as Stroudsburg at the Water Gap. It is rare even in Lancaster and Reading, where *flannel cakes*, the regional term of Eastern Pennsylvania, is still in general use.

Bag school has an even more limited range. It is common in Philadelphia and in Chester, less so in northern Delaware and in West Jersey. It is known in Lancaster, Harrisburg, and Reading, but not widely used. It may well be of rather recent date and has vigorous rivals in *play hookey* and *play truant*. See Figure 22.

All in all, the Philadelphia area has been hospitable to importations from literary English; in recent times it has also adopted an occasional New York City word. On the other hand, Philadelphia always has been a center from which words have spread westward to the Alleghenies and southward along Delaware and Chesapeake Bay.

The Pennsylvania German Area

Some expressions of Pennsylvania German origin are current not only in the still bilingual area in the eastern part of the state but also in sections where Pennsylvania German is now little used or extinct, as in Western Pennsylvania, in the Shenandoah Valley, and in the Palatine settlements on the Yadkin in North Carolina. To the examples noted above we may add the following: *saddle horse* (39) for the near-horse (Pa. Ger. *saddelgaul*), in the Great Valley, in the Shenandoah Valley, and on the Yadkin; *hommie!* (37), a call to calves, also an affectionate term for a calf or a lamb (Pa. Ger. *hammi*), which is current from the Lehigh to the Juniata and southward to the Shenandoah Valley; *vootsie!* (38), a call to pigs, from the Great Valley to the Alleghenies and on the upper reaches of the Potomac in Maryland and in West Virginia; *fat-cakes* (45) for doughnuts (Pa. Ger. *fettkuche*), from the

Great Valley to the Alleghenies; *fossnocks* (45) for a kind of doughnut (Pa. Ger. *fasnachskuche* 'Shrove-tide cakes'), from the Great Valley to the Alleghenies; *thick-milk* (47) for curdled milk (Pa. Ger. *dickemilich*), from the Delaware Valley to the Alleghenies, and to some extent even in the Pittsburgh area. See Figures 23 and 24.

The phrase *till we get there* (89), in the meaning 'by the time we get there,' which is current from the Great Valley to the Alleghenies and on the upper Potomac in West Virginia, also has partly a German background. The meaning of *till* is here extended to render German *bis* as in *bis wir hinkommen*. (German *bis* usually means 'till, until.')

Saw buck (22) is the usual word for the saw horse in Pennsylvania east of the Alleghenies (also on the upper Potomac and on the Yadkin in North Carolina), except for the immediate vicinity of Philadelphia. It is not current on Delaware Bay. This geographic spread in itself suggests a Pennsylvania German model, which we readily recognize in Pennsylvania German *Sägbock*. There are also some instances of *wood buck* in this area as a rendering of Pennsylvania German *holsbock*. The *saw buck* of the Hudson Valley has a 'Holland Dutch' background.

Western Pennsylvania

The Pittsburgh area has very few strictly local expressions. From the mid-eighteenth century to the Revolution this area was little more than an outpost of the English settlements on the seaboard. After the Revolution the population increased by leaps and bounds through influx from the seaboard and from abroad, and Pittsburgh and Wheeling rapidly became centers of trade dominating the upper Ohio Valley and northern West Virginia. Hence the vocabulary of the Pittsburgh area was disseminated throughout these sections of the 'West,' and some of these words will doubtless turn up far down the Ohio Valley and in the middle part of the states of Ohio, Indiana, and Illinois. See Figure 25.

Among the local words we may mention *doodle* (14) for the haycock, which we encounter from the crest of the Alleghenies to the Ohio state line and again in a well-defined area on the lower course of the Kanawha in West Virginia; *carbon oil* (24) for kerosene, from the Alleghenies westward into Ohio (beside the regional *lamp oil*); *cruds* (47) for cottage cheese and *cruddled milk, crudded milk* (47) for curdled milk (of Ulster Scot origin), from the Alleghenies to the Ohio State line; and *grinnie* (59) for the chipmunk, from the valley of the Allegheny to Wheeling.

Expressions that occur in Western Pennsylvania, in northern West Virginia, and in adjoining parts of Ohio are: *sugar camp* (61) for the sugar maple grove, in Western Pennsylvania and all of northern West Virginia; *sugar grove* (61) for the sugar maple grove, from the Allegheny River to the Kanawha (also in central Pennsylvania and on the upper reaches of the Potomac); and *closet* (12) for the outdoor toilet.

Gunny sack (19) for the burlap bag is found only in the westernmost part of Pennsylvania and farther west.

Baby buggy (64) for the baby carriage is also primarily an Ohio Valley word, although it is also used in central Pennsylvania alongside the Philadelphia *baby coach*. It is very common in the Pittsburgh area and the adjoining counties of Ohio and on the lower Kanawha (Charleston).

THE SOUTH MIDLAND

Contrary to a widespread belief, the South Midland, comprising the Appalachians and the Blue Ridge south of the James River, has rather few unique regional and local expressions. The great body of words that have been regarded as peculiar to this region occur also either in the North Midland or in the Southern area. This whole area was settled late, roughly between 1750 and 1800, by expansion southward from the North Midland and westward from the Southern piedmont. Hence Midland and Southern expressions often occur side by side, or one or the other of several regional synonyms has come into general use. These contributions to the regional vocabulary of the South Midland are discussed elsewhere; here we shall consider only those expressions that are confined to the South Midland, whether as innovations or as survivals from early times. See Figure 26.

One of the striking South Midland innovations is the term *milk gap, milking gap* (15) for a rail enclosure where the cows are milked. We find it in Western North Carolina and Virginia (south of the James), and in all of West Virginia except the upper reaches of the Potomac and the counties bordering on the Ohio north of the mouth of the Kanawha. Not a single instance of this expression has been recorded outside this area.

Sugar orchard (61) for the sugar maple grove is current in approximately the same area. In northern West Virginia it competes with the North Midland *sugar camp*.

Another South Midland expression is *clabber milk, clabbered milk* (47), which is here more common than the simple Southern *clabber*. It is found as far north as the northern watershed of the Kanawha. See Figure 27.

Like some of the general Midland features, expressions of the South Midland have sometimes been carried down to the Atlantic in the valleys of the Cape Fear and the Yadkin-Peedee.

So we find *jacket* (27) for a man's vest and *fire board* (8) for the mantel shelf not only in the Southern Appalachians (from the Kanawha to South Carolina) but also in the corridor between the Cape Fear and the Peedee. *Jacket* is clearly a Midland word, since we find relics of it on the upper Potomac and in south-central Pennsylvania. *Fire board*, too, is of Midland origin; otherwise we would encounter relics of it somewhere in the conservative Southern area.

Ridy-horse (22) for the seesaw has very much the same spread as *jacket* and *fire board*, but there is a significant gap on the Yadkin (a stronghold of Midland usage) between the coastal sector and the Blue Ridge sector of its area, and there are relics of it on Albemarle Sound and on Chesapeake Bay, all of which leads to the conclusion that in the coastal sector *ridy-horse* is an old Southern expression, and that the South Midland probably derives it from that source.

Two sections of the South Midland, the Kanawha Valley and Western North Carolina, have some interesting local expressions. On the Kanawha we find *check* and *jack-bite* (48) beside the Southern *snack* for a bite between meals, *hobbies* (44) for small hand-shaped corn cakes, and *masculine* (33) as a polite word for the bull—the last two only south of the Kanawha.

In Western North Carolina simple folk call the living room in their homes the *big-house* (7); *brute* (33) is the polite word for a bull, *hickory* (19) a common term for the ox goad. The earthworm is known as the *red-worm* (60A). These expressions are not found elsewhere in the Eastern States. See Figure 28.

It should be noted in conclusion that a considerable number of North Midland expressions have survived in the English spoken on the Yadkin, including some of Pennsylvania German origin: *grist of corn* (19); *hay mow* (14) for the barn loft; *belling* (82) for the mock serenade; *saw buck* (22) for the saw horse; *saddle horse* (39) for the near-horse; *rain worm* (60A) for the earthworm; the hog call *vootsie!;* and the phrase *sick on the stomach* (80).

THE SOUTHERN AREA

The South is more diversified in speech, both regionally and socially, than either the North or the Midland. Localisms abound, especially in the coastal areas. The Virginia Piedmont has attained a degree of regional unity; perhaps also the piedmont of South Carolina below the Pee-dee. Another fairly unified area appears to be developing in the upper piedmont of North Carolina.

The boundary between the Southern area and the Midland area has been described above (p. 27). It runs in an arc from the Atlantic coast in central Delaware through Baltimore to the Blue Ridge, then along the Blue Ridge to the James River, where it swings out into the piedmont and runs in a southerly direction through North Carolina, reverting to the Blue Ridge in South Carolina. It is most clearly marked in its middle sector, which separates the Virginia Piedmont from the Valley of Virginia.

The Southern speech area comprises the greater part of Delamarvia (the southern two thirds of Delaware and the Eastern Shore of Maryland and Virginia), Virginia east of the Blue Ridge, the eastern half or more of North Carolina, and all of South Carolina except the Blue Ridge province. Although very little material is now available from Georgia and the Gulf States, it is fairly clear that the Southern

speech area extends all the way to East Texas (probably to the valley of the Brazos River).

Speech boundaries within the Southern area are rather more clear-cut than elsewhere in the Eastern States because this area has remained largely agricultural and because its population, derived largely from Colonial stocks, has clung to the soil.

The chief subareas of the South are: (1) the highly diversified Chesapeake Bay area, (2) the relatively unified Virginia Piedmont, and (3) the Carolinas east of the Midland boundary, with several distinct subdivisions. It is important to note, however, that the Carolinas and Chesapeake Bay have some features in common.

The main traits of the inner dialectal structure of the South and the relation of the South Midland to the South are suggested in Figures 29-38 by means of representative isoglosses.

It may well be that the South Midland, which has very few distinctive terms of its own but shares some of its vocabulary with the North Midland and some of it with the South, may have to be regarded in the end as a subarea of the South rather than of the Midland; but it is here treated as a part of the Midland.

Types of geographic distribution of regional words within the South are illustrated in Table III. Some terms are current throughout the South, some in the South and the South Midland; others are restricted to the Virginia Piedmont, to the Carolinas, or to the Southern tidewater. In addition, there are many local expressions which are discussed in their proper places below.

THE SOUTH

We shall first consider certain words that are found in all of the South, or the greater part of it, but not to any extent in the South Midland. See Figure 29.

Lightwood (8), usually pronounced to rime with *lighted*, is the regular term for kindling wood from Chesapeake Bay to Georgia. In Maryland west of the Bay it occurs only from Annapolis southward (beside *kindling*). *Lightwood* has not spread into the Midland except for the Shenandoah Valley, where it stands by the side of the Midland *pine*.

From Maryland to Georgia an armful of fire

TABLE III

THE SOUTHERN AREA

× regular — fairly common . rare	South Midland			South					
				Virginia Maryland					The Carolinas
	Western N. C.	West Virginia	Valley of Virginia	Piedmont	Tidewater	Eastern Shore	Albemarle Sound	Cape Fear	South Carolina
(1) The South and the South Midland									
light-bread (44)	×	×	×	×	×	×	×	×	×
clabber (47)	×	×	—	×	×	×	×	×	—
snack (48)	×	—	—	×	×	×	×	—	—
middlins (46)	×	×	—	×	×	×	×	—	×
ash cakes (44)	—	·	·	×	×	×	—	—	—
(hay) shocks (14)	×	×	×	×	×	·	×	×	—
(corn) shucks (56)	×	×	×	×	×	—	×	×	×
you-all (43)	—	—	×	×	×	—	×	×	×
waiter (82)	—	—	×	×	×	—	×	×	—
pallet (29)	×	—	×	·	×	×	×	×	×
gutters (11)	×	·	×	·	×	×	×	×	—
(barn) lot (15)	×	—	·	×	·	·	×	×	
roll the baby (64)	—	—	×	×	—	—	·	×	×
salad (55)		—	·	×	×	·	×	×	
rock fence (16)	×	×	×	×	×	—	·		
(2) The South									
low (36)	—	·		×	×	×	×	×	×
hasslet (37)	—			×	×	×	×	×	×
lightwood (8)			—	×	×	×	×	×	×
turn of wood (19)				×	×	×	×	×	—
co-wench! (37)				×	×	×	×	×	×
(3) Virginia and the South Midland									
garden house (12)				—	—	×	·	×	
wesket (27)				—	×	—	·		
lumber room (10)				—	×	—	·		
soft peach (54)	·		·	—	×	·			
nicker (36)	·	—	×	—	—				
snake doctor (60)	·	—	×	×	·	·			
come up! (38)	—	—	—	×	·	·			
batter bread (44)				·	×	×			
(4) The Carolinas and the South Midland									
whicker (36)	—				—	×	×	×	×
johnny cake, a griddle cake (44)	—	·		·	×		—	—	—
clabber cheese (47)	×	—		·	·	×	×	—	
breakfast strip (46)	×	—		·	·	×	×	—	
kerosene (24)	×			—		×	×	×	
woods colt (65)	×	×	—			—	×	×	
goop! (38)	—			·			×	×	×
(5) The Southern Coast									
curtains (9)		·	·	·	×	—	×		·
spider (17)			—	·	×	×	×		
mosquito hawk (60)			—	×	×	×	×		
press peach (54)			—	—	×	×	×	×	
piazza (10)			—	—	×	×	×		
earthworm (60)			—		×	×	×		

wood is universally called a *turn of wood* (19). This Southern expression has spread to the Valley of Virginia and is not unknown in Western North Carolina by the side of the Midland *load of wood.*

String beans are generally called *snap beans* (55A) south of the Potomac. In southern Maryland and on the Eastern Shore of Virginia—but not of Maryland—*snap beans* is current to some extent beside the usual *string beans. Snap beans* has crossed the Blue Ridge in Virginia and is a recent competitor of the Midland *green-beans* on the Yadkin in North Carolina.

In all of the Southern area cows are said to *low* (36) at feeding time. *Moo* is not unknown, to be sure, but it is largely confined to city folk. *Low* (which rimes with *so*) has not crossed the Blue Ridge.

The Southern call to cows is *co-wench!, co-inch!,* or *co-ee!* (37). The last variant predominates in Virginia, the first two everywhere else. *Co-wench!* is in general use in Delamarvia; in Maryland west of the Bay it is found only south of Annapolis. The Midland call *sook!* has been carried rather farther into the piedmont of Virginia and North Carolina than most Midland expressions, perhaps as the result of the introduction of stock raising from the western parts of these states into the plantation country.

Hasslet (37) is the usual Southern folk term for the edible inner organs of a pig. It is in regular use on Delamarvia and from the Potomac southward to Georgia. In Maryland west of the Bay it survives only in the two southernmost counties of St. Marys and Charles. It has not entered the Shenandoah Valley but has been carried westward into the corridor that leads to the Cumberland Gap.

Chittlins (37), denoting the small intestines of a pig, has a very similar geographic spread.

Some regional expressions of the South still have vigorous local competitors. Thus we find that the regional phrase *clean across* (28) 'all the way across' is encroaching upon the local expressions *jam across* in the Virginia Tidewater and *slam across* in Eastern North Carolina.

THE SOUTH AND THE SOUTH MIDLAND

The Southern speech area is so highly diversified geographically that the number of regional expressions that are current in all parts of it is relatively small. On the other hand, words that are used in the entire area, or in any considerable part of it, often appear in the South Midland as well. See Figure 30.

The South has many distinctive names for foods and dishes, and especially for things made of pork and corn—the traditional hog and hominy. Many of these terms are current throughout the Southern area and a large number of them have wide currency in the South Midland as well.

From Chesapeake Bay to the western parts of Virginia and the Carolinas, *ash cake* (44) and *hoe cake* (44) are used or remembered as words for hand-shaped corn cakes baked before an open fire. *Egg bread* (44) for a special kind of corn bread is current in the same area, and so is *cracklin bread* (44) for corn bread containing *cracklins* (crisp bits of rendered pork fat).

The term *corn dodger* (44) is known throughout the South and the South Midland, but in two different meanings. On the Eastern Shore and in the eastern part of the Carolinas it means a corn dumpling, elsewhere a small corn pone of irregular shape, baked in a pan.

Breakfast bacon, middlins, and *light-bread* are Southern expressions that have become established in all of the South Midland and have attained a degree of currency even as far north as the Pennsylvania state line.

Breakfast bacon (46) is the most widely used word for smoke-cured bacon in the South and the South Midland, where the simplex *bacon* means the brine-cured variety (salt pork). In Delaware, Maryland, and northern West Virginia *breakfast bacon* and *bacon* are used side by side in this sense.

Middlin(s) and *middlin meat* (46) are the regular designations for salt pork throughout the South and the South Midland. These terms have gained currency as far north as the Pennsylvania line, but in western Maryland, the Valley of Virginia, and northern West Virginia the Midland term *side meat* is also still used.

Wheat bread baked in loaves is apt to be called simply *bread* in the Midland and the North. In the South and the South Midland, however, *light-bread* (44) is the usual designa-

tion, and this compound word is encountered up to the Pennsylvania line, although the simplex *bread* is common enough in this sense in Delaware, Maryland, and West Virginia.

Clabber (47) is the regular term for curdled sour milk everywhere south of the Pennsylvania line. In Maryland and Virginia we find relics of the older *bonny-clabber,* and in the South Midland *clabbered milk* is in common use beside *clabber.* This Southern expression has become fully established in the Ohio Valley, probably because Pennsylvania had such a confusing variety of local terms.

For a bite of food between meals the South and the South Midland as far north as the Kanawha River use *snack* (48). This expression has also been adopted in part in the Shenandoah Valley and in northeastern West Virginia, where it now competes with the Midland *piece* and *piece meal.*

Butter beans (55A) is the Southern word for the lima bean or a small variety of it. The expression is common in all of Virginia and North Carolina, less so in Maryland. South Carolina seems to lack it.

Garden greens are generally known as *salad* or *salat* (55) from the western shore of Chesapeake Bay southward. In the Valley of Virginia and in the western part of the Carolinas the Midland *greens* is still common by the side of Southern *salad.*

The large number of terms connected with food and cooking that have found their way into the South Midland is a striking phenomenon. It can hardly be accounted for on the basis of settlement history; it reflects rather the strong influence of the plantation country upon the culture of the upland during the nineteenth century.

Some everyday farm words of the South are also firmly rooted in the South Midland or parts of it, and several of them are found as far north as the fork of the Ohio at Pittsburgh. The Midland term or terms, however, usually occur alongside of the Southern ones.

The loose piles of hay in the meadows at haying time are called *shocks* (14) from Chesapeake Bay to South Carolina and also in the South Midland; this term predominates also in north-

ern West Virginia and the Ohio Valley as far up
as Wheeling and Pittsburgh. The Midland *cock*,
however, is still fairly common in the Valley of
Virginia and is used to some extent elsewhere in
the South Midland. Moreover, *cock* has nearly
eliminated *shock* on Delamarvia and has considerable currency west of Chesapeake Bay to
the mouth of the James.

In the South as well as the South Midland
and the Shenandoah Valley the leaves on an ear
of corn are called *shucks* (56). In Maryland west
of the Bay the line between Southern *shucks* and
Midland *husks* is quite sharp, the city folks of
Baltimore using the Midland term. On the Eastern Shore we find the local term *caps* between
the Chester River and the Nanticoke, separating
the Midland *husks* from the Southern *shucks*.
The Ohio Valley has *husks* down to the mouth
of the Kanawha, and this Midland term is still
fairly common in northeastern West Virginia.

Rock fence (16) is another Southern term that
is fully established in the South Midland and
the Shenandoah Valley. In West Virginia the
Southern *rock fence* and the Midland *stone fence*
occur side by side on the Monongahela and the
upper reaches of the Potomac. The Midland
term has been carried southward along Chesapeake Bay, nearly eliminating the Southern
rock fence north of the Potomac and restricting
its use on Delamarvia.

Whet rock (23) is current in the greater part
of the *rock fence* area, except for Chesapeake
Bay and Albemarle Sound, where *whet stone*
and several local expressions are used, either
exclusively or predominantly.

From the Rappahannock southward *lot, barn
lot, stable lot* (15) are the usual terms for the
barnyard, and these expressions are current in
all of the South Midland as well as in parts of
northern West Virginia, but not in the Shenandoah Valley. In West Virginia north of the
Kanawha *barn yard* occurs beside the Southern
lot and it predominates in the Ohio Valley. All
of the Chesapeake Bay area has only *barn yard*
or *farm yard*, terms that are not unknown in
coastal North Carolina and on the Yadkin.

The South Midland shares with the South a
preference for polite names for the bull (33).
Nearly all of these are local in character.

Except for an occasional *troughs, water troughs*,
or *eaves troughs* one hears in Virginia and the
Carolinas only *gutters* (11) for the well-known
contrivance on the roof of a house. The Southern *gutters* has become established in the Valley
of Virginia and in the western part of the Carolinas, but not in West Virginia, where the Midland terms *spouts* and *spouting* prevail. These
Midland words are also current in all of Maryland beside *gutters*.

Other expressions that are used throughout
the South and the South Midland are *pallet,
waiter, branch*, and the well-known *you-all*.

Pallet (29) for an improvised bed is known
and used from the western shore of Chesapeake
Bay southward, and westward to the mouth of
the Kanawha. In West Virginia the northern
watershed of the Kanawha forms the boundary.

Waiter (82) is the common folk word for the
best man and the bridesmaid in Virginia and the
Carolinas. In Maryland the expression is now
rare. It is not common in West Virginia, but
scattered instances of it occur even as far north
as the Monongahela.

In Virginia and the Carolinas *roll the baby*
(64) is the regular expression for wheeling a
baby in its carriage. In Maryland the Midland
wheel is commoner than *roll*, in Western North
Carolina *ride* (which also appears in Tidewater
Virginia and in Eastern North Carolina).

Branch (30) is as distinctly Southern as *run*
is Midland and *brook* Northern. In a broad belt
extending from Delaware Bay to the Shenandoah
Valley and the upper reaches of the Potomac
branch and *run* are both in common use for a
small stream, and the same situation obtains in
the Virginia Tidewater. In West Virginia, on the
other hand, there is a rather clear line of demarcation between the *branch* and the *run* areas.
Here *branch* is regular south of the Kanawha,
run to the north of it.

You-all (43), a sort of generous plural form, is
used throughout the South and the South Midland beside the neutral plural *you*. In the South
Midland the distinctive Midland plural form
you'ns survives in the speech of the simple folk
by the side of the more common *you-all*. In the
Ohio Valley this Southern form does not seem
to have taken root.

In similar fashion we find by the side of the neutral possessive adjective *your(s)* the generous form *you-all's*.

THE VIRGINIA PIEDMONT

The Piedmont of Virginia is a highly distinctive speech area. The nucleus of this area contains the old seaports situated at the fall line of the rivers that empty into Chesapeake Bay: Alexandria on the Potomac, Fredericksburg-Falmouth on the Rappahannock, Richmond on the James, and Petersburg on the Appomattox. From these cities the area extends westward to the Blue Ridge, northward to Annapolis (or Baltimore) in Maryland, and southward into the piedmont of North Carolina.

The Virginia Tidewater north of the James has been hospitable to Piedmont terms, although it often preserves old local expressions; the low country south of the James—the so-called South Side—has largely resisted the incursion of Piedmont terms. It is dominated by Norfolk.

Virginia Piedmont expressions have rarely crossed Chesapeake Bay onto the Eastern Shore, but they have often spread to the Valley of Virginia, and not infrequently into the corridor that leads westward from the head of the James, by way of the New River into West Virginia, by that of the Holston River and the Cumberland Gap to Tennessee and Kentucky. Some Piedmont terms have been adopted by the entire South Midland. The dynamic character of the Virginia Piedmont in cultural matters from the Revolution to the Civil War and after is clearly evident in the dissemination of its regional vocabulary across old settlement boundaries and across state lines.

Characteristic farm terms of the central part of the Virginia Piedmont area are *corn house, cow house, cuppin, hovel, line horse,* and *wheel horse.* See Figures 31 and 32.

Corn house (14) for the corn crib is in regular use in the Virginia Piedmont as well as in the Tidewater area north of the James and on the western shore of Maryland up to the Pennsylvania line. It is found also on the lower Shenandoah and, though sparingly, on the Eastern Shore. (Cf. *corn house* in New England and in the Low Country of South Carolina.)

Cow house (15) for the cow barn is restricted to a smaller area. It has not crossed the Potomac.

The old compound *cuppin* (15) is found in all of the Virginia Piedmont. It has become established in the southern peninsula of Maryland and on the Northern Neck, but not in the remainder of Tidewater Virginia. It is yielding ground to the modern compound *cow pen.* Occasionally one hears *cow cuppin.*

Hovel and *hover* (36) are distinctive Piedmont words for the chicken house or roost. These terms have found their way into the Tidewater area north of the James and into southern Maryland.

In the Virginia Piedmont the near-horse is most commonly known as the *line horse* or *wheel horse* (39), especially in the James Valley. These expressions do not appear outside the state, nor have they become established in the Tidewater section.

Way! and *yay!* (38) as calls to stop a horse are confined to a much smaller area lying between the middle course of the James and the Potomac.

The chicken call *coo-chee!, coo-chick!* is also heard only in a part of the Piedmont, from the Rappahannock to the Roanoke in North Carolina, but it has been carried down the points of land to Chesapeake Bay.

The Piedmont has its own hog call which appears in the variations *chook, choke, chuck, choog, kəchoo, kəchook* (38). These calls are used also in the Tidewater area north of the James and in southern Maryland, and to some extent also on the Eastern Shore beside the more common Chesapeake Bay call *wook.*

Other Piedmont expressions are *croker sack* (or *crocus sack*), *hoppergrass, old-field colt,* and the phrase *school breaks up* (at a certain hour).

Croker sack (19) is the usual expression for a burlap bag between the James and the Roanoke above the fall line, and the term occurs also on the upper Rappahannock and in southern Maryland beside the more common *(sea-)grass sack.*

Hoppergrass (61) is a common variant of *grasshopper* in folk speech from the Rappahannock to the Roanoke.

A child born out of wedlock is an *old-field(s) colt* (65) from the Valley of the James to that of the Roanoke—the Virginia counterpart to the *woods colt* of the Carolinas.

By the side of the regional expressions *school lets out* (north of the James) and *school turns out* (south of the James) there is a distinctive Piedmont expression *school breaks up* or *school breaks* (83) in most of eastern Virginia and in adjoining parts of North Carolina.

Among the Virginia Piedmont expressions that have spread considerably beyond their home area we may mention *batter bread, soft peach, lumber room, garden house,* and *wesket.* See Figure 33.

Batter bread (44), denoting a soft corn bread containing egg, is now current in nearly all of Virginia (and very little outside of it). North of the upper Rappahannock and south of the lower James, however, *egg bread* is still the usual term.

Soft peach (54) for the freestone peach is used in almost precisely the same area. Relics of the Chesapeake Bay term *open peach* appear on the points of land between the James and the Potomac.

Lumber room (10) is current for a storeroom in rather large parts of the South, but the Virginia Piedmont and Tidewater are clearly its stronghold, and the Piedmont is its probable center of dissemination. In the Carolinas *plunder room* predominates, a term that has also a degree of currency in Virginia.

Wesket (27) for a man's vest is common from the lower Neuse to the lower James and is widely known to older people throughout Virginia and adjacent parts of West Virginia and Maryland. The Valley of Virginia clearly received *wesket* from the Piedmont. The Midland *jacket,* which is still in common use in Western North Carolina and adjoining parts of Virginia as well as on the upper reaches of the Potomac, survives only in scattered relics in the Valley. Since Albemarle Sound certainly did not import *wesket* from the Virginia Piedmont, we must assume that this term has been current in both the Piedmont and the Tidewater of Virginia from the earliest times. It is a significant fact that the Eastern Shore of Maryland lacks this expression.

Garden house (12) as a polite term for the outdoor toilet has a very similar geographic spread. It is common from the lower Rappahannock to the Neuse and in the Shenandoah Valley. Although *garden house* is no longer common in the Piedmont, the Shenandoah Valley certainly derives it from that section of Virginia. The Piedmont now uses *johnny house* and *jack house.*

Within the Southern speech area *snake doctor* (60A) is distinctly a Virginia Piedmont word for the dragon fly. We find it regularly in all of the Virginia Piedmont and adjoining parts of North Carolina and Maryland, but only rarely on Chesapeake Bay, where *mosquito hawk* prevails. *Snake doctor* is also in regular use in the Shenandoah Valley and quite common in the southeastern half of West Virginia by the side of the Midland *snake feeder.* Since *snake doctor* is indigenous to both Eastern Pennsylvania and the Virginia Piedmont, we must recognize a double source for it in the Valley and the Appalachians.

Some of the farm terms of the Virginia Piedmont have found their way into the South Midland, among them *nicker, turn of corn, come up!,* and *co-sheep!*

The South has two expressions for the friendly noise of a horse at feeding time, *whicker* and *nicker* (36). *Whicker* is the usual expression along the coast from southern Delaware to Georgia and in the greater part of the Carolina piedmont, *nicker* in the Virginia Piedmont and in the Tidewater area from the James northward to Baltimore. From the Virginia Piedmont *nicker* has spread westward all the way to the Ohio Valley, northward to the fork of the Ohio in Pennsylvania, and southward in the Blue Ridge and the Appalachians to Georgia. *Nicker* now dominates this vast area; only relics of the Midland *whinny* and the coastal *whicker* are found here and there.

The fact that *whicker* is still current beside *nicker* on the points of land north of the James leaves no doubt but that *nicker* has spread east as well as west from the Virginia Piedmont.

Co-sheep! (38) as distinct from the Midland call *sheep!* is characteristic of the Virginia Piedmont south of the James River; the Rappahannock Valley has *kə-nan!* or *nannie!* The *co-sheep!* of the Appalachians south of the Kanawha may be due to Virginia influence.

The call *get up!* and clucking serve to start horses or to hasten their pace in the South as elsewhere in the Eastern States. In addition we find the regional call *come up!* (38) from the Virginia Piedmont westward and southward, but not on the Southern coast. That the Virginia Piedmont is the area from which this call was disseminated is not certain but quite probable.

The phrase *turn of wood* for an armful of wood has general currency in the Southern area, but *turn of corn* (14) as a synonym of the Midland *grist of corn* is found only in the Piedmont of Virginia and in the part of the South Midland lying to the south of the Kanawha and the Roanoke. Since the phrase *turn of wood* is not used in the South Midland, *turn of corn* is probably an importation from the Virginia Piedmont rather than a local creation.

Plum peach (54) for the clingstone peach is in common use in a broad belt extending in a southwesterly direction from the Rappahannock to Georgia. This belt comprises the Virginia Piedmont, the Blue Ridge south of the James, and the Appalachians south of the Kanawha. There can be little doubt of the Virginia Piedmont origin of this term since the entire Southern coast and the greater part of the Carolinas have *press peach*.

Scrich owl (59) for the screech owl is current in the same belt, but is found also in the Virginia Tidewater and in southern Maryland. The Virginia origin of this pronunciation would seem to be clear.

Peckerwood (59) for the woodpecker is common in the folk speech of the Virginia Piedmont and adjoining parts of North Carolina. It appears again in the westernmost parts of Virginia and North Carolina, i.e. within the belt of Virginia influence in the Appalachians.

The examples just mentioned show that Virginia Piedmont expressions have traveled southwestward into the Blue Ridge and the Appalachians, along routes that lead to Kentucky and to Tennessee. Some of them have also become established in West Virginia south of the Kanawha.

North of the Kanawha, it seems, only such Southern expressions as were current over a much larger part of the Southern speech area—in Virginia as well as in the Carolinas—have struck root. But there is at least one clear case of a Virginia Piedmont term that has spread all through the Appalachians and well beyond into the Ohio Valley. That term is *nicker* (see above).

THE CAROLINAS

The Carolinas sometimes form a unit over against the Virginia Piedmont area. Not infrequently "Carolina words" appear as far north as the lower James, and again on the Eastern Shore of Chesapeake Bay. What happened in such cases is that expressions that were current on the entire Southern coast or the greater part of it were carried inland in the Carolinas, whereas they were stopped short at the fall line in Virginia or pushed back to Chesapeake Bay by Virginia Piedmont expressions. See Figures 34 and 35.

Whicker (36) is a striking illustration of this process. In the sense of 'whinny' it is in regular use in the Carolinas (except for a narrow strip of northwestern North Carolina), the adjoining Norfolk area south of the lower James, and again in the greater part of Delamarvia. On the points of land north of the James it has been largely replaced by the Piedmont term *nicker*, which also dominates Maryland west of the Bay and has even spread to the Eastern Shore.

Johnny cake (44) for a corn griddle cake is another example. We find it throughout the Carolinas, on Delamarvia, and in Maryland west of the Bay, but not in Virginia, except for the Northern Neck.

Other Carolina words are *breakfast strip, clabber cheese, woods colt, kerosene,* and the hog call *piggoop!*

From the lower James southward *breakfast strip* (46) is a common term for breakfast bacon, and *clabber cheese* (47) for cottage cheese. The latter also has some currency in the westernmost part of Virginia and in West Virginia by the side of the Midland *smear case.*

Woods colt (65) is the Carolina counterpart of the Virginia *old-field colt* for an illegitimate child. The term is not common on Albemarle Sound or in the Low Country of South Carolina and Georgia; on the other hand, it is in general use throughout the Appalachians and in the

Ohio Valley from Wheeling downstream. *Woods colt* may well be a creation of the South Midland that found its way down the river valleys to the Atlantic.

The Carolinas have their own range of hog calls: *goop!*, *woop!*, and *piggoop!* (38). These calls are heard from the Neuse River southward and westward to the Blue Ridge.

The Midland terms *coal oil* and *lamp oil* that found their way into Virginia as trade terms are rarely heard in the Carolinas except along the Virginia line. Carolinians say *kerosene* (24), as do New Yorkers and New Englanders. Did the Carolinas get this product by boat from Northern ports?

Aside from the north-central tier of counties which belong to the Virginia Piedmont area, North Carolina has three fairly distinct speech areas: a western, a northeastern, and a southeastern. The western half of the state belongs to the South Midland. The northeastern quarter, which extends from the Neuse to the lower James in Virginia and centers on Albemarle Sound, is a rather distinctive subarea of the Southern coast. The southeastern quarter, comprising the valleys of the Cape Fear and the Peedee, shares some features with Albemarle Sound and some with the Carolina Piedmont. The speech of this section has few—if any—unique characteristics, but is a blend of coastal and South Midland speech.

For lack of a dominant and stable center of population and trade these three areas of North Carolina have remained rather distinct. Expressions that are common to all parts of the state and, on the other hand, not current in Virginia or South Carolina—real Tarheelisms—are exceedingly scarce. These two words may perhaps be so regarded: *tow sack* and *biddie!*

Tow sack (19) for a burlap sack is in general use throughout the state and very little outside its boundaries—mostly around Norfolk, Virginia.

The chicken call *biddie!*, *widdie!* (38), though used in New England and on Delamarvia, is nevertheless characteristic of North Carolina, since it is not used across the state line in Virginia or south of the Peedee in South Carolina.

The expression *He lay* (or *laid*) *out of school* (83), which is current in all except the north-

eastern part of the state, has certainly been disseminated from the North Carolina piedmont, down the Cape Fear and Peedee and up into the mountains.

The materials now in the collections of the Linguistic Atlas are insufficient for dealing in detail with the speech of South Carolina and Georgia at this time. The samples taken in different parts of South Carolina and adjoining parts of Georgia permit only a number of tentative general statements.

South Carolina falls into three sections of very unequal size: (1) the small Blue Ridge section in the westernmost part of the state, which belongs to the South Midland; (2) the Peedee or Georgetown section, which is part of the Cape Fear–Peedee Corridor leading from the North Carolina piedmont to the sea; and (3) the remaining greater part of the state, comprising the Charleston area and most of the piedmont, which we may call the South Carolina speech area *par excellence*. To what extent the Low Country (Charleston area) differs from the Up-country remains to be determined.

In the coastal area of South Carolina and Georgia—on the so-called sea islands—the simple Negro folk, living in compact settlements, speak a unique type of English, which came into being as a jargon of the slave trade. This Negro dialect, called Gullah, is greatly simplified in its grammatical forms and in its system of sounds and contains a good many African words and idioms.

THE COAST

The Southern tidewater area from the head of Chesapeake Bay to Georgia is highly diversified in speech. It preserves the localisms of colonial times to a much larger extent than other sections of the Eastern States unless it be the New England coast facing the open Atlantic. Here on the bays and wide inlets of the tidal rivers of a drowned coast, settlements were planted in the seventeenth century, beginning with the first decades of it on Chesapeake Bay, with the last decades in the Carolinas (Albemarle Sound and Charleston). Expansion up the rivers was slow and communication among the settlements difficult for several generations. In this isolation local types of speech developed in the various parts of Chesapeake Bay, on Albemarle Sound and the Neuse, and in the Low Country of South Carolina.

In South Carolina the Low Country came to dominate the piedmont; in Virginia the piedmont overshadowed the tidewater by the middle of the eighteenth century, while in North Carolina piedmont and tidewater more nearly balanced each other until the Civil War. As a result we find that in South Carolina the speech of the Low Country has reshaped piedmont speech, that in Virginia the speech of the piedmont has encroached upon the tidewater, while in North Carolina the eastern part of the state has remained distinct in its speech from the western part. Only the Cape Fear Valley shows a blending of tidewater and piedmont speech, probably because the produce of the North Carolina piedmont was shipped down the Cape Fear River from the fall line port of Fayetteville to the seaport of Wilmington. This traffic brought piedmont words down to tidewater.

Although the Southern coast with all its wealth of local expressions offers a rather confusing picture, there are three fairly clear breaks in it: one along the lower James, one along the Neuse, and the third along the Peedee. North of the lower James lies the Chesapeake Bay area, south of it the Albemarle Sound area, while the Peedee separates the Cape Fear area from the Charleston area. These four subareas of the coast clearly reflect settlement areas.

Before dealing with these subdivisions we shall comment on a number of terms that are current along the entire Southern coast or the greater part of it, but not to any extent in the piedmont.

We find, first of all, the weather terms *breeze up* (7), *northeaster*, and *norwester* (common also on the New England coast); and *creek* (30) for a 'salt-water inlet, as in New England. *Curtain* (9) for the roller shade is current in the Southern tidewater from the Cape Fear northward—and again on Delaware Bay and in New England; similarly, *spider* (17) for the cast-iron frying pan, from the Potomac to the Peedee (and in the entire New England settlement area). Two other expressions that are widely used in New England appear in scattered sections of the

Southern coast: *angleworm* (60) for the earthworm, on the Potomac, the lower Neuse, and the lower Peedee; and the phrase *sick to the stomach* (80), on Delamarvia and from Albemarle Sound to the Neuse. All these expressions have survived independently on the Southern coast and in New England.

Expressions that have remained restricted to tidewater on Chesapeake Bay but have been carried from the coast up into the Carolina piedmont are *press peach, mosquito hawk, piazza,* and *earthworm.*

Press peach (54) for the clingstone peach and *mosquito hawk* (60A) for the dragonfly have the same type of distribution. They range from Chesapeake Bay to Georgia and well up into the piedmont in the Carolinas, but survive in Virginia only on the points of land on Chesapeake Bay.

Piazza (10) for a porch is in common use on the coast from the James to Georgia and in the piedmont of the Carolinas. Southern Maryland has relics of this term. (Note that *piazza* is also widely current in New England and the Hudson Valley but not in the Midland.)

The Carolinas and Georgia are the only part of the Eastern States where *earthworm* (60) is a folk word. Elsewhere it is a book word or a city word. *Earthworm* is used by the common people from the mouth of Chesapeake Bay southward. In North Carolina we find it along the shore and in the eastern part of the piedmont, in South Carolina in the Low Country and in the entire piedmont. It occurs also in Gullah.

The Chesapeake Bay area is a decentralized agricultural area without a dominant center.

Baltimore, situated near the head of the Bay, had a late start shortly before the Revolution. It developed as a grain port for the rich farm lands of Maryland west of the Bay, the lower Susquehanna Valley, and the Shenandoah Valley, and extended its trade area westward to the Ohio Valley during the first half of the nineteenth century. The Eastern Shore and the lower part of Chesapeake Bay never came under the influence of Baltimore to any extent.

The Eastern Shore of Maryland and Delaware—the peninsula of Delamarvia—has been

under the influence of Philadelphia, as the southward progress of such Midland expressions as
worm fence (16), *stone fence* (16), *husks* (56), *to
hull beans* (55A), *jag of corn* (19), *spouting* (11),
and *hot-cakes* (45) demonstrates. On the western
shore of the Bay such Midland terms are usually
stopped short at Baltimore, whose speech has remained largely Southern.

The lower part of the Bay, on the other hand,
has come under the influence of the Virginia
Piedmont, although Piedmont expressions have
not crossed the Bay in large numbers.

Among the expressions that are current in all
of the Chesapeake Bay area or the greater part
of it are *hand irons, (sea-)grass sack, guano sack,
nigh-horse, base-born child,* and *tin-panning.*

The folk word *hand irons* (8) for the andirons
is used by older persons in all of Delamarvia, on
the Potomac, the Rappahannock, and in the
Virginia Tidewater north of the James. We find
it also north of Delaware Bay in West Jersey and
in the northern counties of Pennsylvania. In
northern Pennsylvania *hand irons* is clearly of
New England descent. Delaware Bay, adjoining
the Chesapeake Bay area, has doubtless had this
expression from the earliest times.

(Sea-)grass sack (19) for a burlap bag has nearly
the same spread, i.e. from Delaware Bay to the
Rappahannock. The expression is well established on lower Chesapeake Bay and is not uncommon on Albemarle Sound, which is part of
the Norfolk trade area. The synonymous *guano
sack* (19) is largely confined to Maryland, but
has spread to the Shenandoah Valley, presumably as a Baltimore trade word.

Nigh-horse (39) for the near-horse, too, is
current both on Delaware Bay and on Chesapeake Bay, but in very uneven distribution. It
is no longer common except in southern New
Jersey, southern Delaware and on the Northern
Neck of Virginia; the Midland *near-horse* has
taken its place in nearly all of Maryland.

Base-born child, or simply *base-born* (65), for
a bastard, and *tin-panning* (82) for a mock
serenade occur in scattered fashion as relics on
both sides of the Bay, the latter only in Maryland.

West of the Bay we find certain local expressions; Maryland has *open-stone peach* or *open-
seed peach* (54) for the freestone peach, *snake
waiter* (60A) for the dragonfly (only south of
Annapolis); the Virginia Tidewater has *jam
across* (28) for 'clear across' between the Rappahannock and the James, *chamber* (7) for a downstairs bedroom-living room, and *ground worm*
(60) for the earthworm on the Middle Neck and
the Eastern Shore.

The Eastern Shore of Maryland and southern
Delaware have many local expressions. Here we
find *hand horse* and *huther-horse* (39) for the
near-horse, *corn stack* (14) for the corn crib,
caps (56) for the corn husks, *cocky-horse* (32)
for the seesaw, *scrooch owl* (59) for the screech
owl, *cossie!* or *cussie!* (37) as a call to calves, and
among the simple folk the interesting *mongst-ye*
by the side of the Southern *you-all.* See Figure 36.

Three historical factors make the Eastern
Shore of Maryland a rather distinct subdivision
of the Chesapeake Bay area: (1) the preservation
of many local expressions, (2) the importation
of Midland terms from the Philadelphia area,
and (3) the failure to accept Virginia Piedmont
features that have spread into the tidewater area
west of the Bay.

The coastal area from the lower James to the
Peedee has certain expressions that are not found
on Chesapeake Bay or in the Charleston area:
hum, pop lash, slam across, shivering owl. See
Figure 37.

Hum (36) for 'moo' is heard only in this
section of the Eastern States. *Slam across* (28) for
'clear across' and *shivering owl* (59) for the
screech owl are equally unique. *Pop lash* (19) for
the ox whip, though familiar enough in Eastern
New England, does not occur elsewhere in the
South. These expressions hug the coast, but are
sometimes found as far inland as Raleigh and
Fayetteville.

Within this coastal belt of North Carolina
the Albemarle Sound area is a well-defined subdivision extending from the James River in
Virginia to the Neuse, and inland to Raleigh.
The settlements on Albemarle Sound were the
first to be established on the soil of North Carolina, and the planters of this northeastern section
of the state dominated the political scene until
the Revolution. Later the piedmont came into
prominence, but this oldest part of North Caro-

lina has zealously preserved its identity. Intimate trade relations of long standing with the port of Norfolk, Virginia, have tended to keep it apart from the rest of the state, and a soil-bound population has fostered the preservation of local speech ways.

Among the local expressions of this section are *trumpery room* (10) for a storeroom, *whet seed* (28) for the whetstone, *cookie* (45) for a doughnut, *Sunday baby* or *Sunday child* (65) for an illegitimate child. The chicken call *cootie!* (38) is heard only from Albemarle Sound to the mouth of Chesapeake Bay, *hicky-horse* (22) for the seesaw only between the Sound and the Neuse, and the calf call *kədub!* or *kədubbie!* occurs only on Albemarle Sound. See Figure 38.

The Cape Fear area, including the valleys of the Cape Fear and the Peedee, has very few local characteristics. It shares regional expressions either with the Albemarle Sound area or with the piedmont, whence it has imported a fairly large number of South Midland expressions, such as *quarter till ten* (4), *big-house* (7), *fire board* (8), *jacket* (27), and *little piece* (39). *Savannah* (29) for low-lying grass land, current from the mouth of the Neuse to the mouth of the Peedee, is the only unique Cape Fear expression that has come to my attention.

South Carolina to the south of the Peedee River is yet to be investigated systematically. Field work is in progress now. Available samples of the speech of this area point to a distinctive South Carolina vocabulary.[3]

COMBINATIONS OF MAJOR SPEECH AREAS

It is, of course, to be expected that any two of the three major speech areas will have certain expressions in common that are not found in the remaining area. In the random sample of the vocabulary of the Eastern States presented in this book there are about twenty expressions that are shared by the North and the Midland, about twenty that are common to the Midland and the South, and about half that number are shared by the geographically separated Northern

and Southern areas. These instances will be briefly discussed here.

THE NORTH AND THE MIDLAND

The North and the Midland have the following expressions in common: *hay cock* (14) over against Southern *hay shock; hay mow* (14) against *loft; stone* in *stone wall, stone fence* (16) against *rock fence; grist of corn* (19) against *turn of corn; burlap* (19) against several local Southern expressions; *whet stone* (23) against *whet rock; moo* (36) against *low; whinny* (36) against *nicker* and *whicker; wishbone* (37) against *pully-bone, pull-bone;* the hog call *pig!, piggie!* (38) against several local Southern calls; *near-horse* (39) against several local Southern expressions; *bacon* (46) against *breakfast bacon* and *breakfast strip; cling(-stone) peach* (54) against *plum peach* and *press peach; free-stone peach* (54) against several local Southern terms; *string beans* (55) against *snap beans;* and *corn husks* (56) against Southern *corn shucks.*

More precise statements concerning the geographic spread of these expressions and their relative frequency in the various subareas are provided in Chapter III. Table IV gives a summary of these facts.

In the South Midland most of these terms are in competition with Southern terms. On the other hand, the Eastern Shore of Chesapeake Bay has adopted these expressions from the Midland to a considerable extent. Some terms, notably *whet stone, wishbone, cling-stone peach,* and *free-stone peach,* have taken a foothold in other parts of the South as well and are thus coming to be used throughout the Eastern States. See Figures 39 and 40.

THE SOUTH AND THE MIDLAND

The Midland shares the following expressions with the South: *dog irons* or *fire dogs* (8) for the andirons; *paling fence* (16) for a picket fence; *bucket* (17) for the metal pail; *spicket* or *spigot* (18) for the water faucet; *singletree* or *swingletree* (21) as against the Northern *whiffletree* or *whippletree; seesaw* (22) as a folk word; *comfort* (29) as against the Northern *comforter* or *comfortable* for a heavy quilt; *pully-bone, pull-bone* or *pulling bone* (37) for the wishbone; *corn*

---

[3]The field work has now been completed by Dr. Raven I. McDavid, but the materials he collected were not accessible to me until after the book went to press.

pone or pone bread (44) for corn bread; roasting ears (56) for sweet-corn; pole cat (59) for the skunk; ground squirrel (59) for the chipmunk; the folk word granny or granny woman (65) for the midwife; the salutation Christmas gift! (93) for Merry Christmas!; the adverb right (74) in

TABLE IV

THE NORTH AND THE MIDLAND

× regular
— fairly common
. rare

	South		Midland				North			
	All of the South	Eastern Shore	South Midland	Western Pennsylvania	Eastern Pennsylvania	West Jersey	Hudson Valley	Upstate New York	Western New England	Eastern New England
clothes press (9)	—	.	×	—			.	×	—	—
hay cock (14)	×	—	—	×	×		×	×	×	×
hay mow (14)		—	×	×	×		×	×	×	—
stone wall, stone fence (16)	.	—	.	×	×	×	×	×	×	×
grist (19)		—	×	×	×	×	×			
burlap (19)		—		×	×	×	×	×	×	×
whet stone (23)	—	×	—	×	×	×	×	×	×	×
buck 'ram' (34)		—	×	×	×	.	—	×	×	×
moo (36)			—	×	×	×	×	×	×	×
whinny (36)	.		.	×	×	×	×	×	×	×
pluck (37)	.	.			×	—	—	×	—	
wishbone (37)	—	—		.	—	×	—	×	×	×
pig! (38)	×	×	—	—		×	×	×	×	×
near-horse (39)	.	—	.					×	—	×
sheaf (41)		—	.	×	×	—	×	—		
bread 'wheat bread' (44)	×	—	×	×	×	×	×	×	×	×
bacon (46)	.	×	.	×	×	×	×	×	×	×
cling(-stone) (54)	—	—		×	×	×	×	×	×	×
free-stone (54)	—	—		×	×	×	×	×	×	×
string beans (55)	.	×		×	×	×	×	×	×	×
corn husks (56)	—	.	×	×	×	×	×	×	×	×

such expressions as right smart, right good as against Northern quite; and the folk use of agin (89) in the sense of 'by the time,' as in agin he gets there. See Figures 41 and 42.

The boundaries between bucket, singletree, and comfort and the corresponding Northern terms pail, whiffletree, and comforter, comfortable are sharp, and they follow the boundary between the Midland and the North very closely.

Nearly all the other expressions listed above are yielding ground in the North Midland to the Northern expressions, which are more fully supported by literary usage than the old Midland and Southern terms. Thus granny and Christmas

gift! have been largely abandoned in Pennsylvania, and ground squirrel and pole cat have vigorous competitors in chipmunk and skunk throughout most of the North Midland. The Philadelphia area has been the most hospitable to these innovations and is passing them on to the Eastern Shore. The mountainous south-central part of Pennsylvania, on the other hand, has retained the older expressions most faithfully.

Even in the South the better educated among the younger generation have given up, or are giving up, such expressions as paling fence, pully-bone, granny, and Christmas gift! in favor of picket fence, wishbone, midwife, and Merry Christmas!

On the other hand, it is interesting to observe that seesaw, which is a true folk word in the Midland and the South, is replacing regional terms in the North.

A fuller account of the terms that are shared by the Midland and the South will be found in Chapter III. Table V shows the geographic spread of these expressions and their relative frequency in the several subareas.

TABLE V

THE MIDLAND AND THE SOUTH

× regular
— fairly common
. rare

	South				Midland				North
	South Carolina	North Carolina	Virginia Piedmont	Eastern Shore	South Midland	Western Pennsylvania	Eastern Pennsylvania	West Jersey	
dog irons, fire dogs (8)	×	×	×	.	×	—	.	.	.
paling fence (16)	×	×	×	×	×	×	×	—	
bucket (17)	×	×	×	×	×	×	×	×	
spicket (18)	—	×	×	×	×	×	×	×	
singletree (21)	×	×	×	×	×	—	×	×	
seesaw (22)	×	×	×	×	—	×	×	—	×
comfort (29)	×	×	×	×	×	×	×	×	
pully-bone (37)	×	×	×	×	×	.	.	×	
corn pone (44)	×	×	×	×	×	×	—		
roasting ears (56)	×	×	×	×	×	×	—	.	
pole cat (59)	×	×	×	×	×	×	×	.	
ground squirrel (59)	×	×	×	—	×	×	—	.	
granny (woman) (65)	×	×	×	×	×	—	.		
right smart (74)	×	×	×	×	×	×	×	×	
agin I get there (89)	×	×	×	×	—	.			
Christmas gift! (93)	×	×	×	×	—	—			

THE NORTH AND THE SOUTH

The North and the South, geographically separated as they are, have fewer expressions in common than either the North and the Midland or the Midland and the South. Moreover, nearly all these expressions are strictly folk words and are confined to certain subareas of the North and the South.

The expressions that occur in parts of the North and the South are: *quarter to* (4) as against *quarter of* and *quarter till; curtains* (9) for the roller shades; *piazza* (10) for a porch; *gutters* (11) as against *eaves troughs, eaves spouts,* and *spouting; corn house* (14) for the corncrib; *spider* (17) for the cast-iron frying pan; *low* (36) in the South and *loo* in the North for 'moo'; *hasslet, harslet* (37) for the inner organs of a pig; and the sheep call *nannie!* (38). See Figure 43.

The distribution and frequency of these terms are described in Chapter III and summarized in Table VI.

Only two of these expressions, *quarter to* and *gutters,* are gaining ground. Both of them occur also in the coastal section of the Midland—on Delaware Bay—and may well be old there too.

ALL THREE MAJOR AREAS

The Eastern States have, of course, the greater part of the vocabulary in common. Our concern has been with that segment of the vocabulary which is restricted either geographically or socially. We have had occasion to point out the drift from local to regional and from regional to general usage in many instances. We have also observed the replacement of folk words by expressions taken from common speech or cultivated speech or the literary language.

These general trends are strikingly illustrated by the following expressions which are current in all three of the major areas, or large parts of them, but are still paralleled by regional or local terms in certain areas: *saw horse* (22), *vest* (27), *creek* (30) for a fresh-water stream, *sidewalk* (31), *ram* (34), *setting hen* (36), *get up!* (38), *bundle* (41) for a sheaf, *doughnut* (45), *pancake* (45), *cottage cheese* (47), *sugar maple* (61), *midwife* (65), *best man* (82), and *Merry Christmas!* The details are presented in Chapter III.

TABLE VI

THE NORTH AND THE SOUTH

× regular — fairly common . rare	South				Midland		North			
	South Carolina	North Carolina	Virginia Piedmont	Eastern Shore	South Midland	North Midland	Hudson Valley	Upstate New York	Western New England	Eastern New England
quarter to (4)	—	—	×	—		.	—	—	—	—
curtains (9)	.	—	—	—		.	.	—	×	×
piazza (10)	×	×	.	—			—	×	×	×
gutters (11)	×	×	×	—		—	×	.	—	×
corn house (14)	—	.	×	—			.	—	×	×
spider (17)	—	—	.	—		.	.	—	×	×
low, loo (36)	×	×	×	×	.		—	—	—	—
harslet (37)	×	×	×	×	—		—	—	—	×
nannie! (38)	—	—	—	×	.		.	—	—	—

CHAPTER III

REGIONAL AND LOCAL WORDS IN TOPICAL ARRANGEMENT

INTRODUCTION

IN THE preceding chapter regional and local words current in the Eastern States are presented and discussed by areas. Each area, large or small, is there characterized in terms of vocabulary, and the boundaries of the various expressions that are peculiar to it are used to delimit its extent.

In the present chapter the regional and local vocabulary is arranged from the point of view of meaning. All synonyms for one and the same thing or situation are here treated together under one heading, so that the geographic variations in vocabulary can be seen at a glance.

The dissemination of these synonymous words and expressions is described as far as possible in terms of the speech areas that have been delimited in the preceding chapter. The reader will want to keep in mind Figure 3, "The Speech Areas of the Eastern States," and to refer to it again and again.

Whenever it seemed desirable to give a more precise indication of the area in which a word is current, the names of bays, rivers, watersheds, mountain ranges, and other topographical features have been employed to orient the reader. Figure 1 shows most of the geographical terms that have been so used as well as the names of the cities to which references are made in the descriptions.

The social distribution of words is also carefully noted. Some are used only by the simple folk—especially the strictly local expressions; some are restricted to the cultured. Others are current among the simple folk and the large middle class, or among the cultured and the middle class. Others again can be heard from all the people in a given area. Whenever no comment is offered on social distribution it is to be assumed that the word has general currency within the stated geographic limits.

Care has been exercised to point out whether a given expression is in general use, common, infrequent, or rare; also, whether it is spreading or receding, an innovation or a relic. In some cases the apparent focus of dissemination has been identified—at least tentatively.

Striking trends from local to regional usage and from regional to national currency are duly noted. The general trend in the American vocabulary is unmistakably in these directions.

It will be observed that some words occur in two or more geographically separate areas, partly as the result of independent importation from the British Isles, partly as survivals in conservative areas.

Although pains have been taken to describe the geographic and the social spread of each word treated here as accurately as possible, many details—especially scattered occurrences—have not always been mentioned. The need for brevity and a desire to emphasize the more striking features of distribution have prompted this simplification. It should be pointed out in passing that the isoglosses in the figures for Chapter II represent a further simplification of statement for the sake of clarity and convenience.

The wealth of detail recorded for the *Linguistic Atlas* is exhibited in the figures that are included in this chapter. The reader should bear in mind that more than 1,200 informants were interviewed in the Eastern States and that all statements made below concerning the currency of words rest upon this extensive record of usage.

quarter of eleven (4)

Of, to, and *till* are all used over large areas in this phrase.

In the Northern area, on Delaware Bay, and on Chesapeake Bay *of* and *to* stand side by side in this expression. *Quarter of* predominates in the Boston area and in the Hudson Valley, elsewhere *of* and *to* seem to be in balance.

The greater part of the Southern area (Eastern Virginia, northeastern North Carolina, and the Low Country of South Carolina) has exclusively *quarter to*, the South Midland *quarter till*. The Midland *till* has been carried seaward along the Cape Fear and the Peedee rivers and even competes with the Southern *to* on the Neuse.

Pennsylvania presents a picture of great confusion. In the central part of the state the characteristic Midland *till* is still common, but it is yielding ground in the east to *of*, which now predominates in Philadelphia and the southeastern part of the state; and in the Pittsburgh area *of* and *to* are gradually superseding *till*. See Figure 44.

(The wind is) rising (7)

Along the Atlantic coast, from New Brunswick to Cape Fear in North Carolina, the wind is said to *breeze up, breeze on* (less commonly simply to *breeze*) when it gets stronger. This is one of a number of seafaring terms that are current the full length of the Atlantic coast but are known only to those who live within easy reach of the sea. See Figure 45.

living room (7)

In all the Eastern states *living room* and *sitting room* (*settin' room* among the common folk) are the usual names for the room in which the family gathers evenings, and receives and entertains friends. *Sitting room* is now rather a rural expression. *Living room* is fully established in the cities and among the younger generation in the country.

Only the larger houses have (or had) a 'best' room for formal occasions such as weddings, funerals, and the reception of honored guests, which is known as the *parlor* from Maine to the Carolinas. The old-time *parlor* is now largely a thing of the past. Some now call it the *front room*.

All these terms are current nearly everywhere in the Eastern States, but with varying frequency.

In the simple homes of the piedmont and the mountains of North Carolina (also on the Peedee in South Carolina, rarely in West Virginia) the living room is called the *big-house* or the *great-house*, on the Eastern Shore of Virginia the *big-room*. See Figures 46 and 47.

kindling wood (8)

In the Southern area kindling wood is called *lightwood* (usually pronounced like *lighted*), in the Midland *pine, fat-pine, pitch pine, rich-pine*. The Philadelphia area has *kindling (wood)* by the side of *pine*, and this expression is in general use in Maryland west of Chesapeake Bay. In Delamarvia the Southern *lightwood* is firmly established, except for the northern part, which falls within the Philadelphia area.

Northern usage has not been recorded for the Atlas. See Figures 4 and 29.

andirons (8)

The andirons in the fireplace are generally known as *fire dogs, dogs,* or *dog irons* in the greater part of the South, the South Midland, and in southwestern Pennsylvania. *Dog irons* predominates from the lower James River (the Norfolk area) to the lower Neuse in North Carolina and in the South Midland, *fire dogs* in South Carolina and the greater part of North Carolina.

Scattered instances of *fire dogs* occur also in Eastern Pennsylvania, and the term is not unknown in New England; but the usual expression in Pennsylvania and the North is *andirons*, which has also become well established on Chesapeake Bay and on the Potomac. As a literary term *andirons* is current also in Southern cities.

In the *andirons* area the common folk not infrequently say *hand irons*, especially (1) in an area extending from Delaware Bay to the Rappahannock in Virginia and (2) in the northern counties of Pennsylvania. See Figure 48.

mantel shelf (8)

The shelf over the opening of the fireplace is known as the *mantel* or *mantel piece* in most parts of the Eastern States. (These terms also denote the entire decorative frame of the opening, the uprights together with the shelf.) In eastern Virginia and adjoining parts of North Carolina, except for the central part of the Virginia Piedmont, *shelf* is widely used instead of, or by the side of, *mantel (piece)*.

The South Midland, including the drainage basin of the Kanawha, has the distinctive expression *fire board*, which has spread down to the Atlantic between the Cape Fear and the Peedee rivers. See Figure 27.

In the vicinity of Raleigh, North Carolina, the strictly local term *frontis* is in use.

roller shades (9)

Roller shades are a recent invention. The term *(roller) shades* has general currency in the Hudson Valley, the Virginia Piedmont, and the greater part of the Carolinas, and it is widely used in urban areas elsewhere. But in large parts of the Eastern States people still pull down the *curtains* or the *blinds*.

Curtain is widely used in this sense (1) in New England and the New England settlement area, (2) in the Philadelphia area, and (3) on Chesapeake Bay and in the coastal part of northeastern North Carolina. Scattered instances of it have also been noted in the Midland.

The Midland term is *blinds*. In the Philadelphia area and on Delamarvia *blinds* competes with *curtains;* in the remainder of Pennsylvania and in all of the South Midland *blinds* has complete sway. There this term is never used as a synonym of shutters; only the *curtains* area has *blinds* in this sense. See Figure 49.

clothes closet (9)

Throughout the New England settlement area and the North Midland, including the Shenandoah Valley and northern West Virginia, *clothes press* is still a common term for the clothes closet in rural areas. On Narragansett Bay, where *closet* is the usual designation for the pantry, and in Western Pennsylvania and the adjoining counties of Ohio and West Virginia, *clothes press* is current among all social classes in the country as well as in the cities. On the other hand, the urbanized areas around Boston, in the Lower Connecticut Valley, in the lower Hudson Valley, and around Philadelphia now use *(clothes) closet* almost entirely. Since the Southern area has no trace of *clothes press,* the common occurrence of this expression on the Eastern Shore must be due to earlier Philadelphia influence, even though this term is now rare there. See Figures 50 and 51.

store room (10)

Many houses have a room in the attic or the cellar for storing old furniture and utensils. In the South Atlantic States we find a variety of terms to denote it: *lumber room, plunder room, trumpery room, junk room, catch-all.*

Lumber room is the Virginia Piedmont and Tidewater term, which is now current also on the Eastern Shore of Virginia (but not of Maryland) and in the Valley of Virginia. The greater part of North Carolina and adjoining parts of South Carolina have *plunder room,* and this term is not uncommon, by the side of *lumber room,* in Virginia south of the James. From Albemarle Sound to the lower Neuse *trumpery room* is current, on Delaware Bay, *catch-all.*

The expressions for this storeroom were not systematically recorded in the Middle Atlantic States and in New England, except for the eastern half of Pennsylvania. *Store room* appears to be the usual term in the Philadelphia area, *junk room* from the Susquehanna westward. *Junk room* is in use also in the Pennsylvania settlements of the piedmont of North Carolina and on the Cape Fear River by the side of *plunder room.* See Figure 52.

porch (10)

The screened porch and the sleeping porch are recent additions to man's comfort; they are known everywhere as *porches.* The unscreened porches of earlier days are also widely called *porches,* but other names are current, too: *piazza, stoop, veranda, gallery,* sometimes with different shades of meanings.

Piazza is found (1) in all of New England and, though less commonly, in the Hudson Valley and on Long Island; (2) in the Carolinas and south of the lower James in Virginia; (3) in southern Maryland west of Chesapeake Bay. The occurrence of *piazza* in southern Maryland permits the inference that this expression was once current all the way from Chesapeake Bay to the Georgia coast and that in the section of the Virginia Tidewater lying between the Potomac and the James, which is under Piedmont influence, the term has been given up.

The old-time *piazza* is usually long and narrow and sheltered by a roof supported by pillars.

Stoop is in general use in the Dutch settlement area—the Hudson Valley, northern New Jersey, and Long Island; it is common in Western New

England and the New England settlements of New York State and northern Pennsylvania and has spread into Eastern New England to the very door of Boston. From Narragansett Bay to Cape Cod and on the coast of Maine *stoop* is known, but little used.

Stoop is one of the few Dutch words that have become established beyond the limits of the Dutch settlement area. The reason for the adoption of *stoop* in New England is that the Dutch type of entry to the house, the raised platform, became fashionable in New England. To this day *piazza* and *stoop* mean different things in the New England area. See Figures 7 and 43.

gutters (on the roof) (11)

Gutters is in regular use on all social levels (1) in the Southern area, (2) in the Hudson Valley, Long Island, and nearly all of New Jersey, and (3) in Eastern New England. In southwestern Connecticut and in Philadelphia and vicinity *gutters* is now very common, but older regional expressions are still used by many. Elsewhere *gutters* is strictly a trade name.

Most parts of the North and the Midland still possess vigorous regional terms.

Eaves troughs (sometimes *eaves troths*) is current in all of New England, except the coastal section from Cape Cod to Maine, and in the New England settlement area. Scattered instances of *eaves troughs, water troughs,* and simply *troughs* occur on Delaware Bay, Chesapeake Bay, the Carolina coast, and in western Virginia and North Carolina, mostly in the speech of older people who have not yet adopted *gutters.* Moreover, *eaves troughs* is rather common in west-central West Virginia, especially in the Ohio Valley section of it, where the *eaves troughs* of the New England settlements of Marietta and vicinity across the river supported this older Southern term.

The North Midland and all of West Virginia have the expressions *the spouting* and *the spouts,* the latter being most frequent in West Virginia.

A related *eaves spouts* is common in the Upper Connecticut Valley and to the east thereof, except for the coastal area; and relics of it are found in Rhode Island, on Cape Cod, and on Nantucket, all parts of Eastern New England.

Whether the *eaves spouts* of the northern counties of Pennsylvania and the Western Reserve of Ohio is a direct descendant of this New England expression or, at least in part, a blend of the New England *eaves troughs* and the Pennsylvania *spouting, spouts* is an open question. It is a very striking fact that the New England settlements in New York State have only *eaves troughs,* whose original home is in southwestern New England. See Figures 53 and 54.

privy (12)

Privy and *back-house* are current everywhere for the old-fashioned outdoor toilet.

The more common regional terms are: *outhouse,* mostly in the New England settlement area; *water closet,* in New England and in the Philadelphia area (occasionally elsewhere); *closet,* in the Ohio Valley; *toilet,* in parts of New England; *garden house,* in Virginia and northeastern North Carolina; *johnny (house), jack house,* in Virginia; *necessary,* in the Boston area and in parts of the South. See Figure 55.

loft (14)

Barns are built in many different ways in different sections, depending in part upon tradition and prevalent crops and in part upon the site of the farm.

The upper part of a barn is called the *loft* in the greater part of the Eastern States: regularly so (1) in the Southern area and in the mountains south of the Kanawha, and (2) in New England and its offshoots; less commonly in the North Midland.

Loft is not current in central Pennsylvania and in the adjoining part of West Virginia, and it is infrequent in other parts of Pennsylvania and most of New Jersey. In some of the New England coast towns *loft* is reserved for the sail loft.

In most of Pennsylvania the loft is called the *overhead,* in the Pennsylvania German section also the *over-den* (cf. German *Tenne* 'barn floor').

The smaller New England barns often have a raised platform over the cow stalls or at one end of the barn for storing hay or grain, which is known as the *scaffold* (usually pronounced *scaffle*). This expression is found also on the

Mohawk and in the northern counties of Pennsylvania.

In Worcester County, Massachusetts, and in the Upper Connecticut Valley a platform right under the sloping sides of the roof is called the *high-beams,* less commonly the *great-beams* (pronounced *grett-beams*). *Great-beams* occurs also on the southeastern prong of Long Island. The hay is said to be *on the high-beams* or *in the high-beams.*

In the North Midland, in the Shenandoah Valley, and in West Virginia north of the Kanawha *(hay) mow* is in general use for the upper floor of a hay barn, and this expression is current also in New York State and to some extent in northwestern New England.

Many New England barns have compartments for storing hay that run from the barn floor to the roof. These are known as *bays* throughout the New England settlement area except for Cape Cod, Narragansett Bay, and the Maine coast, where *ground mow* is current.

It should be noted that in some sections the term *(hay) mow* is also extensively applied to any stack of hay in the barn, whether it rests on the barn floor or on a raised platform. See Figures 6 and 56.

corn crib (14)

Indian corn is often stored in sheds with flaring sides and a projecting roof. In the Midland and the entire New England settlement area this structure is called a *corn crib,* usually shortened to *crib* in Rhode Island. The simplex *crib* is characteristic of all of North Carolina and adjoining parts of Tidewater Virginia (south of the James), and of westernmost Virginia and South Carolina.

The Virginia Piedmont, the Tidewater area north of the James, and the Western Shore of Maryland have the distinctive term *corn house* to the exclusion of *corn crib.*

In New England the two expressions stand side by side, but only scattered relics of *corn house* are found in the New England settlement area.

Two local expressions are worth noting, the *crib house* of southern New Jersey and the *corn stack* of southern Delamarvia (southern Delaware to Cape Charles). See Figure 57.

hay cock (14)

For the temporary small heaps of hay in the meadow two regional terms are widely current, *cock* in the New England area and the North Midland, *shock* in the Southern area and in the South Midland. The Midland *cock,* however, is still common in the Valley of Virginia, not uncommon in Western North Carolina, and relics of it have survived in central West Virginia. Moreover, this Midland term has spread all the way down to the mouth of Chesapeake Bay on Delamarvia and to the James River on the western shore of the Bay.

The Southern *shock,* on the other hand, has become established in the greater part of the South Midland and bids fair to replace *cock* altogether in that section. On the Eastern Shore *shock* is no longer common, and it is clearly losing ground in Maryland west of the Bay.

Other terms for the haycock, more local in character, are: *heap* (1) in parts of New England and (2) in the Pennsylvania German area (cf. Pennsylvania German *Haufe*); *tumble,* scattered in northern New England; *doodle,* (1) in Western Pennsylvania and (2) on the lower Kanawha in West Virginia; *hand stack,* scattered in Pennsylvania; *pile,* (1) on the Atlantic coast from Delaware to Georgia and (2) in Eastern Pennsylvania. See Figures 58 and 59.

hay stack (14)

Cone-shaped hay stacks can be seen throughout the Eastern States, and they are regularly known by that name. Haystacks with a rectangular base are much less common, except in certain areas. These house-shaped stacks have distinctive names in certain sections. See Figure 60.

In an area including all of Virginia, except the Middle Neck and the South Side (the Norfolk area), all of Maryland, as well as Delaware Bay and the Lower Delaware Valley, these rectangular stacks are called *ricks.* Scattered instances of *rick* have been noted in West Virginia and in westernmost North Carolina.

The Dutch settlement area (western Long Island and the Hudson and Mohawk valleys) has *barrack,* a term of Dutch origin. This type of stack has a square base and a roof that slides on four corner posts. Stacks of this construction can also be seen east of Narragansett Bay and are locally known as *Dutch caps* or *hay caps*.

cow pen (15)

The enclosure adjoining the cow barn or cow shed is generally called a *cow pen* north of the Mason and Dixon's line as well as in large parts of the South. But the Southern area and the South Midland have in addition a variety of regional and local terms. See Figure 61.

In the Virginia Piedmont and the adjoining parts of Maryland and North Carolina the old compound *cuppin* (sometimes *cow cuppin*) is still current, and many remember it as an older word for the cowpen.

In Delamarvia and on Albemarle Sound *(cow) pound* still predominates, and in a belt directly west of the *pound* area on Albemarle Sound one hears *cow brake* (from the James to the Neuse).

The Appalachians and the Blue Ridge south of the James have *milk gap, milking gap,* one of the few expressions in the southern mountains that cannot be traced back to Pennsylvania or the Southern area.

In addition to these terms, *cow lot* and *milk lot* turn up in scattered fashion in different parts of the South and the South Midland.

In the North only Eastern New England and eastern Long Island have local expressions for the cowpen, the former *cow yard,* the latter *pightle* (riming with *title*). In all the vocabulary gathered for the Linguistic Atlas *pightle* is the only expression that is confined to Long Island.

barn yard (15)

The yard adjoining or surrounding the barn is regularly called *barn yard* north of the Potomac, *lot* (or *stable lot, barn lot, farm lot*) to the south of it.

In West Virginia the Midland *barn yard* and the Southern *barn lot* stand side by side; in the Shenandoah Valley *barn yard* is in general use, and the Midland expression is now common between the Potomac and the Rappahannock and in Tidewater Virginia. Elsewhere in the Southern area *barn yard* occurs in scattered fashion. It seems that *barn yard* is on the way to nation-wide currency. See Figure 62.

picket fence (16)

Fences with pointed or blunt upright slats which commonly surround the dwelling and the garden are known as *picket fences* in the New England settlement area, and as *paling fences, paled fences,* or simply as *palings* in the Midland and the Southern area. The variant *paled fence* is characteristic of the Philadelphia area.

Picket fence appears as a modern term in large parts of the Midland and the South, especially in the Ohio Valley, on Chesapeake Bay, in northeastern North Carolina, and in the Charleston area in South Carolina. See Figure 63.

rail fence (16)

The old-fashioned rail fence built of overlapping rails laid zigzag fashion is simply called a *rail fence* in the Southern area, in New York State, and in the northern counties of Pennsylvania. This term is also widely current in West Virginia and is in regular use in the mountains farther south. In New England this type of fence is commonly known as a *Virginia rail fence* to distinguish it from the *post-and-rail fence* of New England.

The Midland term for the zigzag fence is *worm fence,* an expression that predominates in Pennsylvania, West Virginia, New Jersey, and Delamarvia and has made its way into northern Virginia.

Sporadic terms for this kind of fence are *zigzag fence* and *snake fence.* See Figure 64.

Other types of fences are built of rails: the *post-and-rail* fence of New England, also known as the *Connecticut rail fence,* in which the rails are inserted in sturdy posts; the *herring-bone fence=stake-and-rider fence=buck fence* (Eastern Pennsylvania)=*rip-gut fence,* in which the rails are supported by crossed stakes.

stone fence (16)

Fences built of loose stones around fields and pastures are known as *stone walls* in the New England settlement area as far west as central New York State, as *stone fences* in the North Midland, and as *rock fences* farther south. *Stone fence* now predominates in all of Maryland, but in West Virginia the Southern *rock fence* is now more common than the Midland *stone fence.*

In parts of North Carolina *rock wall* stands by the side of *rock fence,* in northwestern New Jersey *stone row* by the side of *stone fence* and *stone wall.* See Figure 65.

pail (17)

The well-known metal container is called a *pail* in the entire New England settlement area and in the Hudson Valley, a *bucket* in all of the Midland and the South. However, on the New England coast north of Boston *bucket* is still used beside *pail* in this sense (sporadically also elsewhere in New England). On the other hand, *pail* has spread southward to central New Jersey and is now also current in Philadelphia beside *bucket.*

In parts of the Southern area *pail* has survived as the name of a wooden milk or water container which has one long stave serving as a handle.

Bucket, in turn, survives in New England in such compounds as *well bucket* and *fire bucket* (but cf. *cedar pail*).

Note also Northern *swill pail,* and Midland and Southern *slop bucket.* See Figures 66 and 67.

frying pan (of cast iron) (17)

The flat-bottomed cast-iron frying pan is now often called simply a *frying pan,* especially in urban areas. However, two older expressions, *skillet* and *spider,* are still extensively used for the cast-iron pan to distinguish it from the modern sheet-metal frying pan.

Skillet is current in all of the Midland from New Jersey to western South Carolina and westward. It is also the old term in the Virginia Piedmont, but it has here been largely supplanted by *frying pan.*

Spider occurs in two large separate areas: (1) in the New England settlement area (all the way to the Western Reserve of Ohio), and (2) in the tidewater area from the Potomac southward to the Peedee in South Carolina. It appears also on the Jersey coast from Sandy Hook to Cape May. See Figure 68.

faucet (18)

The water *faucet* is known by that name only in the Northern area. The entire Midland and the South have *spicket* (occasionally *spigot*).

Faucet, to be sure, is not entirely unknown in this sense in the Midland and the South. See Figure 69.

ox goad (19)

Oxen are little used as draft animals nowadays, but many of the older country folk still remember the ox goad, a stout pointed stick with a lash. There are many different terms for it in different parts of the Eastern States: *goad* (sometimes *goard*) in New England and the North Midland; *gad* in Western New England, on Long Island, in northern Pennsylvania, in northern West Virginia, and on Delaware Bay; *pop lash* on Narragansett Bay (with scattered instances elsewhere in New England), in eastern New Jersey, and on the North Carolina coast; *wattle* in southern Pennsylvania from the Susquehanna to the Monongahela; and *hickory* in the western part of the Carolinas. See Figure 28.

Elsewhere *whip* or *switch* appears to have been used.

paper bag (19)

Paper bag and *paper sack* are both widely used in the Eastern States.

Poke is current, often by the side of *bag* or *sack,* in a large area extending from central Pennsylvania westward, and southward to the Carolinas. In Virginia the Blue Ridge forms the eastern boundary of the *poke* area, in North Carolina the Yadkin.

To the east of the *poke* area, in the bilingual Great Valley of Pennsylvania (from Reading to Frederick in Maryland), the Pennsylvania German term *toot,* riming with *foot,* is in common use in the English spoken there. See Figure 70.

burlap bag (19)

Burlap sack or *bag* is the most common term in the Eastern States for the rough loose-woven sack in which potatoes and other farm produce are shipped. It is regularly current throughout the North and the North Midland, and not uncommon in Tidewater Virginia and on the Kanawha. However, most of the Southern area and parts of the Midland have vigorous regional and local terms.

Sea-grass sack, grass sack is current on the coast from Delaware Bay to Albemarle Sound and also on the Western Shore of Chesapeake Bay north of the James River.

Croker sack, crocus sack is in common use (1) in the southern part of the Virginia Piedmont, (2) in South Carolina and Georgia (also in Wilmington at the mouth of the Cape Fear), and (3) on Martha's Vineyard off Cape Cod.

Tow sack is the North Carolina term. It is common throughout the state and rare outside of it, except around Norfolk, Virginia.

Guano sack is common in Maryland, both east and west of the Bay, and in the Shenandoah Valley—presumably as a Baltimore trade name. (Much guano was imported by way of Baltimore and distributed to the farm lands from there.)

Gunny sack is the regular term for the burlap bag in the Ohio Valley from Wheeling downstream. Scattered instances of it have been noted in Eastern Pennsylvania, in Metropolitan New York, and in New England. See Figure 71.

grist of corn (19)

The quantity of corn a farmer has (or had) ground at one time at the gristmill is (or was) called a *grist of corn,* a *turn of corn,* or a *jag of corn.*

Grist occurs in the North and the North Midland, *turn* in the Virginia Piedmont and the South Midland. The boundary between *grist* and *turn* runs along the Kanawha in West Virginia and along the James in the Valley of Virginia, but the Midland *grist* survives on the Yadkin and the upper Cape Fear River in North Carolina.

Jag of corn is current in all of Pennsylvania, on Delaware Bay, in Maryland, and on the upper reaches of the Potomac in West Virginia. In Delaware and Maryland, where *grist* is not current, *jag* means a *grist*. But in Pennsylvania and southern New Jersey a *jag* is less than a *grist;* here *jag* is applied to a part load of anything carried on a wagon. See Figure 72.

armful (of wood) (19)

An armful of wood that one carries to the stove or the fireplace is called an *armful,* an *arm load,* a *load,* or a *turn of wood.* See Figure 73.

Armful is the regular expression in the North. In the North Midland *armful* is now more common than the old Midland *arm load* and *load,* but in the South Midland it is less common.

Load and *arm load* are found throughout the Midland except for western Virginia. In West Virginia the simple *load* predominates, as it does in North Carolina west of the Yadkin; in Pennsylvania and southern New Jersey *load* and *arm load* are equally common, but *armful* has replaced them almost completely in the Pittsburgh area and in the Pennsylvania German section.

The Southern area regularly has the expression *turn of wood* (cf. *turn of corn*).

tongue (of a wagon) (20)

The shaft between the two horses hitched to a farm wagon is called the *tongue* in all parts of the Eastern States, but there are also several regional and local terms.

In New England and the Hudson Valley *pole* is in common use. In the remainder of New York State it is less common. *Pole* occurs also on the Atlantic coast from Sandy Hook in New Jersey to Cape Charles in Virginia, and especially in the Virginia Tidewater north of the James. Sporadic instances appear in the Philadelphia area and in Maryland west of the Bay.

The heavy pole of the old oxcart has the special designations *neap* in the Lower Connecticut Valley, in Litchfield County, Connecticut, and in the Berkshires; and *neb* in Essex County, Massachusetts (Salem, Rockport). See Figures 74 and 75.

hauling (wood) (21)

In the Midland and the South *hauling* is the regular term for transporting bulky articles, such as wood, on a wagon or a truck. Along the Southern coast, less often in the piedmont, *carrying* is used by the side of *hauling,* on the North Carolina coast also *carting.*

Hauling is generally known also in the North, but the regional expression *drawing* or *carting* comes more readily to the lips of the common folk in the countryside. The expression *drawing wood* is current (1) in all of New England (except only the southeastern sector extending from the New London area to the Plymouth area, Cape Cod, and the islands offshore), (2) in all of New York State except the Metropolitan area, and (3) in the northern counties of Pennsylvania. The area of *carting* extends in an unbroken belt along the shore from Cape Cod to southern New Jersey. In Connecticut *drawing* competes with it, but not in southeastern Massachusetts, Long Island, Metropolitan New York, and New Jersey. *Carting* is also common in Upland Maine with its Plymouth Colony settlements and in the Loyalist settlements on the St. John in New Brunswick. It is not unknown in other parts of New England where *drawing wood* is the usual expression. See Figure 76.

From Marblehead to the southern tip of Maine and on the lower Merrimack the expression *teaming wood* appears to be the usual one.

singletree (21)

The bar to which the traces of a horse are fastened is called a *singletree* or a *swingletree* in all of the South and the Midland, a *whiffletree* or a *whippletree* in the North. Only central New Jersey has a local expression, *swiveltree,* several instances of which have been noted also on the upper Ohio.

In the North Midland *singletree* is now almost universal. The older *swingletree* does, however, survive on the Delaware and in southern New Jersey. In the South and the Southern Appalachians *singletree* and *swingletree* stand side by side, but *singletree,* a counter-term to *doubletree* (shortened from *double swingletree*), is gaining ground and already predominates decidedly in the Virginia Piedmont.

Whiffletree is the usual form of the Northern expression; *whippletree* is not uncommon in Western New England, in Upstate New York, and in northwestern Pennsylvania and the Western Reserve of Ohio, but there is a trend to *whiffletree* here too. See Figure 77.

stone boat (21)

The wheelless horse-drawn vehicle made of heavy planks, which is used for dragging stones from the fields, is known as a *stone sled* or *drag sled* in the Midland and as a *stone boat* in the North, except for the coastal area of New England, which has *drag* or *stone drag.*

Stone boat is a Connecticut Valley and Hudson Valley expression that was carried westward to the Great Lakes. In Pennsylvania and Ohio it has spread rather farther south than other New Englandisms, especially in the Pittsburgh area.

In the entire Connecticut Valley we find both the "western" *stone boat* and the "eastern" *(stone) drag;* also on Long Island and in East Jersey. See Figure 78.

seesaw (22)

The word *seesaw* is used everywhere, but in the New England settlement area other expressions are more widely current than *seesaw.* The same is true of parts of the South and the South Midland. It is only in Pennsylvania, and the greater parts of northern Maryland, Virginia, and South Carolina that *seesaw* is not paralleled by other terms.

Teeter, teeter board, teetering board are characteristic of New England and the entire New England settlement area to the Great Lakes. We find these expressions also in the New England settlements around Marietta and even on the West Virginia side of the Ohio.

On the lower Hudson, on Long Island, and in New Jersey *teeter (board)* is uncommon. Here we encounter *teeter-totter,* an expression that occurs also in the New England settlements of New York State, Pennsylvania, and Ohio. In New England *teeter-totter* can now be heard only on the Housatonic and west of the Green Mountains, but its predominance in northern New Jersey and its widespread use in the New England settlement area lead to the inference that it was formerly more widely current in Western New England.

It is fairly clear that *teeter (board)* is supplanting the earlier local expressions in New England: *tinter* in New Haven and on the lower Connecticut River; *dandle* in Rhode Island; *tilt, tilting board, tilter board* in Essex County, Massachusetts, and on the coast of Maine; *teedle board, tiddle board* on Cape Anne. However, on Cape Cod, Buzzards Bay, Martha's Vineyard, Nantucket, and on Aquidneck (Newport) in Narragansett Bay the Plymouth Colony expression *tilt, tilting board* is still firmly established; and Block Island has its *tippity-bounce* beside *tilt.*

The expressions for the seesaw in New England illustrate admirably the general trend in the development of the vocabulary of the Eastern States: the old (Colonial) local expressions are yielding ground to the regional term *teeter (board)*, which in turn is being supplanted by the national (literary) expression *seesaw* in urbanized areas.

In the Southern area and in the Appalachians *seesaw* is in rather general use on all social levels. The most widespread regional term is *ridy-horse (riding horse)*. It occurs (1) in the Appalachians from central West Virginia southward, and (2) in the coastal area of the Carolinas between the Neuse and the Peedee; and (3) relics of it occur on Albemarle Sound and on upper Chesapeake Bay.

Local expressions are: *cocky-horse, cock horse* in southern Delaware and in adjoining parts of the Eastern Shore of Maryland, and around St. Marys in southern Maryland; *hicky-horse, hick horse* between Albemarle Sound and the lower Neuse. See Figure 79.

bob sled (22)

Bob sled is the regular term in the Midland and the North for a coasting sled consisting of two short sleds or *bobs* that are fastened together, tandem-fashion, with a heavy board. This expression is also applied to a heavy horse-drawn sled consisting of two *bobs*.

In New England *bob sled* is not in general use and when it is used refers mostly to the horse-drawn sled. We find instead three regional terms in rather well defined geographic distribution. *Double runner* is current in the entire coastal area from Narragansett Bay to New Brunswick, including Worcester County in Massachusetts and all of New Hampshire except the northern third. *Double ripper*, occasionally shortened to *ripper* or *double rip*, is found in all of Connecticut and in western Massachusetts. *Traverse sled*, which is probably of Canadian French origin, is the regular term in Vermont and adjoining parts of New Hampshire and has found its way into eastern New Hampshire and Upland Maine, where it competes with the coastal term *double runner*.

None of these New England terms seems to have survived west of the Hudson, although an isolated *rips* was recorded in Binghamton, New York. See Figure 80.

saw horse (a rack for cutting wood) (22)

Saw horse, often shortened to *horse,* is in rather general use throughout the Eastern States except for the greater part of Pennsylvania east of the Alleghenies and western Maryland, and the Dutch settlements, where *saw buck* dominates.

Saw buck, wood buck, sometimes simply *buck,* are characteristic of the entire German settlement area in Eastern Pennsylvania, western Maryland, the Shenandoah Valley, the upper reaches of the Potomac in West Virginia, and on the Yadkin in North Carolina. These expressions are clearly modeled on German *Sägebock, Holzbock.* Scattered instances occur also in Western Pennsylvania.

Saw buck also has rather general currency in the entire Dutch settlement area from Long Island and eastern New Jersey to Albany, whence it was carried westward into the rest of New York State, into the Housatonic Valley, along Long Island Sound in Connecticut, and into western Vermont. Here *saw buck* has the Dutch prototype *zaagbock.*

Although *saw buck* is now used all the way from Western New England to the Shenandoah Valley, it was disseminated from two separate focal areas, the Dutch on the Hudson and the Pennsylvania German on the Lehigh and the Susquehanna.

In the Alleghenies the saw horse is sometimes called a *(wood) jack*. In southern Ohio we find *rack, wood rack* in this sense. There is no trace of these terms farther east. See Figure 81.

coal scuttle (23)

The following expressions occur in marked regional distribution: *coal hod, coal scuttle, coal bucket, coal pail.*

Coal hod is the regular expression in New England and has survived to some extent in parts of the New England settlement area (on the upper Susquehanna, in the Western Reserve). It is common in all of Maryland and is not unknown between the Potomac and the Rappahannock and on the lower Shenandoah. Furthermore, it occurs in the New England settlements around Marietta and in the adjoining part of West Virginia.

Coal scuttle has general currency in two separate areas: (1) from the Mohawk to Delaware Bay, including all of the Hudson Valley, Long Island, New Jersey, and the Philadelphia area; and (2) from the Potomac southward to the northern counties of North Carolina and westward to the New River in West Virginia.

From the Hudson Valley *coal scuttle* has spread into western Connecticut (to New Haven) and into the New England settlement area (as far as the Western Reserve), where it is now more common than the New England *coal hod;* and to New Brunswick, carried there by New York and New Jersey Loyalists.

The greater part of Pennsylvania has *coal bucket,* and this term is common in all of the Midland area as well as in the greater part of North Carolina. The Low Country of South Carolina, however, seems to have *coal scuttle.*

Coal pail appears here and there in the Northern *coal scuttle* area. See Figure 82.

whet stone (23)

The two common expressions are *whet stone* and *whet rock. Whet rock* is current in the South, except for the tidewater area, and in the South Midland; *whet stone* is in general use in the North Midland and in the North. *Whet stone,* however, is also the usual term on Chesapeake Bay and in northeastern North Carolina, and is used to some extent throughout the *whet rock* area. See Figure 83.

Two local terms are found on the south Atlantic coast: *whet seed* on Albemarle Sound, *whet* or *whetter* in parts of Delamarvia (especially southern Delaware) and from the Neuse to the Cape Fear River in North Carolina.

In New England and in East Jersey the emery-coated wooden whetter is known as a *rifle.*

kerosene (24)

There are striking regional expressions for the kerosene that superseded candles and whale oil for illuminating the home in the latter part of the nineteenth century.

Kerosene is in general use (1) in the North and (2) in the Carolinas.

From Pennsylvania to Virginia we find two other terms: *coal oil* in Pennsylvania east of the Alleghenies and thence southward to the Rappahannock and to Cape Charles; *lamp oil* in Pennsylvania west of the Alleghenies, in West Virginia, and in the Virginia Piedmont. *Coal oil,* to be sure, is used to some extent also in the Ohio Valley. The present spread of *coal oil* and *lamp oil* must be connected somehow with the marketing areas of this product of Pennsylvania and northern West Virginia.

The Pittsburgh area has, in addition to *lamp oil,* the local expression *carbon oil.* See Figure 84.

batteau (24)

Batteau is the name of a large flat-bottomed boat which was formerly used on the rivers for taking the farm or plantation produce to the market towns or to shipping points. The term is found on the Atlantic coast from Sandy Hook in New Jersey to Georgia. It is common on the Delaware and on Chesapeake Bay. In South Carolina *batteau* is used in the piedmont as well as in the tidewater section. The occurrence of *batteau* on the Yadkin in North Carolina reminds us of the intimate trade connections that existed between the North Carolina piedmont and the Low Country of South Carolina from the latter part of the eighteenth century till the coming of the railroads. See Figure 85.

vest (27)

Vest is current everywhere, but the common folk in the South and the South Midland are more likely to call this part of a man's suit a *wesket* or a *jacket.* See Figure 86.

Wesket can be heard among the simple folk in all of Virginia and adjoining parts of West Virginia, in northeastern North Carolina, and, if less frequently, in Maryland west of the Bay.

Jacket is common in the piedmont and the Blue Ridge of North Carolina and in adjoining parts of South Carolina, Virginia, and West Virginia. Scattered instances of *jacket* in central Pennsylvania and its common use along the upper reaches of the Potomac in West Virginia make it highly probable that the term is of Pennsylvania origin. In this case, as in so many others, earlier Pennsylvania usage is better preserved in the southern mountains and the North Carolina piedmont than in Pennsylvania itself.

clear across (28)

Instead of, or by the side of, the common expression *clear across* (the bed), we encounter in the Southern area *clean across* from the Potomac to the Peedee, *jam across* between the Rappahannock and the James, and *slam across* from the lower James to the Cape Fear. In the South Midland *plum across* is in general use. See Figure 87.

pallet (29)

Pallet is the regular name of an improvised bed on the floor throughout the Southern area and in the South Midland (as far north as the northern watershed of the Kanawha). In the southern part of Delamarvia *lodge* is used in this sense. See Figure 88.

comfort (29)

The thick cotton-padded quilt is known as a *comfort* in the Midland and the South, as a *comforter* or as a *comfortable* in the North.

Comforter is the usual term in Eastern New England and in Manhattan, *comfortable* in southwestern New England, in the Hudson Valley, on Long Island, in East Jersey, and in New York State. However, *comforter* is scattered all through the *comfortable* area, and *comfortable*, in turn, is not unknown in the Delaware Valley beside *comfort*.

In the mountains of central Pennsylvania *hap*, one of the few Scotch-Irish words, is in common use beside *comfort*.

Tied quilt and *tie* are used by some in New England to distinguish the heavy quilt from the thin sewed *quilt*. See Figure 89.

bottom land (29)

In the Midland and the South *bottom lands* and *bottoms* are the most common expressions for low-lying flat meadow lands and fields along large and small watercourses. *Bottom lands* is more common in the North Midland, *bottoms* in the South and the South Midland.

In New York State and the adjoining counties of Pennsylvania *flats* is the regular designation. This term is used to some extent also in northern East Jersey and in Eastern Pennsylvania as well as in the Virginia Piedmont and Tidewater.

Low-lands is characteristic of Maryland, Delaware, and southeastern Pennsylvania but occurs sporadically also on the southern coast and in New England. See Figures 90 and 91.

Other regional expressions are *intervale* or *interval* in New England (except for the southwestern part); *low-grounds* in the Virginia Piedmont and the greater part of Eastern North Carolina; *savannah*, from the lower Neuse to the Peedee, for low-lying grassland.

salt creek (30)

The salt-water inlets of small streams that empty into the sea are known as *creeks* from Maine to Cape Fear in North Carolina. See Figure 92.

creek (30)

Creek is the most common word for a small fresh-water stream in the Eastern States. It is current everywhere except in the greater part of New England, where *brook* or *river* are the usual terms.

Outside New England, Long Island, and Metropolitan New York *brook* is rare as a common noun, but it appears in the proper names of many streams in the New England settlement area as far west as Erie, Pennsylvania.

The Midland term for a smaller stream is *run*, but in Pennsylvania and the northern half of West Virginia *creek* is now the common noun. However, *run* occurs in the names of many streams in this area. As a common noun, *run* is now characteristic of an area extending from Delaware Bay to the James River (except Lower Delamarvia) and westward to the Shenandoah and the upper reaches of the Potomac in West Virginia. It is also fairly common along the Neuse in North Carolina.

In the South and in the South Midland as far north as the Kanawha Valley *branch* is the usual designation of the tributary of a *creek* or a *river*. *Branch* is also current on Delaware Bay beside *run*.

The Dutch word *kill* for a small watercourse survives only in the names of certain creeks or rivers in the Dutch settlement area, such as the *Batten Kill* in Vermont, the *Catskill Creek* in New York, and the *Schuylkill River* in Pennsylvania. See Figure 93.

sidewalk (31)

Throughout the Eastern States *sidewalk* is in general use, excepting only the Philadelphia trade area, which extends westward to the Alleghenies, northward to the fork of the Susquehanna, and southward on Delaware Bay and Chesapeake Bay. Here the Philadelphia term *pavement* is current. See Figure 20.

bull (33)

The plain term *bull* is current everywhere, and in the North Midland and New York State other expressions are rare. In New England, the South, and the South Midland, however, the plain term is not used by older folk of one sex in the presence of the other. Even many of the younger generation prefer the veiled expressions of the Victorian era. See Figure 94.

New England expressions for the bull are: *sire, animal* or *male animal, critter, toro* (New Hampshire and Vermont), *seed ox* (rare), *gentleman cow, gentleman ox* (found also on Chesapeake Bay), and *masculine* (riming with *fine,* on Nantucket).

Southernisms are equally varied: *male* and *male cow* in Virginia, adjoining parts of North Carolina, and on Delamarvia (occasionally also in New England); *beast, stock beast, male beast* in the coastal section of the Carolinas; *stock brute, male brute* in westernmost North Carolina; *steer* from southern Maryland to Albemarle Sound; *ox* in the Virginia Tidewater, central West Virginia, and sporadically elsewhere; *gentleman cow* on Chesapeake Bay (also in New England); and *masculine* (riming with *fine*) in southern West Virginia (also on Nantucket). West Virginia further contributes *Durham, jock,* and *major.*

Some of these expressions are now rare or are used only jestingly, but in the Southern area such expressions as the *male,* the *beast,* and the *brute* are common, and if one used the plain word *bull* to a lady, one might be in trouble.

ram (34)

Ram is current everywhere in the Eastern States as the name of the male sheep, but outside the Southern area *buck* and *buck sheep* occur by the side of *ram,* especially in rural sections. In the Pennsylvania German settlement area one can also hear *sheep buck,* which is modeled on the German *Schafbock.* See Figure 95.

moo (36)

In the North and the Midland the gentle noise cows make at feeding time is usually called *mooing (mewing,* by some). This expression is used also by some of the younger generation in the South, but the usual expression from Baltimore southward is *low* (riming with *so*).

In the lower James River Valley *low* is sometimes changed to *lower.* This is an overcorrection on the model of *four,* which has a folk pronunciation riming with *so* beside the cultivated pronunciation.

Low occurs also in southern New England. *Loo,* a variant of it, is fairly common in rural New England and has survived to some extent in northern Pennsylvania and central New York State. See Figure 96.

From Albemarle Sound to the Peedee Valley in South Carolina the expression *hum* is current beside *low,* which here usually means 'bellow.'

bellow (36)

For the loud noise cows make, especially when their calves are taken from them, New England says *bellow, beller,* the Midland *bawl.* Bawl is in general use in West Jersey, in Pennsylvania (aside from the northern counties and parts of the Pennsylvania Dutch area), and in Virginia and the Carolinas from the Blue Ridge westward. See Figure 16.

In Eastern North Carolina *low* seems to have this sense.

whinny (36)

Three terms, or groups of related terms, are current for the gentle noise made by horses at feeding time: *whinny (whinner, winny, winner), whicker (wicker, whinker),* and *nicker* (rarely *nickle*). These expressions show a rather clearcut geographic distribution.

Whinny and *whinner* are the usual expressions in New England (aside from Rhode Island, the Plymouth area, Martha's Vineyard, and Nantucket), New York State, New Jersey, the greater part of Pennsylvania, and adjoining parts of Ohio. Aside from the Blue Ridge, only scattered instances of *whinny* have been noted south of Pennsylvania, which appear to be recent importations from the literary language.

Nicker is in general use in a large area extending from Chesapeake Bay westward to southern Ohio and Kentucky and from there southward through the Appalachians as far as Georgia. It is in regular use in all of Virginia except the Norfolk area south of the lower James. The Virginia Piedmont would seem to be the original center from which *nicker* spread out. Interestingly enough, there are some relics of *nicker* in New England.

Whicker is now used in four separate areas: (1) in southeastern New England, from the lower Connecticut to Cape Cod and the islands offshore, an area that centers on Narragansett Bay; (2) in Maine, which derived part of its population from the Plymouth and Cape Cod areas; (3) on the lower Susquehanna; and (4) in the southern two thirds of Delamarvia, in the Virginia Tidewater (especially south of the James), and in the Carolinas (except for the westernmost parts). It seems that the *whicker* area on the Susquehanna has been separated in rather recent times from the far-flung Southern *whicker* area by the encroachment upon Delamarvia of *whinny* from the Midland and of *nicker* from the Western Shore of Chesapeake Bay.

In the Carolinas *whicker* is well established, but in New England it is yielding ground to *whinny,* and in Tidewater Virginia *nicker* is taking its place.

Laugh, a Germanism, is still current in the Great Valley of Pennsylvania, but it is being replaced by *whinny.* See Figure 97.

setting hen (36)

Clook (less commonly *cluck*) is an expression of Pennsylvania German origin that is extensively used for the setting hen in Pennsylvania from the Delaware to the Ohio. It is rare beyond the boundaries of the state.

wishbone (37)

The V-shaped clavicles of a fowl are variously known as *wishbone, pully-bone, pull-bone (pulling bone),* and *lucky-bone.* All these terms have reference to the popular practice of pulling the bone apart to have one's wish if one is lucky enough to get the larger half of it.

Wishbone appears to be a Northern expression which now also predominates in the North Midland and has come to be rather widely used in Maryland and Virginia west of Chesapeake Bay. In the Carolinas it is pretty well confined to cultivated speech.

The usual Southern and South Midland expression is *pully-bone, pull-bone.* This term is also current among the older folk in the North Midland, notably in southern New Jersey and southwestern Pennsylvania, but *wishbone* has taken its place in the greater part of Pennsylvania and in the Baltimore area even in the speech of the common man. *Pull-bone* is characteristic of southern New Jersey, Chesapeake Bay, the Potomac Valley, and the Charleston area of South Carolina.

Lucky-bone is the usual folk word between the Kennebec and the Merrimack in northern New England and has some currency also in eastern Virginia. See Figure 98.

Calls to Cows in the Pasture (37)

Each of the three major areas has its distinctive call. *Boss!, bossie!,* sometimes preceded by *co* or *come,* is used in all of New England and the New England settlements of New York State, northern Pennsylvania, and Ohio, as well as in the Hudson Valley; *sook!, sookie!, sook cow!* in the Midland, from the Susquehanna westward, and southward to northern Georgia; *co-wench!, co-inch!, co-ee!* in the South, from Delaware Bay to Georgia. See Figures 99 and 100.

Beside these regional calls, whose present spread reflects the major settlement areas of the Eastern States, a number of more local calls have survived: *co!* in Eastern New England, on Long Island Sound, and in southern New Jersey; *coaf!* on the New England coast; *kush!, kushie!* (with the vowel of *bush*) in northern New Jersey (from Bergen County to Sandy Hook), with scattered instances on the Delaware and in the Hudson Valley; *woo!, wookie! (whookie!, hookie!)* in the Pennsylvania German settlements on the Lower Susquehanna and from there southward to the head of the Shenandoah, as well as in northern West Virginia (the upper Potomac and Monongahela), with scattered instances in the Ohio Valley; finally, the German calls *komm da!* on the Lehigh and *seh!* on the Susquehanna.

Calls to Cows during Milking (37)

The call *so!* is current nearly everywhere in the Eastern States from Maine to Georgia and westward to the Ohio. However, it is not used in Virginia, except in the southwestern part. It is uncommon in adjoining parts of North Carolina, in Maryland west of the Bay, and in south-central Pennsylvania. See Figure 101.

This area has the related *saw!*, which is current everywhere south of Pennsylvania, except Delamarvia, and in south-central Pennsylvania also (as far north as the fork of the Susquehanna). In the greater part of this large area *so!* and *saw!* stand side by side.

Other calls have survived here and there: *hoist!* (with the vowel of *high*) and the shortened *hie!* in New England (now rare) and in southernmost New Jersey; *sto!* in the Albany area, doubtless of Dutch origin; and the Pennsylvania German *stehn!* in the Palatine settlements.

The call proper is often followed by the name of the cow or the local affectionate appellation for a cow, such as *boss(ie)*, *wench*, *sook(ie)*, *kush(ie)*, *tytie* (the last two in northern New Jersey). Compare the cow calls above.

Calls to Calves (37)

There are three regional calls: *bossie!* in New England and the New England settlements, *sookie!* in the Midland, and *cossie!* or *cussie!* in the South. However, the Midland call has encroached upon the Virginia Piedmont and on all of South Carolina and Georgia.

Co-calfie! competes with *cossie!* in parts of eastern Virginia and North Carolina, *cubbie!* predominates on the Eastern Shore of Virginia and in the Norfolk area, *co-dubbie!* on Albemarle Sound.

The Pennsylvania German call *hommie!* or *hommilie!* is still current beside *sookie!* from the Lehigh to the Shenandoah and westward to the Alleghenies. Northern New Jersey has *tye!*, which must be of Dutch origin. On the upper Delaware (in Pennsylvania and in the Catskills) several instances of *kees!*, *kish!* have been recorded (cf. the cow call *kush!*).

It is interesting to see that none of the local calls of the Atlantic seaboard have survived west of the Alleghenies; there *bossie!* and *sookie!* alone are current. See Figure 102.

hasslet (37)

The edible inner organs of a pig, calf, or sheep butchered on the farm are widely known as the *hasslet (harslet)*, the *pluck*, or the *liver and lights*.

Hasslet occurs in three separate areas: (1) the entire Southern area and parts of the South Midland (but not the Shenandoah Valley), (2) Eastern New England exclusive of Rhode Island and eastern Connecticut, and (3) the lower Hudson Valley.

Pluck is current, in uneven distribution, from New Hampshire to Virginia. It is common .in Rhode Island, Connecticut, western Vermont, and the New York counties east of the Hudson; also in the New England settlements on the upper Susquehanna, on Delaware Bay, and in Maryland west of the Bay. (The Eastern Shore has *hasslet*.)

Liver and lights is of common occurrenc_ (1) in the Maryland counties adjoining Pennsylvania and on Delaware Bay, and (2) in Western North Carolina.

In the greater part of the Midland a comprehensive term to include liver, kidneys, heart and lungs (lights) is lacking, and the urban population in other sections is largely unfamiliar with the regional expressions. We have no national term and presumably never will have one since butchering on the farm is going out.

It is of some interest to note that Aquidneck Island in Narragansett Bay (the Newport area) has the distinctive expression *pig's squin* for the edible inner organs of a pig. See Figure 103.

chittlins (37)

Chittlins is the name of the small intestines of a pig in the Southern area, where they are eaten by the simple folk. The trisyllabic *chitterlings* is rare.

Calls to Pigs (38)

The call *pig!*, *piggie!* is current throughout the New England and Midland areas, except for the Pennsylvania German settlements.

The German call *voots!*, *vootsie!*, *vootie!* (with the vowel of *put*) is in rather general use from the Lehigh to the Shenandoah and the upper Potomac, and westward to the Alleghenies, and relics of it have survived on the Yadkin in North Carolina.

Two other calls occur in parts of the North Midland: *poo-ie!* in the Delaware Valley, especially on the Jersey side, and *hoo-ie!, hoa-ie!, woo-ie!* in northern Delaware and on the lower Susquehanna. Both of them are also in common use in a well-defined area centering on Wheeling, West Virginia, presumably derived from the Delaware Valley.

In northeastern New England and on Nantucket, Martha's Vineyard, and Block Island *chook!, choke!* has survived.

Chook!, choke! is in general use in the Virginia Piedmont and occurs also on both sides of Chesapeake Bay and to some extent on the North Carolina coast as far south as the Neuse. Other variants of this call in the South are *choog!, chuck!, kə-chook!, kə-choo!*

On the Eastern Shore and between the lower James and the Neuse *wook!, wookie!, woak!* predominates.

In North Carolina south of the Neuse, in South Carolina, and in Georgia entirely different calls are in regular use: *goop!, piggoop!* (with the vowel of *loop*), and *woop!, woopie!* The diversity of Southern usage is very striking. See Figure 104.

Calls to Sheep (38)

Urbanized areas such as eastern Massachusetts, the lower Hudson and Long Island, and the Philadelphia-Baltimore area no longer have knowledge of a sheep call, and rural areas where sheep raising never was common, such as the Low Country of South Carolina, have never had a current expression. Even in sections that once raised sheep many people have forgotten the call.

The geographic distribution of the sheep calls is rather complicated, partly because of this situation, but the major speech areas come out fairly clearly nevertheless. The New England area has *kə-day! (kə-daik!, kə-dack!, kə-dick!)* and *nannie!, kə-nan!;* the Midland has *sheep!, sheepie!;* the Southern piedmont has *co-sheep!* (which has been carried westward into the Blue Ridge and the Appalachians south of the Kanawha, where it competes with the Midland *sheep!, sheepie!*),

and the Southern tidewater from Chesapeake Bay to Georgia has *nannie!, kə-nan!* (like the New England area).

Of the New England calls, *nannie!* and its variants have the wider spread. It is (or was) current all the way from Maine and Cape Cod to the Western Reserve. *Kə-day!* and its variants are common in the Connecticut Valley, the Green Mountains, and in Upstate New York. Narragansett Bay alone has *cade!,* which is here also the name for a pet sheep.

In the South *nannie!* and its variants are in general use on both sides of Chesapeake Bay, on the Rappahannock, in coastal North Carolina, and on the Peedee. This coastal call has been carried westward into the Blue Ridge of North Carolina and westernmost Virginia, where it competes with the Midland *sheepie!* and the Virginia Piedmont call *co-sheep!* See Figure 105.

Calls to Chickens (38)

The calls *chick!* and *chickie!* are current throughout the Eastern States, but in certain sections other expressions are used as well (sometimes restricted to hens). See Figure 106.

Biddie! (widdie!) occurs in three separate areas: (1) from the Connecticut Valley eastward to Cape Cod and Maine, (2) from southern Delaware southward to Cape Charles, and (3) in North Carolina and on the Peedee.

The call *kip!,* surely of Dutch origin, is used in the Hudson and Mohawk valleys, in the Catskills, and in Bergen County, New Jersey. Eastern Long Island and lower Narragansett Bay have *coop!* (with the vowel of *book*). The German *bee!* is still common in the Pennsylvania German area. The Virginia Piedmont and Tidewater south of the Rappahannock have *coo-chee!, coo-chick!,* the points of land between Albemarle Sound and the mouth of the James *cootie!* (with the vowel of *put*).

Neither the *biddie!* of New England nor the *coo-chee!* of Virginia has been carried westward.

Calls for Driving Horses (38)

The call *get up!* (in various pronunciations), chirping, and clucking are in rather general use throughout the Eastern States, but there are also a number of regional expressions.

In Virginia and adjoining parts of Maryland, West Virginia, and North Carolina the more usual call is *come up!*, which may be followed by *sir*. On lower Chesapeake Bay and especially in Eastern North Carolina *go along!* and *go on!* are used in this sense, but in New England they are employed to hasten the pace. See Figure 107.

Calls to Stop a Horse (38)

The most common call is *woa!* It is the only form of the call one hears in the Midland and the greater part of the South. It is also widely used in New England and the Hudson Valley by the side of the variant *whoa!*, but is uncommon in the New England settlements to the west, where *whoa!* predominates. Outside the New England settlements *whoa!* is exceedingly rare.

Another variant, *hoa!*, is fairly common in western Connecticut and in Greater New York City, and in the Southern coastal area from Chesapeake Bay to the Neuse. Yet another call, *waw!*, is frequently heard in the Virginia Tidewater (especially on the Rappahannock) and between the Roanoke and the Neuse in North Carolina.

The variety of calls is especially great in New England and in eastern Virginia. The former has *woa!*, *whoa!*, and *hoa!*, the latter, *woa!*, *waw!*, and *hoa!*, and in addition, *way!* on the James and *yay!* on the Potomac and the Eastern Shore. Beyond the mountains it seems that only *woa!* and the New England *whoa!* survive. See Figure 108.

near-horse (39)

The left horse of a (plow) team is known as the *near-horse (near-side horse)* in a large area extending from the Connecticut River to the Potomac and the Kanawha, excepting only the southwestern half of Pennsylvania.

In Eastern New England *nigh-horse* predominates (*near-horse* being uncommon), and this term, though yielding ground to *near-horse*, is still extensively used in Western New England and the entire New England settlement area. *Nigh-horse* is also fairly common on Delaware Bay and on the Northern Neck of Virginia; and scattered instances have been noted in coastal North Carolina and Georgia.

Another expression, *lead horse (leader)*, is fully

established in two large detached sections of the Midland: (1) in southwestern Pennsylvania, from the lower Susquehanna westward, and (2) in the Blue Ridge and the Appalachians south of the James and the Kanawha.

In parts of the German settlements in Eastern Pennsylvania, in the Shenandoah Valley, and on the Yadkin the near-horse is called the *saddle horse*. This term is modeled on the German *Sattelgaul*.

Several other expressions occur in the South: *line horse* and *wheel horse* in the Piedmont of Virginia; *hand horse* and *huther-horse (hither-horse)* on the Eastern Shore of Maryland and in southern Delaware. See Figures 109 and 110.

a little way (39)

He lives a little way(s) down the road is an utterance one hears in all of the Eastern States. In the greater part of the Midland, however, many are more apt to say *a little piece* instead of *a little way(s)*. This expression is also in common use in Delamarvia and between the Cape Fear and the Peedee. See Figure 111.

The expression *a little piece* is especially common (1) on the Susquehanna and on Delaware Bay, whence it may have spread into Delamarvia, (2) in the northern half of West Virginia, and (3) in Western North Carolina, whence it spread down to the coast between the Cape Fear and the Peedee. On the other hand, it has been almost eliminated in the Valley of Virginia.

Pennsylvania is clearly the original home of this expression. Whether the German expression *ein klein(es) Stück* had something to do with the preservation of it in the Midland is not clear.

second crop (of hay) (41)

Second crop is the regular expression employed with reference to hay and clover in the South and the Midland. *Second cutting* competes with it only (1) in the coastal area from Delaware Bay to the Neuse in North Carolina, and (2) in the Ohio Valley.

In the New England settlement area usage is complicated and in flux. *Second crop* is regular in Maine and New Hampshire, but much less common in other parts of New England; in the Hudson Valley again it is in fairly general use.

Second cutting competes with *second crop* in New York State and is now also used by some in western Connecticut.

Western New England as well as Rhode Island and eastern Massachusetts has the old expression *rowen crop* or *rowen* (riming with *plowin'*) for the second crop of hay or clover. *Rowen* is still well established here in this sense, but in New York State it denotes the uncut growth that develops after the first cutting of the grass. This meaning of *rowen* and of the related *rowet* of the New Hampshire coast is not unknown in New England.

The following rare relics are of historical interest: *aftermath* in the New England area and on Delamarvia; *aftergrass* in New Brunswick and northeastern Maine; scattered cases of *aftercrop*, *aftercutting*, *aftergrowth*, and *lattercrop* in the New England settlement area. See Figure 112.

sheaf (41)

In the Southern area and in the South Midland *bundle* is the regular word for a sheaf of wheat. Elsewhere in the Eastern States *bundle* and *sheaf* occur side by side, the former predominating in the entire New England settlement area, the latter in Pennsylvania and adjoining parts of West Virginia. In Philadelphia and its immediate vicinity *sheaf* is used to the exclusion of *bundle*, and in the adjoining Pennsylvania German section to the west *sheaf* is much more common than *bundle*. (The Pennsylvania German term is homophonous with *shape*.)

Sheaf predominates in all the larger cities of the North and the Midland, partly because it is the literary term. In the South *sheaf* is almost entirely restricted to cultured speakers. See Figure 113.

you-all (43)

The form *you* is used as a plural in all parts of the Eastern States. By the side of *you*, the greater part of the Midland and all of the South have the specific, emphatic, or 'generous' plural forms *you'ns*, *you-all*, and *mongst-ye*. All these forms have a possessive case: *you'ns's*, *you-all's*, *mongst-ye's*. See Figure 114.

You-all is current throughout the South and the South Midland (in all of West Virginia, except the northwestern section around Wheeling and Parkersburg).

You'ns is the Midland form and occurs in the folk speech of Pennsylvania west of the Susquehanna, in large parts of West Virginia, and in the westernmost parts of Virginia and North Carolina.

The form *mongst-ye* is common in the folk speech of the central part of Delamarvia, and rare instances are found from the mouth of Chesapeake Bay to Albemarle Sound.

wheat bread (in loaves) (44)

In the North and the North Midland, where wheat bread is consumed more commonly than any other variety of loaf bread, it is generally known simply as *bread*. If a more specific term is needed to distinguish it from rye bread or corn bread, *wheat bread* is used in the greater part of the area, *white-bread* in Eastern New England.

In the South and the South Midland this type of bread is commonly known as *light-bread*, in the coastal area also as *loaf bread*, as distinct from *pone bread* for corn bread. (But some Carolinians speak of a *pone of light-bread*.)

The expressions *yeast bread*, *east bread*, current in Eastern New England and on Chesapeake Bay, and the *raised-bread*, *riz-bread* of Eastern New England refer to the homemade loaf. See Figure 115.

corn bread (in cakes) (44)

Beside the national term *corn bread*, which now predominates in the urbanized areas and is widely used by the better educated in most rural areas as well, several regional expressions are still firmly established in the speech of the common man and the simple folk. See Figure 116.

In New England, except for Rhode Island, and in the entire New England settlement area *johnny cake* appears to be holding its own, and there are relics of it in Metropolitan New York and in most parts of New Jersey. (For *johnny cake* in the sense of 'griddle cake' see below.)

In the valley of the Susquehanna, in all of Pennsylvania lying to the west of it, and in all the Atlantic states south of Pennsylvania *pone*, *corn 'pone*, and *pone bread* are widely used, but *corn bread* is gaining ground. Relics of *pone* in the Philadelphia area indicate that this term was formerly current throughout the South and the Midland. (It is of Algonkian origin.)

corn griddle cake (44)

Griddle cakes made of corn meal, with or without an admixture of flour, baked in varying sizes and in varying thickness on a griddle or in a frying pan, formerly also on a board before the open fire, are a Southern favorite. They are known under a great variety of terms, some regional, others local; some are in common use among all classes of people, others are folksy, old-fashioned, or obsolescent.

One of the more widely used terms is *johnny cake,* which is current in several unconnected areas: (1) in the Carolinas, (2) in Maryland, southern Delaware, and the Northern Neck and Eastern Shore of Virginia, (3) in central West Virginia. This expression is unknown in the greater part of Virginia and the Midland area. In New England and the New England settlement area *johnny cake* means 'corn bread,' but in Rhode Island it refers to a corn griddle cake, which is known as a *Rhode Island johnny cake* in the adjoining parts of Connecticut and Massachusetts.

In the southern part of the Eastern Shore of Maryland and in coastal North Carolina *johnny cake* competes with *johnnikin,* on which it is probably built up, as the *Dictionary of American English* suggests.

Another common Southern expression for a corn griddle cake is *hoe cake.* It is in general use in the Carolinas and in all except the west-central part of Virginia, at least in folk speech or as an old-fashioned term. It does not occur east of Chesapeake Bay, and is rare even in southern Maryland and uncommon in the *johnnikin* area on the coast of North Carolina.

On the lower Susquehanna and in northern Delaware griddle cakes made of corn meal are known as *corn cakes,* and this term now competes in Maryland with *johnny cake,* in the Shenandoah Valley and the Northern Neck of Virginia with *hoe cake.*

In the Midland and farther north griddle cakes made of corn meal are rarely served, and hence there are no local terms. The only exception is Rhode Island (see above).

In the South Midland (most of West Virginia, western Virginia, Western North Carolina), and in the Northern Neck and the northern Piedmont of Virginia the term *corn dodger* is applied to a small corn cake (two or three in one pan); in West Virginia south of the Kanawha the corresponding term is *hobby.* In parts of this area *hoe cake* and *johnny cake* are also current, denoting a thinner cake.

In the eastern part of the Carolinas and on the Eastern Shore of Maryland *corn dodger* means a dumpling, usually steamed with vegetables. Here the corn griddle cake is a *johnny cake,* a *johnnikin,* or a *hoe cake.*

Another term for a small corn cake formerly baked in the embers of the fireplace is *ash cake,* which is current on both sides of Chesapeake Bay from Baltimore southward, and in all of Virginia and the Carolinas. It is not common in Virginia west of the Blue Ridge, where *dodger* seems to take its place, or in coastal North Carolina; it is rare in West Virginia. See Figures 117, 118, and 119.

cracklin bread (44)

In the Carolinas, in Virginia, and to some extent also in southern Maryland *cracklins,* small pieces of rendered pork fat, are sometimes mixed with corn meal to make *cracklin bread* or *fatty-bread.*

The term *cracklin bread* is current throughout this area; *fatty-bread* is common between the lower James and the Roanoke rivers, uncommon elsewhere.

batter bread (44)

A soft cake of corn meal and eggs, baked in a pan, is served in the Carolinas, in Virginia, and in southern Maryland. It is called *batter bread* in the greater part of Virginia, *egg bread* in the Carolinas, and *egg bread* or *egg pone* in southern Maryland and the southern part of the Eastern Shore of Maryland. Another term, *spoon bread,* is current in scattered communities on Chesapeake Bay (Baltimore to Norfolk), on the lower Shenandoah, and on the Cape Fear in North Carolina (Wilmington). See Figure 33.

doughnut (45)

The national term *doughnut* is current everywhere in the Eastern States, but other expressions are in use in certain sections either as synonyms of *doughnut* or for a special kind of doughnut.

The sweetened unraised variety, usually ring-shaped or twisted, is known in Eastern New England simply as a *doughnut,* the raised variety as a *raised doughnut* or *riz doughnut* (the latter in folk speech).

In the Dutch settlement area the unraised variety is a *cruller,* the raised variety a *doughnut.* This usage is common also in Western New England, in all of New Jersey, in southeastern Pennsylvania, in Baltimore, and on the upper Potomac. The term *cruller* is clearly derived from Dutch *krul,* which means 'curl.' Several instances of *crull* have been noted in northern West Virginia and in Western North Carolina, areas that were in part settled from Eastern Pennsylvania; but they may be shortenings of *cruller.*

The unraised variety has also other names: *fried-cake* (in most parts of New England; and in the entire New England settlement area in New York State and northern Pennsylvania, where *cruller* has not taken hold), *nut cake* (New Hampshire and Maine), *rings* (on Nantucket), *fat-cake* (in the Pennsylvania German area, modeled on German *Fettkuchen*), *fossnocks* (in the Pennsylvania German area, shortened from *Fastnachtskuchen*), the Dutch *olicook* (in the Hudson Valley), and *cookie* (in northeastern North Carolina).

Of all these terms only *doughnut* and *fried-cake* seem to have survived west of the Alleghenies. See Figure 120.

pancake (45)

For a thin wheat cake cooked on a griddle or in a pan the term *pancake* is current in all the Eastern States, but with varying frequency. It is rare in Eastern New England, uncommon in central Pennsylvania and the Blue Ridge of Virginia, and not too common in the piedmont of Virginia and North Carolina. On Chesapeake Bay and in the tidewater of the Carolinas *pancake* usually denotes a large pancake containing eggs.

Other terms for this type of cakes are regional or local.

Griddle cake is characteristic of Eastern New England as far west as the Connecticut Valley; it is used to some extent also in Metropolitan New York, the Hudson Valley, East Jersey, and parts of Pennsylvania. New Hampshire and Maine, however, have preserved *fritter* in this sense.

Pancake, which is fully established in western Connecticut now, but which may have come in from the Hudson Valley, is making its way into Eastern New England. The common *pancake* of northern Maine and New Brunswick was doubtless introduced by New York and New Jersey Loyalists.

Hot-cake is largely confined to Delaware Bay and the Delaware Valley in Pennsylvania.

Flannel cake (flannen cake) seems to be an old Pennsylvania term. It is in regular use from the Susquehanna to the Alleghenies and in the adjoining part of Maryland, including Baltimore. It has been carried southward into the Blue Ridge and along Chesapeake Bay, and westward to the upper Ohio River. In the Pennsylvania German area and the vicinity of Philadelphia *flannel cake* still has some currency but has been yielding ground to *hot-cake* and *pancake.*

The characteristic term south of the Potomac is *batter cake (batty-cake),* and this Southern term has been carried westward into the Blue Ridge and into the valley of the Kanawha in West Virginia. The term is known also in Baltimore and in southern New Jersey, and scattered instances have been recorded near Wheeling on the upper Ohio. See Figure 121.

salt pork (46)

The fat sides of pork pickled in brine were, and still are in some sections, one of the staple foods on the farm or plantation.

The most common regional terms are *salt pork, side meat* and *side pork, middlin(s)* and *middlin meat.*

Salt pork is current in New England and in the New England settlements of New York State as far west as the Finger Lakes. In the Hudson Valley it competes with *side pork, side of pork, side of bacon, side of meat.*

The most common expressions in the North Midland are *side meat, side pork,* and *flitch (of bacon, of side meat). Side meat* is a familiar

term from New Jersey and northern Delaware
to northern West Virginia and Ohio (and
doubtless farther west); it has also considerable
currency in eastern North Carolina and South
Carolina as well as in the Blue Ridge of Virginia,
competing here with the Southern *middlin*. In
the *side meat* area of the Midland some speakers
use the phrases *side of meat, side of pork,* or *side
of bacon,* especially on the upper Ohio River and
in parts of New Jersey. *Side pork* is characteristic
of the Hudson Valley, the New England counties
of Pennsylvania, and western New York State,
where it would seem to be a blend of New England *salt pork* and Midland *side meat*.

In the heart of Pennsylvania, from the Delaware to the Allegheny River, the expressions
flitch of bacon and *flitch of side meat* are widely
used for salt pork, and some in this area apply
the term also to smoked *side meat*. *Flitch* has not
spread beyond the boundaries of the state, although some of our informants on Delaware Bay
are familiar with it.

The South and the South Midland, with the
exception of the greater part of South Carolina,
have *middlin(s)* and *middlin meat*. These terms
are in general use in southern Delaware and in
all of Maryland, and from there southward to
the Peedee in South Carolina.

In northern West Virginia, in the Blue Ridge
of Virginia, and in Eastern North Carolina *side
meat* and *middlin* stand side by side.

Less common terms are: *fat-back* (the upper
part of a side of bacon) in the western parts of
the Carolinas and the Virginia Piedmont; *pork*
(for short) from Albemarle Sound to the Neuse
in North Carolina; also *sow belly* and *belly meat*
(the lower part of a side), *white-meat,* and *fat-
meat*. See Figures 19 and 122.

bacon (smoked) (46)

Sliced bacon of the sort served with eggs for
breakfast is known simply as *bacon* in the North
and the North Midland, and as far south as the
Potomac and the Kanawha.

In Virginia and southern West Virginia and
adjoining parts of North Carolina *breakfast
bacon* is the usual name, and this expression is
current also in Maryland and northern West
Virginia beside the simple *bacon*.

In the Carolinas *breakfast strip* predominates,
a term used also in eastern Virginia south of
the James River.

Breakfast meat is used by some of the simpler
folk south of the Potomac to whom *meat* means
primarily *pork*. See Figure 123.

clabber (47)

There is no national or literary term for
curdled sour milk. We have instead a number of
regional and local terms: *clabber* and *clabbered
milk, bonny-clabber* and *bonny-clapper, lobbered
milk* and *loppered milk, thick-milk, curdled
milk* and *cruddled milk* (also *crudded milk* and
cruddy milk), and *sour milk*.

Clabber is the Southern expression, *clabber
milk* that of the South Midland. *Clabber* is in
general use south of the Pennsylvania state line;
it is used to some extent even in the southern
counties of Pennsylvania. The Ohio Valley from
Wheeling downstream has *clabber*, less commonly *clabbered milk*, and the latter expression
seems to have replaced *lobbered milk* in the
Western Reserve of Ohio.

Bonny-clabber is still common in the Philadelphia area, *bonny-clapper* (less often *bonny-
clabber*) in Eastern New England (except for
Rhode Island, the New London area, and the
greater part of Maine). *Bonny-clabber* appears
in scattered fashion in central and western Pennsylvania and from there southward to North
Carolina, an area in which it has been largely
replaced by other terms.

From the Connecticut River westward to the
Great Lakes as well as in Rhode Island west of
Narragansett Bay, around New London, on Long
Island, and in northern New Jersey (but not in
Metropolitan New York), *lobbered milk* or *loppered milk* or both are in general use. The variant *lobbered milk* is regular in Rhode Island
and the New London area and in the Rhode Island
towns in the northern part of the Berkshires,
loppered milk in the lower Connecticut Valley
and the southern part of the Berkshires, and on
Long Island. In the Hudson Valley and in Vermont *lobbered* and *loppered* are equally common, while *loppered* predominates in central
New York State and farther west.

Clabber, clapper and *lobbered, loppered* are

all Anglicized forms of Gaelic *hlabar,* meaning 'thick' and 'mud'; the first part of *bonny-clabber* is the Gaelic word for milk. It is of interest to note that in New England relics of *clobbered, clabbered,* and *labbered* have survived by the side of the usual *lobbered* and *loppered.*

Pennsylvania has a number of local terms of entirely different origin. *Curdled milk* occurs in eastern Pennsylvania and Metropolitan New York; *cruddled milk (crudded milk, cruddy milk)* in western Pennsylvania and to some extent also on the Susquehanna. *Cruddled milk* is almost certainly of Scotch-Irish origin (cf. *crud* for cottage cheese in the same area). *Thick-milk,* modeled on Pennsylvania German *Dickemilch,* is also extensively used in Pennsylvania from the Delaware River to Pittsburgh. Relics of *thick-milk* appear also in the Mohawk Valley, probably as a legacy of the Palatine settlers of pre-Revolutionary days. See Figure 124.

cottage cheese (47)

Cottage cheese is the trade name for curds in all the Eastern States; it is especially common in the urbanized areas. The earlier regional terms, however, are still in rather general use, even in the cities.

Maine and adjoining parts of New Hampshire have *curds, curd cheese.* In coastal New England, from the mouth of the Connecticut River to Cape Cod and northward to the Kennebec River, *sour-milk cheese* predominates.

The remaining greater part of New England, except for southwestern Connecticut, has *Dutch cheese,* a term that also competes with *sour-milk cheese* on Narragansett Bay, in the back-country of Boston, and in the Merrimack Valley of New Hampshire. *Dutch cheese,* named with reference to the Dutch in the Hudson Valley, has also become established in the New England settlements of New York State, Pennsylvania, and Ohio, and has spread to some extent into West Virginia from Marietta.

The Hudson Valley expression is *pot cheese,* which is modeled on Dutch *pot kees.* (One of the few remaining bilingual inhabitants of Bergen County, New Jersey, who was interviewed by Dr. Lowman in 1941, uses *pot cheese* in his English, *pot kees* in his Dutch.) This term is now in general use in the Dutch settlement area and has spread eastward into Connecticut (the Housatonic Valley) and the New England settlements of Long Island, and westward to the Delaware and the head of the Mohawk.

Smear case (shmear case, smear cheese), borrowed from the Pennsylvania German *(schmierkäs),* is current throughout the North Midland and has spread to all of Delaware and Maryland and into the Shenandoah Valley. It has even gained a foothold on the Northern Neck of Virginia and on the Kanawha in West Virginia.

In the Southern area *curds (curd cheese)* and *clabber cheese* are widely used, the former on Chesapeake Bay, and the Carolina coast, the latter in the greater part of the Carolinas and in parts of West Virginia. A third term, *homemade cheese,* has considerable currency in western North Carolina and parts of the Appalachians.

It is of interest to note that (1) *curds,* the standard British term, has survived in two entirely separate areas in which English settlers predominated—Eastern New England and the coastal section of the South; and (2) that *pot cheese* and *smear case* have spread beyond the Dutch and the German settlement areas. It is quite clear from the comments of many of our informants that cottage cheese has been a favorite food with the Dutch and the Germans and that, on the other hand, the English settlers have had no liking for it. "We feed it to the chickens" is the common comment of descendants of this stock. See Figures 125 and 126.

a bite (between meals) (48)

Three expressions for eating something between meals are widely used: *bite* in the New England settlement area, *snack* in the Southern area and the South Midland, *piece* in the North Midland. The areas of these three terms overlap a great deal, especially in the thickly populated tract extending from Greater New York City to Baltimore.

Although *bite* is predominantly a New England term, it occurs beside *snack* or *piece* or both all the way from the Hudson Valley to the Potomac. In similar fashion *snack* is not confined to the South and the South Midland but is used also in Philadelphia and enjoys great popularity in Greater New York City and the Hudson Valley.

Piece is in general use in all of Pennsylvania except for Philadelphia and its immediate vicinity, in northern West Virginia, and in the Ohio Valley. It is less common in the Shenandoah Valley and rather rare on the Kanawha, where the Southern *snack* has become established. The Kanawha Valley has also the two local expressions *check* and *jack-bite* beside *snack* and *piece*. Neither of these terms has been noted elsewhere in the Eastern States.

Scattered instances of *piece meal*, in this sense, have been recorded in the Blue Ridge and on the Kanawha.

Piece is not uncommon in the New England counties of Pennsylvania, in parts of Upstate New York, and on the Jersey side of the upper Delaware. Since Pennsylvania expressions rarely spread to these sections and since the word is not current in New England, *piece* may here have a Dutch background. See Figure 127.

cling-stone peach (54)

Cling-stone peach is the regular term throughout the New England settlement area. The Midland has *cling-stone peach* and *cling peach*, the South and the South Midland *press peach* and *plum peach*.

In the Midland *cling-stone peach* is nearly universal between the Delaware and the Susquehanna, *cling peach* in the greater part of Maryland, the Shenandoah Valley, all of West Virginia north of the Kanawha, and Western Pennsylvania. *Cling-stone peach* is found also in southern Maryland, northern Virginia, and in scattered fashion on the southern coast from Tidewater Virginia to Georgia, as a recent importation from farther north. Both *cling-stone peach* and *cling peach* are common in Greater New York City and in western North Carolina.

The old Southern terms are *press peach* and *plum peach*. *Press peach* is used in a widening belt that runs from lower Delaware to Georgia. The greater part of South Carolina and the eastern half of North Carolina have this expression, but in Virginia it is now confined to the points of land on Chesapeake Bay.

Plum peach is the Virginia Piedmont term which has spread in a southwesterly direction into southwestern Virginia, southern West Virginia, and the western parts of the Carolinas, where it is in competition with the Midland word *cling-(stone) peach*. It does not occur north of the Rappahannock. See Figure 128.

free-stone peach (54)

Free-stone peach is current in the greater part of the Midland and in the entire New England settlement area. It is the regular expression in West Virginia and the Shenandoah Valley and has survived to some extent in the westernmost parts of Virginia and the Carolinas. As an innovation it appears now also in Tidewater Virginia and on the North Carolina coasts.

South of the Pennsylvania line a considerable variety of expressions is found in rather bewildering distribution. Maryland west of the Bay regularly has *open-stone peach* or *open-seed peach*, and this term has taken hold in northern West Virginia, probably as a Baltimore trade name; the Eastern Shore has *opening peach* and *open peach*. *Open peach* is found also in a coastal belt extending from the lower James to the Peedee, as well as on the Yadkin in North Carolina. Curiously enough *open-stone peach* and *open-seed peach* turn up again in Western North Carolina.

Soft peach is characteristic of the Virginia Piedmont, *clear-seed peach* and *clear-stone peach* of South Carolina and of a curious belt running northward through the eastern piedmont of North Carolina to the James in Virginia.

In New England *free-stone peach* is the universally accepted term, but on lower Cape Cod (Chatham to Provincetown) *cleave-stone peach* occurs as a relic. A single instance of this term was noted on the southwestern prong of Long Island. Is this the old Plymouth Colony word? See Figure 129 and 130.

greens (55)

Garden greens regularly go by this name in the North Midland, in Delamarvia, and in all of Maryland west of the Bay except for the peninsula south of Annapolis. In the South Midland also, *(garden) greens* is the usual term, and it appears to be gaining ground there. In the entire coastal section of North Carolina and South Carolina *greens* is common—and certainly old; in Tidewater Virginia it is quite rare except on the Northern Neck, and in the Piedmont of Virginia it is not used at all.

The distinctive Virginia Piedmont term is *salad*, more commonly pronounced *salat* in the speech of the folk. It is universal here and predominates over *greens* in adjoining parts of Maryland and North Carolina as well. In the greater part of the Carolinas *salad* and *greens* stand side by side, many persons using both terms. In the Virginia Tidewater *salad* has almost eliminated *greens*, but it has not crossed the Bay to the Eastern Shore. See Figure 131.

shelling (beans) (55)

Removing beans from the dry pods is called *shelling* nearly everywhere in the Eastern States. *Hulling* occurs beside *shelling* in large parts of the Midland (from the lower Susquehanna westward), and this expression predominates in the greater part of Maryland and in the northern third of West Virginia. See Figure 132.

string beans (55)

Three terms for string beans are current over large areas: *string beans* north of the Potomac, *snap beans* south of it, and *green-beans* in the West Midland from the upper Ohio to the Carolinas. *String beans* occurs also in the eastern part of the Carolinas (but not on Albemarle Sound) and is gaining a foothold on the Northern Neck of Virginia and in the Pittsburgh area.

Snap beans is the regular term in most of Virginia and in adjoining parts of North Carolina east of the Blue Ridge. It competes with the Midland *green-beans* in westernmost Virginia and in western North Carolina and South Carolina, and with *string beans* on the Northern Neck of Virginia and on the Carolina coast.

Green-beans dominates the mountains of North Carolina and all of West Virginia, and it is still common on the upper Ohio and its tributaries. On the eastern flank it is yielding ground to *snap beans* south of the Potomac, and to *string beans* north of it. There are relics of *green-beans* in central Pennsylvania. The term survives also in the Catskills. See Figure 133.

lima beans (55)

Butter beans is a common expression for lima beans in all of the Southern area. Many people in this section differentiate between the large *lima beans* and the smaller *butter beans*.

corn husks (56)

The cover leaves of an ear of corn are called *husks* in the North and the North Midland, *shucks* in the South and the South Midland. Northern West Virginia is a transition area. The middle part of Delamarvia has the word *caps* in this sense, which here separates Midland *husks* from Southern *shucks*. *Caps* is probably an innovation that arose along the dividing line between *husks* and *shucks*. See Figure 134.

sweet-corn (56)

For sweet-corn served on the cob *roasting ear* is the usual term in all of the South as well as in the Midland from the Susquehanna westward. In the North Midland other terms are encroaching upon the original domain of *roasting ear*. See Figure 135.

screech owl (59)

Of all the owls the common little screech owl is the best known and is the object of various superstitions. The term *screech owl* is current in all parts of the Eastern States, but on Delamarvia and south of the Potomac other variants of this word and two other expressions have a wider currency than *screech owl*.

Scrich owl and the less common variants *squich owl, squinch owl* are current in Virginia east of the Blue Ridge and in the adjoining parts of North Carolina; also in the westernmost parts of the Carolinas and Virginia and adjoining sections of Kentucky and West Virginia, probably as an importation from the Virginia Piedmont.

Southern Delaware and adjoining parts of the Eastern Shore of Maryland have *scrooch owl* in common with parts of the Carolinas and West Virginia.

Shivering owl (occasionally *shiveling owl*) occurs on the Carolina shore from Albemarle Sound to the Peedee.

In the Midland an occasional *squeech owl* turns up besides the regular *screech owl*, and around Cape May in southern New Jersey the term *winnering owl* is current, which was probably brought here by early settlers from New England. One instance of this expression was recorded at the mouth of the Connecticut River, another on the eastern point of Long Island— the only cases of *winnering owl* recorded outside New Jersey. See Figure 136.

woodpecker (59)

The variant *peckerwood* is common in the folk speech of the Virginia Piedmont and can be heard also in the mountains of North Carolina.

Similarly, *hoppergrass* for *grasshopper* is found in the Piedmont of Virginia.

skunk (59)

The regular Southern term for the skunk is *pole cat*, an expression that is common also in Pennsylvania west of the Susquehanna and in the South Midland. *Pole cat* doubtless was formerly more common in the Midland; the Northern term *skunk* (of Indian origin), supported by literary usage, has made its way into the Midland and even into the Southern area.

It may be of some interest to point out that the Pennsylvania German term *Pisskatz* clearly was suggested by the Pennsylvania English term *pole cat*. See Figure 137.

chipmunk (59)

The chipmunk is regularly so called in the North; the South and the South Midland just as regularly use *ground squirrel*.

In the North Midland the present situation is rather confused. *Chipmunk* predominates in Eastern Pennsylvania, *ground squirrel* in the Pittsburgh area and the Ohio Valley. In the Philadelphia area (on the Delaware, the lower Susquehanna, and the Juniata) an older expression, *ground hackie,* is being replaced by *chipmunk*. *Chipmunk* is also crowding out *ground squirrel* in central Pennsylvania and in southern New Jersey; it has made its way down the Eastern Shore, and through Maryland to the Shenandoah Valley, supported by literary usage.

Scattered relics of two old local terms occur: *grinnie* around Pittsburgh, *chickery* south and east of Philadelphia. Sporadic terms are *chippie* and *chip squirrel*. Pennsylvania German has *Fenzemaus* [fentsəmaus]. See Figure 138.

earthworm (60)

The most common words for the earthworm in the Eastern States are *fish worm, fishing worm,* and *angle worm*. See Figures 139 and 140.

Fish worm is common (1) in the upper Connecticut Valley and Worcester County, Massachusetts, (2) in the Dutch settlement area, and (3) in West Virginia. *Fishing worm* predominates (1) in an area extending from the lower Susquehanna southward on either side of Chesapeake Bay, including all of Delamarvia except the southern tip, (2) in Western Pennsylvania and adjoining parts of Ohio and West Virginia, and (3) in the Virginia Piedmont and adjoining parts of North Carolina. *Fish bait* and *bait worm* occupy smaller areas within the extensive *fish worm* and *fishing worm* areas of the Midland and the South, namely, (1) south-central Pennsylvania and adjoining parts of Maryland and (2) the western piedmont of North Carolina and adjoining parts of Virginia.

In New England and the New England settlements *angle worm* is in general use as a regional term by the side of several local expressions. It is not common in the Hudson Valley, but it predominates on Long Island (including Brooklyn) and on the Jersey shore from Newark to Cape May. Small *angle worm* islands are found on the lower Potomac and in Cartaret County, North Carolina, at the mouth of the Neuse.

Earthworm is a folk word in South Carolina, the Cape Fear section, and in a coastal belt extending from the Neuse to the mouth of Chesapeake Bay. In New England *earthworm* is a city word, and it appears as such also in Greater New York City and Philadelphia. It is rare elsewhere in the North and the Midland.

Other expressions for the earthworm are local in character. *Mud worm* is common in the Merrimack Valley in New Hampshire and in Essex County, Massachusetts; *eace worm* appears in Rhode Island west of Narragansett Bay; *angle dog* on the lower Connecticut River is a Windsor colony word; *ground worm* is found on the Eastern Shore of Virginia and the points of land between the Rappahannock and the James; *robin worm* is heard on Pamlico Sound in North Carolina; *red-worm* is the usual expression in the mountains of North Carolina and adjoining parts of Virginia, West Virginia, and Kentucky, and relics of it occur in Pennsylvania, which may be the original home of this term; scattered instances of *rain worm* are found in the Pennsylvania German area (cf. *Regenwurm*), in the German settlements on the Yadkin in North Carolina, in Nobleboro, Maine (a Palatine town), and on Buzzards Bay in Massachusetts, where it must be of English origin (cf. Old English *regenwyrm*).

In addition, *night walker* and *night crawler* are applied to the mature earthworm over large areas.

All of the more common words except *earthworm* are clearly fishermen's terms.

dragon fly (60)

Dragon fly is largely a book word in the Eastern States, and as such it has gained a foothold in urbanized areas from Boston to Baltimore.

The usual regional terms are: *darning needle, snake feeder, snake doctor,* and *mosquito hawk.*

All of the New England settlement area and the Dutch settlement area regularly have *darning needle (devil's darning needle).* This term is also current beside *dragon fly* among cultured Philadelphians, perhaps owing to contacts with Greater New York City. Scattered instances occur on the Northern Neck of Virginia, on the upper Ohio, and, rather more frequently, in the southern half of West Virginia. It is possible that in West Virginia *darning needle* is in part derived from the Northern Neck, but it seems more probable that it came in from the New England settlements on the Ohio (Marietta), which, however, no longer have this term.

The usual Midland expression is *snake feeder.* One hears it on both sides of the Delaware and from there westward to Ohio. East of the Alleghenies it competes with *snake doctor,* in the Pennsylvania German area also with *dragon fly* and several local expressions; west of the Alleghenies *snake feeder* is fully established. *Snake feeder* predominates also in the North Carolina mountains and in adjoining parts of Virginia and South Carolina.

In the southern two-thirds of West Virginia usage is confused. The Midland *snake feeder* does occur, but the Virginia Piedmont expression

snake doctor is more common and, in addition, *darning needle* is heard on the Kanawha and the Guyandot.

In the Virginia Piedmont and the Shenandoah Valley and adjoining parts of Maryland and North Carolina *snake doctor* is the regular term. *Snake doctor* is also common on both sides of Delaware Bay (beside *mosquito hawk*), on the Susquehanna (beside *snake feeder*), and in the greater part of West Virginia (beside *snake feeder* and *darning needle*). The present geographic and social distribution of this expression clearly points to the fact that it has spread from two separate centers, the Virginia Piedmont and the Philadelphia area, and that these two areas have only recently been merged into one. The city of Philadelphia itself now has only the literary *dragon fly* and the New York *darning needle,* but *snake doctor* and *snake feeder* still surround it.

Mosquito hawk occurs along the coast in a widening belt extending from Delaware Bay to Georgia. It is the usual expression in all of Delmarvia and the Virginia Tidewater, in the southeastern half of North Carolina, and in the greater part of South Carolina. On the periphery of the *mosquito hawk* area some informants say that the *mosquito hawk* is larger than the *snake doctor*—an interesting case of secondary differentiation in meaning.

In addition to these regional terms we find a number of local expressions: *spindle* in New Jersey; *snake servant, snake guarder,* and *snake heeder* in the Pennsylvania German area; and *snake waiter* in the southern peninsula of Maryland. See Figures 141 and 142.

sugar maple (61)

Sugar maple is used to some extent in all parts of the Eastern States. In the North Midland east of the Alleghenies, in northern New Jersey, in Greater New York City, and in the Southern area it is the only current expression. Urban areas and sections in which this tree does not grow—southeastern New England and the Southern area— have only the national term *sugar maple.*

Elsewhere rather vigorous regional expressions occur: *rock maple* in Eastern New England; *hard maple* in Western New England and the entire New England settlement area in New York State, Pennsylvania, and Ohio; *sugar tree* in the South Midland and in the valley of the Ohio and its tributaries. West Virginia is the present stronghold of *sugar tree*, but the term is certainly of Pennsylvania origin since we encounter it on the Allegheny, in south-central Pennsylvania, and in the entire Pennsylvania settlement area as far south as the Smoky Mountains in North Carolina. See Figure 143.

(sugar) maple grove (61)

There is a wealth of regional and local terms for the sugar maple grove: *sugar bush, sugar camp, sugar grove, sugar lot, sugar orchard, sugar place; sap bush, sap orchard; maple grove, maple orchard.* See Figures 144 and 145.

New England itself has a variety of expressions. *Maple grove* is little used in areas where such groves are located, but it is common in southern New England from Boston to New Haven, especially in urban areas. Upland Maine and eastern New Hampshire have *sap orchard*, northeastern Vermont and the adjoining parts of New Hampshire *sugar place*, the greater part of Western New England *sugar orchard. Sugar orchard* is used also on the lower Merrimack and, though less commonly, in other parts of Eastern New England. It is rather striking that none of the local New England expressions have survived west of the Hudson River.

The Hudson Valley has *sugar bush* and *sap bush*, both expressions containing the Dutch word *bush, vosh. Sap bush* is practically confined to the Dutch settlement area, but *sugar bush* has invaded the Berkshires and the Green Mountains and firmly established itself in the New England settlement area in New York, Pennsylvania, and Ohio.

From Metropolitan New York to the Potomac and westward to the Alleghenies *maple grove* is in general use; only scattered instances of *sugar bush, sugar orchard, maple orchard, sugar grove,* and *sugar camp* have been noted here.

In Western Pennsylvania, northern West Virginia, and adjoining parts of Ohio *sugar camp* and *sugar grove* are common. The latter is found also in south-central Pennsylvania and on the

upper Potomac in West Virginia. *Maple grove* is rare in this whole area.

Sugar orchard is the characteristic expression in the southern Appalachians from the northern watershed of the Kanawha to the Carolinas. This term is current also in Western New England, as has been noted above.

Although there is much overlapping, the geographic boundaries of most of these terms are rather neatly defined. Large parts of the tidewater and the piedmont of Virginia and the Carolinas have no fixed expressions because the sugar maple is unknown there.

sycamore (61)

The sycamore goes by this name regularly in the valley of the Ohio and its tributaries. East of the Alleghenies *sycamore* is not common except for the Pennsylvania German area. In New England *sycamore* is as distinctly a book word as among the Pennsylvania Germans and in the large urban centers of Philadelphia and New York City.

There are two vigorous regional terms for the sycamore, *button ball* and *button wood*.

Button ball is current in a well-defined area extending from eastern Connecticut to the Finger Lakes in New York State, including the Berkshires and the entire Hudson Valley, all except the eastern prongs of Long Island, and northern New Jersey. The term is also used in the environs of Philadelphia by the side of *button wood*.

Button wood is found in two separate areas: (1) in Eastern New England, including Rhode Island and Massachusetts east of the Connecticut River; and (2) in Pennsylvania east of the Alleghenies together with the greater part of New Jersey. See Figure 146.

The rather clear demarcation line between *button wood* and *button ball* in New England is probably of rather recent origin. Relics of *button wood* on the upper Housatonic in Connecticut and on the eastern prongs of Long Island point to its former currency in the present *button ball* area of Western New England. This inference helps to explain the general adoption of *button wood* in the New England counties of Pennsylvania, which usually agree with the New England settlements in New York State but in this instance are sharply differentiated from it. If the New England settlers from Western New England brought both *button ball* and *button wood* with them, *button ball* could easily become established in New York State, *button wood,* supported by Pennsylvania usage, in the New England counties of Pennsylvania.

Maryland, Virginia, and Carolina usage has not been recorded, but the universal use of *sycamore* in all of West Virginia points to the dominance of that term in the Southern area.

baby carriage (64)

Since the 1870's the baby carriage has replaced the cradle. *Baby carriage* is the regular term (1) in the New England settlement area from Maine to Lake Erie and (2) in the Southern states. On Delaware Bay and in the greater part of Pennsylvania *baby carriage* is less widely used.

Within the Philadelphia trade area, that is, in Delaware, in southern New Jersey, and in southeastern Pennsylvania as far west as the Alleghenies, *baby coach* predominates; west of the Alleghenies, *baby buggy. Baby buggy* is current also in Ohio and on the lower Kanawha in West Virginia. In the southeastern counties of Ohio *baby cab* stands by the side of *baby buggy* and *baby carriage.* See Figure 147.

wheel the baby (64)

Wheel the baby is in universal use in the North and the North Midland, including the Shenandoah Valley and the northern half of West Virginia. It is also the usual expression in the southern half of that state, and in all of Maryland west of the Bay except around St. Marys. See Figure 148.

The Southern area, except for South Carolina, has the two expressions *roll the baby* and *ride the baby* side by side. *Ride* is fairly common in North Carolina, in Tidewater Virginia, and in westernmost Virginia, less so on Delamarvia, around St. Marys in southern Maryland, and in southern West Virginia. In the Virginia Piedmont it is now rare. It has been superseded by *roll,* which is current in the entire Southern area and is gaining ground in the Blue Ridge as well. *Roll the baby* is the only expression used in

South Carolina (except the Peedee Valley, where *ride* survives), and on the Georgia coast.

midwife (65)

Midwife is used throughout the Eastern States, but in the central section of Pennsylvania and everywhere south of Pennsylvania the common folk still say *granny* or *granny woman,* and the better-educated generally know this folk term. The simplex *granny* is characteristic of the Virginia Piedmont and the Charleston area, *granny woman* of North Carolina and West Virginia; elsewhere the two variants occur side by side in varying proportion. Relics of *granny (woman)* occur in Eastern Pennsylvania and in the Pittsburgh area. See Figure 149.

bastard (65)

The neutral expression *illegitimate child* and the blunt term *bastard* are known and used everywhere. Playful and veiled terms, on the other hand, are regional or local in character.

Woods colt is current in the Carolinas, the southern Appalachians, and the Ohio Valley from Wheeling downstream. It is not common on the Shenandoah and the upper Potomac. The Virginia Piedmont, from the James Valley southward, has *old-field colt,* but this expression is no longer widely used. On Chesapeake Bay, especially on the Eastern Shore, we find *base-born (child),* and this term appears also here and there in the Appalachians (but not in the intervening Virginia Piedmont). The playful expression *Sunday baby* or *child* is heard from Albemarle Sound to the mouth of the Neuse.

In the North Midland and the North the veiled *come-by-chance* is widely current in rural sections—in northern West Virginia, on Delaware Bay, on the upper Susquehanna, and in New York State from the Finger Lakes to the upper Hudson. This expression is used also in New England, as one would gather from its common occurrence in the New England settlement area of New York and Pennsylvania, but this point was not systematically investigated in New England. Two other terms are restricted to smaller areas: *ketch-colt* to central New York State, *stolen colt* to the middle part of New Jersey. See Figure 150.

right smart (74)

In the Midland and the South the adverb *right* is common in such expressions as *right good, right smart*. The New England settlement area now lacks this expression, but it is not uncommon in the Hudson Valley and on western Long Island, where the Dutch synonym *recht* supported it. See Figure 151.

sick at the stomach (80)

Four different prepositions are current in the Eastern States in the phrase meaning 'sick at the stomach,' in fairly well defined but partly overlapping areas. See Figure 152.

At the stomach is usual in all of the South and the Midland and is not uncommon in Greater New York City, Connecticut, and Rhode Island. In the greater part of New England and the rest of the Northern area it is exceedingly rare. We shall see that in parts of the South and the Midland other prepositions compete with *at*.

The New England settlement area has predominantly *to the stomach*, northern New England, Upstate New York, and northern Pennsylvania almost exclusively so. In southern New England and in Greater New York City *at* is now fairly common among younger and cultured persons; it is clearly a newcomer here. Outside the New England settlement area we find *to the stomach* on Delaware Bay, on the Eastern Shore, and in coastal points southward to the Neuse in North Carolina. This coastal belt is well known for its conservatism.

The variant *in the stomach* is current in two separate areas: (1) southeastern Pennsylvania, including Philadelphia, and (2) the tidewater area, from southern Maryland to the Neuse in North Carolina.

The variant *on the stomach* is also current in two detached areas: (1) the Pennsylvania German settlement area of Eastern Pennsylvania and the Shenandoah Valley; (2) the Pennsylvania German settlements on the Yadkin in North Carolina, and from there between the Cape Fear and the Peedee all the way down to the coast. This use of *on* in the phrase *sick on the stomach* may rest upon the corresponding German idiom *etwas auf dem Magen haben*, but it may also have been introduced from the synony-

mous English expression *to have something on the stomach*.

It should be noted that in some sections of the Eastern States usage is quite uniform (e.g. *to* in New York State, *at* in most of Virginia), in others diversified and unsettled (e.g. *to* and *at* in New Jersey, *in*, *on*, and *at* on the Susquehanna).

best man (82)

The national term *best man* is current in all the Eastern States, but south of the Potomac it is not common among the simple folk or in rural areas. Here the usual folk word is *waiter*, which applies also to the bridesmaid.

In the Charleston area and on the Georgia coast, however, *groomsman* seems to predominate, and this term is not uncommon west of Chesapeake Bay from Baltimore to Norfolk (including Washington and Richmond). Scattered instances have been recorded also in western Virginia and in West Virginia. See Figure 153.

serenade (82)

The serenading of newlyweds has been largely abandoned, but the memory of this old folk custom still stirs the hearts of the older folk in the rural areas of all the Eastern States.

Serenade is the usual term among the folk in Eastern New England and in the South Atlantic States, and it is widely known and used elsewhere in the Eastern States.

Regional and local terms are numerous: *chivaree* (1) in northern Vermont, New Hampshire and Maine, and in New Brunswick, and (2) in the westernmost part of Virginia and the adjoining part of Kentucky; *horning, horning bee* (1) in Rhode Island and (2) from the Berkshires and the southern part of the Green Mountains to Lake Erie, including the New England settlements in Pennsylvania but not the lower Hudson; *calathump, calathumpian band* (1) commonly in New Haven County, Connecticut (an old Yale College word), and (2) in scattered fashion in the Delaware Valley, on the Eastern Shore, in central Pennsylvania, and on the upper James in Virginia; *skimerton, skimilton* in a well-defined area extending from the Housatonic in Connecticut to the upper Delaware Valley, including the lower Hudson Valley, the Catskills, and northern New Jersey; *bull band, bull banding* in the German settlements of the Great Valley of Pennsylvania; *tin-panning* in Maryland on both sides of the Bay (one of the few expressions confined to Maryland); and, finally, *belling* in large parts of the Midland, especially (1) in a belt running from the West Branch of the Susquehanna to the upper Potomac and the Shenandoah Valley, (2) on the Ohio and the Kanawha, and (3) on the Yadkin in North Carolina. Pennsylvania is doubtless the original home of *belling* in the New World. See Figure 154.

(school) lets out (83)

The expression *school lets out* is current, with varying frequency, in the North, the North Midland (to the Kanawha Valley), and as far south as the James River in Virginia. Moreover, it is not unknown in North Carolina, especially on the Yadkin. See Figures 155 and 156.

In the South and the South Midland the regional term *turns out* is used, predominantly so in the Carolinas, in Virginia south of the James, and in southern West Virginia, less frequently on Chesapeake Bay, rarely in the heart of the Virginia Piedmont.

The Virginia Piedmont has its own expression, *breaks up* or *breaks*, but *lets out* and *turns out* compete with it.

Pennsylvania has the local expression *leaves out*, which is used by the common people, often beside *lets out*, all the way from the Delaware to the Allegheny River, especially in the Pennsylvania German centers.

Another local expression, *school gets out*, is current in Greater New York City and vicinity. Most of New England has *school closes* by the side of *school lets out*.

Elsewhere the expression *school lets out* is universal, or nearly so: in New York State, northern Pennsylvania, on the Ohio, and in most of New Jersey and Maryland.

Rare instances of *school goes out* have been noted on the Lehigh in Pennsylvania, where it clearly reflects the German idiom *geht aus*, but also in the city of Hudson on the Hudson River.

played truant (83)

Played hookey, played truant, and *skipped school* occur side by side, with varying frequency,

from New England to Virginia and westward to the Ohio Valley; and these terms are not unknown in the Carolinas. See Figures 157 and 158.

Regional and local terms are: *hooked Jack* on Cape Cod; *bagged school* in the Philadelphia area (from Delaware Bay to the Susquehanna); and *lay out (of school), laid out (of school)* (1) in Western North Carolina and adjoining parts of Virginia and South Carolina, and (2) in the contiguous easterly parts of North Carolina and South Carolina lying between the Neuse and the Peedee. Scattering instances of *lay out* and *laid out* have also been noted on the James and the Rappahannock.

Since compulsory school attendance is of rather recent date, some if not most of the terms are of recent coinage. It is very significant that the boundaries of the major speech areas, which largely follow settlement boundaries, are not reflected to any extent in the boundaries separating the expressions for playing truant.

I want to get off (85)

The standard phrasing is current everywhere, but in the common speech of the Midland the shorter *I want off* is widely used. One hears it on the Susquehanna and from there westward to the Ohio Valley and southward all through the Appalachians. The preservation in the Midland of this older English construction in which an adverb is joined directly to *want* may in part be due to German influence (cf. *ich will hinaus*). See Figure 159.

by the time I get there (89)

In the North, on the Delaware River, and on Delaware Bay all social groups use this construction exclusively. The greater part of the Midland and the South, however, have retained in their folk speech the expression *agin I get there;* and from the Pennsylvania German area to the Alleghenies one hears *till I get there*.

Agin is most common in the Appalachians, but it has considerable currency among the simple folk, white and black, in the Southern piedmont and along the coast as well. In Pennsylvania *agin* is not unusual west of the Alleghenies. Farther east it is heard now only on the upper Susquehanna and along the Maryland line, i.e. on the northern and southern fringes of the *till* area. See Figure 160.

Merry Christmas! (93)

In the North and in most of the North Midland *Merry Christmas!* is the universal Christmas salutation, and this expression is now freely used by the younger generation in the South and the South Midland, especially in urban areas.

The simple folk of the South and the South Midland still say *Christmas gift!* This salutation is also still heard from older people in southern Pennsylvania (from the Susquehanna westward) and is in rather common use in the Ohio Valley, in West Virginia as well as in Ohio. It seems fairly clear that both the South and the Midland had this expression from early times, and that *Merry Christmas!* has largely displaced *Christmas gift!* in Pennsylvania and on Delaware Bay in fairly recent times. See Figure 161.

belly-gut, belly-bump, belly-bust (95)

Adverbial expressions for coasting 'face-down' on a sled are numerous and display a striking geographic pattern reflecting settlement areas.

Belly-bump, belly-bumper(s), belly-bumping are characteristic (1) of coastal New England and (2) of Eastern Pennsylvania to the Alleghenies; *belly-bunt* predominates in the upper Connecti-cut Valley, in Worcester County, Massachusetts, and in parts of Maine; *belly-gut, belly-gutter* are found from the lower Connecticut to the Great Lakes and on the Allegheny River in Pennsylvania; *belly-wop, belly-wopper(s)* dominates (1) the lower Hudson, Long Island and East Jersey, and (2) Maryland; *belly-bust, belly-buster* occur in the South Midland and in parts of Virginia.

There are also some expressions that are local or individual or occur in scattered fashion: *belly-whack*, sporadically throughout the North; *belly-kachunk*, around New London, Connecticut; *belly-flop, belly-flopper*, in Western New England and on Delaware Bay; *belly-womper(s)*, on the Susquehanna; *belly-bunker*, in Western Pennsylvania; *belly-grinder*, in the Wheeling area; *belly-booster*, in southern Ohio. See Figure 162.

(May I) take you home (97)

The well-known Southern *carry you home* is heard from Annapolis, Maryland, southward. In Virginia it stops short at the Blue Ridge, but in the Carolinas this characteristic expression of the plantation country has spread westward into the mountains. On the Eastern Shore and in southern Delaware, which were plantation country in earlier days, this expression is also current. See Figure 163.

GLOSSARY

(Numbers following F refer to the Figures in the back of the book.)

aftercrop 16, 67; F112
aftercutting 67
aftergrass 16, 67; F112
aftergrowth 16, 67; F112
aftermath 16, 67; F112
agin I get there (by the time)
    48, 79; F160
andirons 51
angle dog 26, 74; F140
angle worm 14, 26, 45, 74;
    F140
animal 19, 62
apple dowdy 20
apple grunt 23
apple slump 23
armful 29, 57; F73
arm load 29, 57; F73
ash cake 39, 68; F119
ash pone F119
at home 17

baby buggy 36, 77; F147
baby cab 77; F147
baby carriage 77; F147
baby coach 33, 36, 77; F20, 147
back-house 53
bacon 39, 47, 70
bag 56
bag school 35, 79; F22, 158
bait worm 74; F139
bannock 22
barn lot 40, 55; F62
barn yard 40, 55
barrack 24, 54; F13, 60
base-born child, base-born 46,
    77; F36, 150
bastard 77
batteau 60; F85
batter bread, 42, 68
batter cake 69; F33, 121
batty-cake 69

bawl 30, 62; F16
bay 15, 54
beast 62; F94
bee! 65; F106
beller 19, 62
belling 37, 79; F154
bellow 19, 62
belly-booster 80
belly-bump 20; F9, 162
belly-bumper(s) 20, 80; F9,
    162
belly-bumping 80
belly-bunker 80
belly-bunt 20, 80; F162
belly-bust 80; F162
belly-buster 80; F162
belly-flop 80; F162
belly-flopper 80; F162
belly-flouncer F162
belly-grinder 80; F162
belly-gut 18, 25, 80; F7, 162
belly-gutter 18, 25, 80; F7, 162
belly-gutting 18
belly-kəchunk 80
belly meat 70
belly-whack 80; F162
belly-womper(s) 80; F162
belly-wop 18, 25, 80; F162
belly-wopper 18, 25, 80; F162
belly-wopping 25
best man 49, 78
biddie! 21, 44, 65; F106
big-house 37, 47, 51; F28, 47
big-room 51; F47
bite 14, 32, 71; F127
blare 23
blinds 28, 52; F16, 49
bob 59
bob sled 59
bonny-clabber 20, 21, 39, 70;
    F2, 10, 124

bonny-clabber cheese F126
bonny-clapper 20, 21, 70; F2,
    10, 124
boss! 14, 24, 63; F99
bossie! (to cows) 24, 63; F99
bossie! (to calves) 64
bottom lands 61; F90
bottoms 61; F90
brake F61
branch 40, 61; F93
bread 39
breakfast bacon 39, 70; F123
breakfast meat 70; F123
breakfast strip 43, 70; F123
breaks (of school) 42, 79; F156
breaks up (of school) 41, 42,
    79; F156
breeze F45
breeze on, breeze up 19, 22, 45,
    51; F45
brook 12, 13, 61; F93
brute 37, 62
buck (ram) 62; F95
buck (saw horse) 59; F81
bucket 13, 47, 48, 56; F42, 66
buck fence 55
buck sheep 62; F95
bull 62
bull band, bull banding 78;
    F154
bundle 49, 67
burlap bag 47, 56
burlap sack 56
butlery 17
butter beans 39, 73
button ball 17, 22, 25, 34, 76;
    F146
button wood 17, 20, 22, 25, 33,
    34, 76; F9, 146
buttry 16; F6, 51
by the time 79

cade 23; F12
cade! 23, 65; F105
calathump 26, 78; F154
calathumpian band 78; F154
cap 40, 46; F36, 134
carbon oil 14, 36, 60; F84
carrying (wood) 57; F76
carry you home 80; F163
carting (wood) 17, 19, 26, 57, 58; F76
catch-all 52
cedar pail 13, 56
chamber 46; F47
check 36, 72; F26
chick! 21, 65
chickery 74; F138
chickie! 65
chims 23
chipmunk 15, 48, 74; F138
chippie 74
chip squirrel 74
chitterlings 64
chittlins 38, 64
chivaree 24, 78; F154
choke! 20, 22, 41, 65
choog! 41, 65; F104
chook! 20, 22, 41, 65; F104
Christmas gift! 48, 80; F42, 161
chuck! 41, 65; F104
clabber 36, 39, 70; F124
clabber cheese 43, 71; F126
clabbered milk 36, 70; F124
clabber milk 36, 70; F124
clean across 38, 61; F87
clear across 61
clear-seed peach 72; F129
clear-stone peach 72; F129
cleave-stone peach 23, 72; F129
cling peach 47, 72
cling-stone peach 47, 72
clobbered milk 71
clook 32, 63
closes (of school) F156
closet (toilet) 36, 53
closet (for clothes) 52
closet (pantry) 17, 23
clothes closet 52
clothes press 52; F50

cluck 33, 63
clucker 33
co! 14, 20, 21, 26, 63; F100
coaf! 14, 20, 21, 63; F100
coal bucket 59, 60
coal hod 16, 25, 59, 60; F82
coal oil 14, 31, 33, 34, 60; F84
coal pail 59, 60
coal scuttle 16, 25, 59, 60; F82
co-boss! 12, 14, 63; F99
co-bossie! 63; F99
cob pie 23
co-calfie! 64
cock 40, 54; F58
cock horse 59; F79
cocky-horse 46, 59; F79
co-dubbie! 64; F38, 102
co-ee! 38, 63; F99
cohog 20, 22, 23
co-inch! 38, 63; F99
come boss! 12, 14, 63; F99
come bossie! 63; F99
come-by-chance 77; F150
come up! 42, 43, 66; F107
come up, sir! 66
comfort 13, 47, 48, 61; F89
comfortable 12, 13, 48, 61; F89
comforter 12, 13, 48, 61; F89
common (park) 20
Connecticut rail fence 55
coo-chee! 41, 65; F106
coo-chick! 41, 65; F106
cookie 47, 69; F120
coop! 23, 65; F106
cooter F32
cootie! 47, 65; F106
corn bread 14, 67
corn cake, corn griddle cake 68
corn crib 19, 54
corn dodger 39, 68; F118
corn husks 73; F40, 134
corn house 19, 41, 49, 54; F2, 31, 32, 57
corn meal pudding 17
corn pone 47, 67; F41, 116
corn stack 46, 54; F57
co-sheep! 30, 42, 65

corn shucks 73; F30
cosset 20
cossie! 46, 64; F102
cottage cheese 49, 71
councilman 20
county seat 20
cow brake 55; F61
cow cuppin 55
co-wench! 38, 63; F29, 99
cow house 41; F31
cow lot 55; F61, 62
cow pen 55
cow pound 55; F61
cow yard 55; F62
cracklin bread 39, 68
cracklins 39, 68
creek (salt) 19, 32, 45, 61; F92
creek (fresh) 13, 49, 61
creeper 23; F68
crib 54
crib house 26, 54; F57
critter 19, 62; F94
crocus sack 41, 57; F71
croker sack 41, 57; F32, 71
crudded milk 36, 70; F124
cruddled milk 36, 70; F124
cruddy milk 70; F124
cruds, crud cheese 20, 36; F126
crull 69
cruller 18, 21, 24, 25, 69; F14, 120
cubbie! 64; F38, 102
culch 22
cuppin 41, 54; F2, 31, 61
curd(s), curd cheese 22, 71; F126
curdled milk 70
curtain (roller shade) 15, 29, 45, 49, 52; F49
cussie! 46, 64; F102

dandle 23, 58; F79
darning needle 12, 14, 26, 34, 75; F5a, 141
devil's darning needle 75
dickie F80
dodger 39, 68; F118
dog irons 47, 51; F48

dogs 51; F48
doodle 35, 54; F25, 59
double rip 59
double ripper 21, 27, 59; F80
double runner 20, 24, 59; F80
double swingletree 58
doubletree 58
doughnut *(raised)* 21, 49, 69
doughnut *(unraised)* 18, 21,
  49, 69
dowdy 20
drag 18, 20, 58; F9, 78
dragon fly 14, 34, 75
drag sled 18, 58
drawing (wood) 17, 57, 58;
  F76
drooth F25
Durham 62
Dutch cap 23, 55; F60
Dutch cheese 18, 21, 24, 71;
  F8, 125

eace worm 23, 74; F140
earthworm 14, 45, 74; F35, 139
east bread 67
eaves spouts 15, 19, 22, 53;
  F11, 54
eaves troths 15, 53; F54
eaves troughs 15, 19, 25, 53;
  F54
egg bread 39, 68
egg pone 68
eel worm F140
emptins 18

farm lot 55; F62
farm yard 40
fat-back 70
fat-cake 35, 69; F120
fat-meat 70
fat-pine 29, 51
fatty-bread 68
faucet 15, 56
fills 17; F75
fire board 36, 47, 51; F27
fire bucket 13, 56
fire bug 33; F142
fire dogs 47, 51; F48

fire fly 17, 33; F142
fish bait 74; F139
fishing worm 74; F139
fish worm 14, 26, 74; F139
flannel cake 33, 34, 35, 69; F21,
  121
flannen cake 69; F21, 121
flats 61; F91
flitch 70; F19
flitch of bacon 32, 69; F19
flitch of side meat 32, 69
fossnocks 35, 69
free-seed peach F129
free-stone peach 47, 72; F129
fried-cake 18, 21, 25, 69; F120
fritter *(pancake)* 20, 22, 69;
  F11
frontis 52
front room 51; F47
frying pan 16, 29, 56
funnel 16
funnel *(stovepipe)* 22; F11

gad 56
gallery 52
garden greens 72
garden house 42, 53; F55
gentleman cow 19, 62
gentleman ox 19, 62
gets out *(of school)* 26, 79;
  F156
get up! 19, 43, 49, 65
goad 21, 56
go along! 66; F107
goard 56
goes out *(of school)* 79; F156
go 'long! 19, 66; F107
go on! 19, 66; F107
goop! 44, 65; F104
grand-sir 22
granny 48, 77; F149
granny woman 48, 77; F149
grasshopper 74
grass sack 41, 46, 56; F71
great-beams 22, 54; F56
great-house 51; F47
green *(park)* 20, 26
green-beans 30, 38, 73; F133

greens 39, 72
griddle cake 19, 69
grinnie 36; F138
grist of corn 37, 47, 57; F39, 72
groomsman 78; F153
ground hackie 74; F138
ground mow 16, 22, 54; F56
ground squirrel 15, 48, 74;
  F138
ground worm 46, 74; F140
guano sack 46, 57; F71
gunny sack 36, 57; F71
gutters 15, 19, 25, 29, 40, 49, 53;
  F53

hand horse 46, 66; F36, 110
hand irons 46, 51; F48
hand stack 54; F59
hap 61; F25, 89
hard clam 27
hard maple 75; F143
harslet, hasslet 20, 21, 38, 49,
  64; F43, 103
hasty-pudding 17
hauling (wood) 17, 57
haw! F108
hay cap 23, 55; F60
hay cock 47, 54; F58
hay mow 37, 47, 54; F39, 56
hay stack 54
heap 54; F59
herring-bone fence 55
hick horse 59; F79
hickory 37, 56; F28
hicky-horse 47, 59; F79
hie! 19, 26, 64; F101
high-beams 22, 54; F56
hither-horse 66; F110
hoa! 66; F108
hoa-ie! 65; F104
hobby 36, 68; F26, 117, 118
hoe cake 39, 68
hog boist 27
hog house 21
hog pen 21
hogshead cheese 20
hog sty 21
hoist! 18, 26, 64; F101

home-made cheese 71
hommie! 35, 64; F102
hommilie! 64; F102
hoo-ie! 65; F104
hookie! 63; F100
hook Jack 23, 79; F158
hook school F158
hoppergrass 41, 74
horning 18, 23, 24, 78; F154
horning bee 78; F154
horse 59
horse and team 20, 21
hot-cake 34, 35, 46, 69; F2, 22, 121
hovel 41
hover 41
hull (beans) 29, 46, 73; F132
hum 46, 62; F37
husk 40, 46, 47, 73; F40, 134
huther-horse 46, 66; F110

illegitimate child 77
Indian bannock 22
Indian pudding 17
interval, intervale 22, 61; F91
ivy 26

jack 59; F81
jack-bite 36, 72; F26
jacket 36, 42, 47, 60; F27, 86
jack house 42, 53; F55
jag (of corn) 31, 46, 57; F72
jam across 38, 46, 61; F87
jock 62
johnnikin 68; F117
johnny cake (corn bread) 12, 14, 67; F116
johnny cake (corn griddle cake) 23, 43, 68; F34, 117
johnny house, johnny 42, 53; F55
junk room 52

kə-boss! 14
kə-choo! 41, 65; F104
kə-chook! 41, 65
kə-dack! 16, 65; F105
kə-daik! 65; F105

kə-day! 16, 65; F105
kə-dick! 16, 65; F105
kə-dub!, kə-dubbie! 47
kə-nan! 42, 65; F105
kees! 24, 64; F102
kellie 24
kerosene 14, 31, 43, 44, 60
ketch-colt 77; F150
kill (creek) 13, 24, 61; F93
killie, killie fish 24
kindling wood, kindling 30, 51
kip! 24, 65; F106
kish! 24, 64; F102
komm da! 63; F100
kush! 24, 26, 63; F100, 101
kushie! 24, 63; F100, 101

labbered milk 71
lamp oil 14, 31, 34, 36, 60; F84
lash 46, 56
lattercrop 16, 67; F112
laugh 63; F97
lay out of school 44, 79; F158
leader 66; F110
lead horse 31, 66; F110
lean-to 20, 21
leaves out (of school) 33, 79; F19, 156
lets out (of school) 42, 79; F155
lie out of school 79; F158
light-bread 39, 67; F30, 115
lightning bug 17, 33
lightwood 37, 51; F4, 29
lima beans 73
line horse 41, 66; F110
little piece 29, 66; F111
little way(s) 29, 66
liver and lights 64
living room 51
load 29, 38, 57; F73
loaf bread 67
lobbered milk 17, 25, 70; F124
lodge 61; F88
loft 23, 47, 53
loo 16, 49, 62; F96
loppered milk 17, 25, 70; F124
lot 40, 55; F62
low (moo) 38, 49, 62; F29, 96

lower (moo) 62; F96
lowery 19
low-grounds 61; F91
low-lands 61; F91
lucky-bone 63; F97
lulling, lulling down 22
lumber room 42, 52; F33, 52

major 62
male 62
male animal 62
male beast 62; F94
male brute 62; F94
male cow 62; F94
mantel 51
mantel piece 51
mantel shelf 51
maple grove 76; F144
maple orchard 76
masculine 23, 36, 62; F94
meat 70
menhaden 21, 27
merry Christmas! 48, 49, 80
mew (moo) 62
middlin(s) 32, 39, 69; F122
middlin meat 39, 69; F122
midwife 48, 49, 77
milk and pudding 17
milk gap, milking gap 36, 55; F26, 61
milk lot 55; F61
milk pail 12
minnies 23
minnims 23
moderate 22
mongst-ye 46, 67; F114
mongst-ye's 67
moo, mooing 16, 38, 47, 62
mosquito hawk 42, 45, 75; F34, 141
mow 54; F56
mud worm 23, 74; F140
mummichim 23
mummichog 20, 23
mush 17

nannie! 42, 49, 65; F105
neap 57; F74

near-horse 15, 31, 46, 47, 66; F109
near-side horse 66; F109
neb 23, 57; F74
necessary, necessary house 19,
    53; F55
nicker 42, 43, 62, 63; F33, 97
nickle 62; F97
nigh-horse 14, 15, 31, 46, 66;
    F109
night crawler 75
night walker 75
northeaster 19, 45
norwester 19, 45
nut cake 69; F120

of eleven 30, 50; F44
old-field(s) colt 41, 77; F150
olicook 24, 69; F120
opening peach 72; F130
open peach 42, 72; F130
open-seed peach 46, 72; F129
open-stone peach 46, 72; F129
orts 23
orts pail 23
out-house 53
over-den 32, 53; F56
overhead 32, 53; F19, 56
ox 62; F94
ox goad 20, 56

pail 12, 13, 48, 56; F5a, 66
pale yard F63
paled fence 15, 55; F41, 63
paling fence 15, 47, 48, 55;
    F41, 63
palings 55; F63
pallet 40, 61; F88
pancake 20, 49, 69
pancake (fritter) 22
pan dowdy 20, 21
pantry 17
paper bag 56
paper sack 56
parlor 51; F46
pavement 33, 62; F20
peckerwood 43, 74
piazza 18, 45, 49, 52; F35, 43
picket fence 15, 48, 55

piece (distance) 29, 39, 47; F111
piece, piece meal 14, 32, 39, 71,
    72; F127
pig! 47, 64
piggie! 47, 64
piggoop! 43, 44, 65; F104
pightle 27, 55; F61, 62
pig pen 21
pig's squin 23, 64; F103
pig sty 20, 21
pile 54; F59
pine 29, 51
pitch pine 29, 51
play hookey 35, 79; F158
play truant 35, 79; F157
pluck 21, 64; F103
plum across 61; F87
plum peach 43, 72; F128
plunder room 42, 52; F52
poggy 21, 23, 27
pogy 20, 21
poke 30, 56; F17, 70
pole 57; F74
pole cat 15, 48, 74; F42, 137
pone 67; F41, 116
pone bread 48, 67; F116
ponhaws 32; F23
poo-ie! 26, 65; F104
pop lash 46, 56
porch 52
porch (kitchen ell) 23, 52
porgy 23, 27
pork 70
post-and-rail fence 55
pot cheese 18, 24, 71; F8, 14,
    125
pound 55; F61
press peach 43, 45, 72; F35,
    128
privy 53
pudding 17
pull-bone 47, 63; F98
pulling bone 47, 63; F98
pully-bone 47, 48, 63; F98

quahog 20, 22, 23
quilt 61
quohog 22

rack 59; F81
rail fence 31, 55
rain spouts F54
rain worm 37, 75; F24, 140
raised-bread 21, 67; F115
raised doughnut 20, 21, 69
ram 49, 62
rare-ripe 23
red-worm 37, 74; F28, 140
Rhode Island johnny cake 23,
    68
rich-pine 29, 51
rick 34, 54; F60
ride the baby 40, 77; F148
riding horse 59; F79
ridy-horse 36, 59; F79
rifle 19, 60; F83
right (adv.) 24, 48, 78; F151
ring 69; F120
rip-gut fence 55
ripper 59
rips 59
rising (of wind) 51
river 61
riz-bread 20, 21, 67; F115
riz doughnut 20, 21, 69
roasting ear 48, 73; F41, 135
robin worm 74
rock fence 31, 40 47, 55; F65
rock maple 20, 22, 75; F143
rock wall F65
roller shades 28, 29, 52
rollichies 24
roll the baby 40, 77; F148
round clam 21, 26, 27
rowen 16, 67; F112
rowen crop 16, 67; F112
rowet 67
run (creek) 13, 32, 40, 61; F18,
    93

sack 56
saddle horse 31, 35, 37, 66;
    F24, 110
salad, salat 39, 73; F131
salt creek 61
salt pork 12, 14, 32, 69; F129
sap bucket 13

sap bush 18, 25, 76; F145
sap orchard 18, 22, 76; F144
savannah 47, 61; F91
saw! 64; F101
saw bench F81
saw buck 25, 35, 37, 59; F81
saw horse 25, 49, 59
scaffle 15, 53; F6
scaffold 15, 53
scrapple 32
screech owl 73
scrich owl 43, 73; F136
scrooch owl 46, 73; F136
sculch 22
scup 21, 23, 27
scupaug 21
sea-grass sack 41, 46, 56; F71
second crop 16, 66
second cutting 16, 66
seed ox 62
seesaw 16, 47, 48, 58, 59
seh! 63; F100
selectman 20
serenade 24, 78
setting hen 49, 63
settin' room 51
shacket 23
shades 15, 29, 52
shafe *(sheaf)* F113
shaffs 17
shafts 17
shavs 17
sheaf 67; F113
sheep! 16, 30, 65
sheep buck 62; F95
sheepie! 16, 30, 65
shelf 51
shell (beans) 29, 73
shire town 20
shiveling owl 73; F136
shivering owl 46, 73; F2, 37, 136
shmear case 71
shock 39, 47, 54; F58
shuck 40, 73; F30, 134
sick at the stomach 14, 78
sick in the stomach 78; F152
sick on the stomach 37, 78; F152

sick to the stomach 14, 45, 78; F152
side meat 14, 32, 39, 69; F122
side of bacon 69; F122
side of meat 32, 69; F122
side of pork 32, 69; F122
side pork 14, 69; F122
sidewalk 49, 62
singletree 13, 47, 48, 58; F41, 77
sire 19, 62; F94
sitting room 50
skillet 16, 29, 56; F68
skimerton 18, 24, 78; F14, 154
skimilton 24, 78; F14, 154
skip school 79; F157
skunk 15, 48, 74; F137
slam across 38, 46, 61; F37, 87
slop 13; F67
slop bucket 56
smear case 18, 32, 71; F18, 125
smear cheese 71; F18
smurring, smurring up 22
smurry 22
snack 14, 26, 32, 39, 71; F127
snake doctor 26, 30, 33, 34, 42, 75; F141
snake feeder 14, 26, 30, 34, 42, 75; F15, 141
snake fence 55; F64
snake guarder 34, 75
snake heeder 34, 75
snake servant 34, 75
snake waiter 46, 75; F141
snap beans 31, 38, 73; F133
so! 24, 64
soft peach 42, 72; F130
sook! 14, 30, 38, 63; F4, 15, 99
sook cow! 63; F99
sookie! *(to cows)* 30, 63; F99
sookie! *(to calves)* 30, 64
sour milk 70
sour-milk cheese 20, 21, 71; F8, 10, 126
sow belly 70
spawn, spawn and milk 24
spicket 15, 47, 56; F42, 69
spider 16, 45, 49, 56; F6, 43, 68

spigot 15, 47, 56; F69
spindle *(dragon fly)* 26, 75; F141
spindle *(of corn stalk)* 22
spindle out 22
spoon bread 68
spoon haunch 23
spoon hunt 23
spoon wood 23
spouting 15, 29, 40, 46, 53; F54
spouts 29, 40, 53; F54
squeech owl 73
squich owl 73; F136
squinch owl 73; F136
stable lot 40, 55; F62
stake-and-rider fence 55
steer 62; F94
stehn! 64
steps 18
sto! 24, 64; F101
stock beast 62; F94
stock brute 62; F94
stolen colt 77; F150
stone boat 17, 18, 20, 58; F5b, 7, 78
stone drag 18, 58; F9, 78
stone fence 14, 31, 40, 46, 47, 55; F39, 65
stone row 14, 26, 56
stone sled 18, 58
stone wall 14, 31, 47, 55; F39, 65
stoop 18, 25, 52; F7
store room 52
string beans 31, 38, 47, 73; F40, 133
sty 21
sugar bush 18, 24, 25, 76; F145
sugar camp 36, 76; F145
sugar grove 36, 76; F145
sugar lot 18, 76; F144
sugar maple 22, 31, 49, 75
sugar orchard 18, 24, 25, 36, 76; F145
sugar place 18, 24, 76; F144
sugar tree 31, 76; F17, 143
Sunday baby, Sunday child 47, 77; F150

suppawn 17, 24; F2, 13
sweet-corn 73
swill 12, 13; F67
swill bucket 13
swill pail 12, 56
swingletree 13, 47, 58; F41, 77
switch 56
swiveltree 13, 26, 58; F77
sycamore 17, 34, 76

team 21
teaming (wood) 23, 58; F76
teedle board 23, 58
teenter 26
teeter 16, 25, 58; F5b, 6, 79
teeter board 16, 25, 58; F5b, 6, 79
teetering board 16, 58, 79
teeter-totter 16, 25, 58; F13, 79
tempest 23; F12
thick-milk 26, 35, 70; F23, 124
thills 17; F75
tiddle board 23, 58
tie, tied quilt 61
tie-up 21
till eleven 30, 47, 50; F44
till I get there 33, 34, 35, 79; F21, 160
tilt 22, 58; F79
tilter 22
tilter board, tilting board 22, 58; F79
tin-panning 46, 79; F154
tinter 26, 58; F79
tippity-bounce 23, 58; F79
to eleven 30, 49, 50; F44
to home 17
toilet 53
tongue (of a wagon) 57
tonic 20, 21
toot (bag) 30, 56; F2, 23, 70
top cow 19; F94
top gallant 26
top ox F94
top steer F94
toro 19, 62; F94

tow sack 44, 57; F71
traverse sled 20, 24, 59; F80
troughs 40, 53
trumpery room 47, 52; F38, 52
tumble (hay cock) 22, 54; F59
tunnel (funnel) 16
turn of corn 42, 43, 47, 57; F72
turn of wood 38, 43, 57; F73
turns out (of school) 42, 79; F155
tye! 14, 24, 26, 64; F102
tytie! 24; F101

veranda 52
vest 49, 60
Virginia rail fence 55
vootie!, voots! 64; F104
vootsie! 35, 37, 64; F24, 104

waiter 40, 78; F153
walling F63
want in 30
want off 30, 79; F15, 159
water closet 53
water pail 12
water spouts F54
water troughs 40, 53; F54
wattle 56
waw! 66; F108
way! 41, 66; F108
webbins 22
well bucket 13, 56
-wench 38, 63; F29, 99
wesket 42, 60; F86
wheat bread 67
wheel horse 41, 66; F110
wheel the baby 40, 77; F148
whet 60; F83
whet rock 40, 60; F83
whet seed 47, 60; F38, 83
whet stone 40, 47, 60
whetter 60; F83
whicker 20, 21, 42, 43, 62, 63; F10, 34, 97
whiffletree 12, 13, 47, 48, 58; F4, 5a,b, 77

whinker 62; F97
whinner 21, 62; F97
whinny 21, 42, 47, 62, 63; F40, 97
whinter F97
whip 56
whippletree 12, 13, 47, 58; F4, 5a,b, 77
white-arsed hornet 23
white-bread 20, 21, 67
white-meat 70
whoa! 16, 66
whookie! 63; F100
wicker 62
widdie! 44, 65; F106
winner 62
winnering owl 74; F136
winny 62
wishbone 47, 48, 63
woa! 16, 66
woak! 65, F104
woo! 63; F100
wood buck 35, 59; F81
wooden pail 13
wood jack 59; F81
woodpecker 74
wood rack 59; F81
woods colt 42, 43, 77; F150
woo-ie! 65; F104
wook! 41, 65; F104
wookie! (to cows) 63; F100, 104
wookie! (to pigs) 65
woop! 44, 65; F104
woopie! 65; F104
worm fence 31, 46, 55; F18, 64

yay! 41, 66; F108
yeast bread 20, 21, 67
you-all 31, 40, 67; F30, 114
you-all's 41, 67
you'ns 31, 40, 67; F114
you'ns's 67
yous F114

zigzag fence 55; F64

THE FIGURES

In Figure 2 and in Figures 4–43 boundaries are drawn for individual regional words, most of which are shown in great detail in Figures 44–162. These word boundaries or isoglosses are employed to set off the major speech areas and their subdivisions. For a fuller statement regarding the significance of the isoglosses and the use made of them see page 11.

Figures 44–163 present a rather full record of the geographic dissemination of different words for one and the same thing. Some figures exhibit all the regional synonyms, others only a selection of them. To prevent misunderstanding, the reader should always consult the text of Chapter III (pages 50-80), to which the numbers in parentheses following the headings of these figures refer.

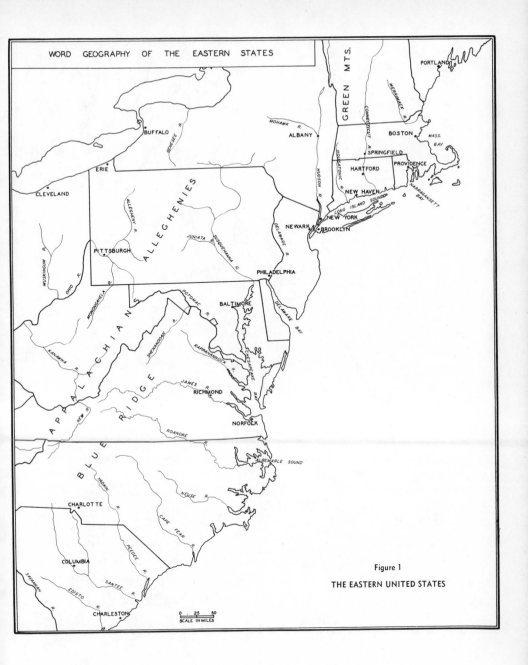

WORD GEOGRAPHY OF THE EASTERN STATES

Figure 1

THE EASTERN UNITED STATES

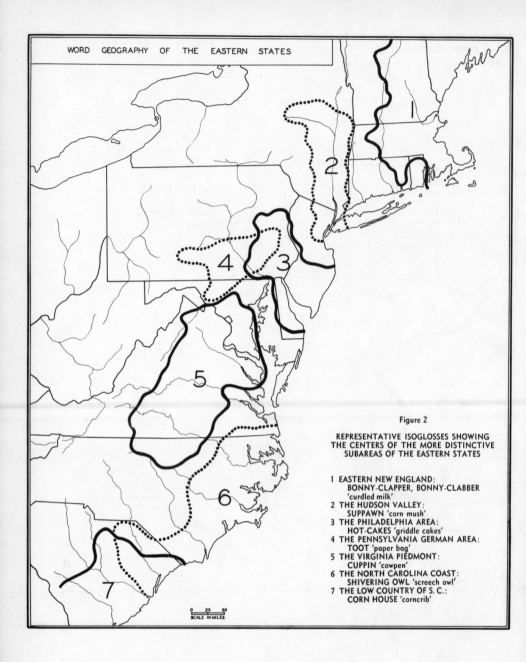

WORD GEOGRAPHY OF THE EASTERN STATES

Figure 2

REPRESENTATIVE ISOGLOSSES SHOWING
THE CENTERS OF THE MORE DISTINCTIVE
SUBAREAS OF THE EASTERN STATES

1 EASTERN NEW ENGLAND:
    BONNY-CLAPPER, BONNY-CLABBER
    'curdled milk'
2 THE HUDSON VALLEY:
    SUPPAWN 'corn mush'
3 THE PHILADELPHIA AREA:
    HOT-CAKES 'griddle cakes'
4 THE PENNSYLVANIA GERMAN AREA:
    TOOT 'paper bag'
5 THE VIRGINIA PIEDMONT:
    CUPPIN 'cowpen'
6 THE NORTH CAROLINA COAST:
    SHIVERING OWL 'screech owl'
7 THE LOW COUNTRY OF S. C.:
    CORN HOUSE 'corncrib'

0   25   50
SCALE IN MILES

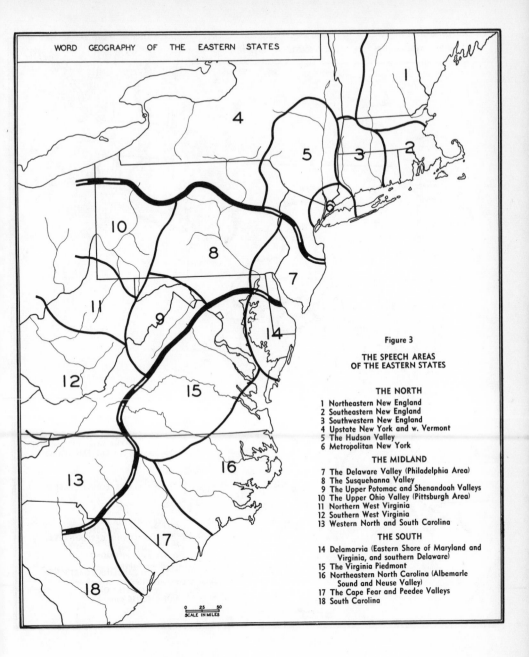

WORD GEOGRAPHY OF THE EASTERN STATES

Figure 3

**THE SPEECH AREAS
OF THE EASTERN STATES**

THE NORTH

1 Northeastern New England
2 Southeastern New England
3 Southwestern New England
4 Upstate New York and w. Vermont
5 The Hudson Valley
6 Metropolitan New York

THE MIDLAND

7 The Delaware Valley (Philadelphia Area)
8 The Susquehanna Valley
9 The Upper Potomac and Shenandoah Valleys
10 The Upper Ohio Valley (Pittsburgh Area)
11 Northern West Virginia
12 Southern West Virginia
13 Western North and South Carolina

THE SOUTH

14 Delamarvia (Eastern Shore of Maryland and
    Virginia, and southern Delaware)
15 The Virginia Piedmont
16 Northeastern North Carolina (Albemarle
    Sound and Neuse Valley)
17 The Cape Fear and Peedee Valleys
18 South Carolina

0   25   50
SCALE IN MILES

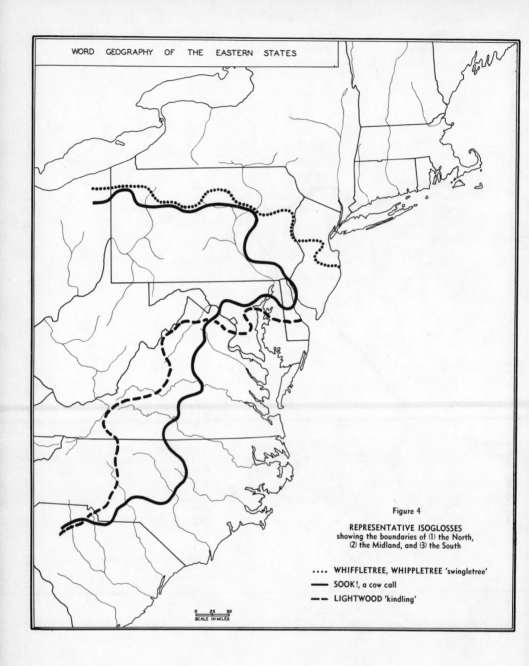

Figure 4

REPRESENTATIVE ISOGLOSSES
showing the boundaries of (1) the North,
(2) the Midland, and (3) the South

.... WHIFFLETREE, WHIPPLETREE 'swingletree'

—— SOOK!, a cow call

– – LIGHTWOOD 'kindling'

0   25   50
SCALE IN MILES

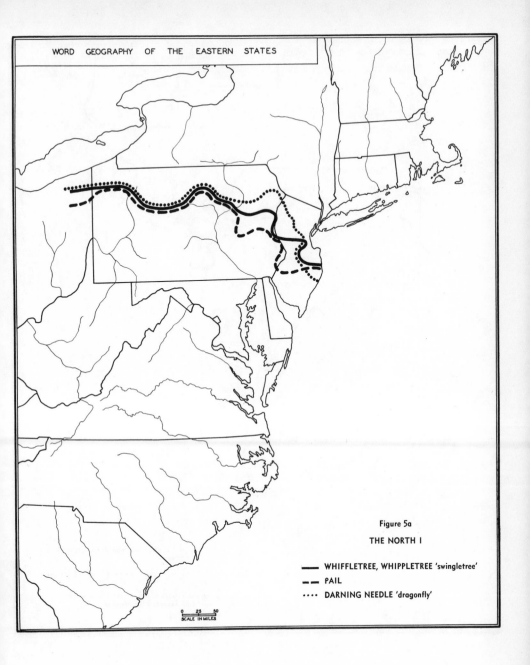

Figure 5a

THE NORTH I

—— WHIFFLETREE, WHIPPLETREE 'swingletree'
– – PAIL
•••• DARNING NEEDLE 'dragonfly'

0 25 50
SCALE IN MILES

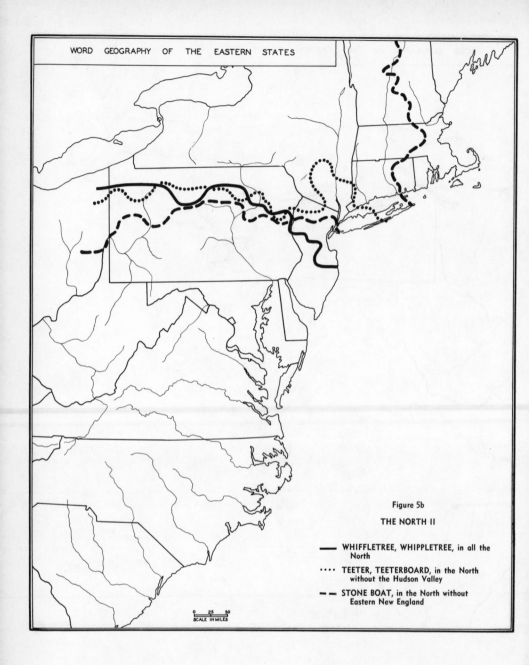

Figure 5b

THE NORTH II

━━━ **WHIFFLETREE, WHIPPLETREE,** in all the North

•••• **TEETER, TEETERBOARD,** in the North without the Hudson Valley

━ ━ **STONE BOAT,** in the North without Eastern New England

0   25   50
SCALE IN MILES

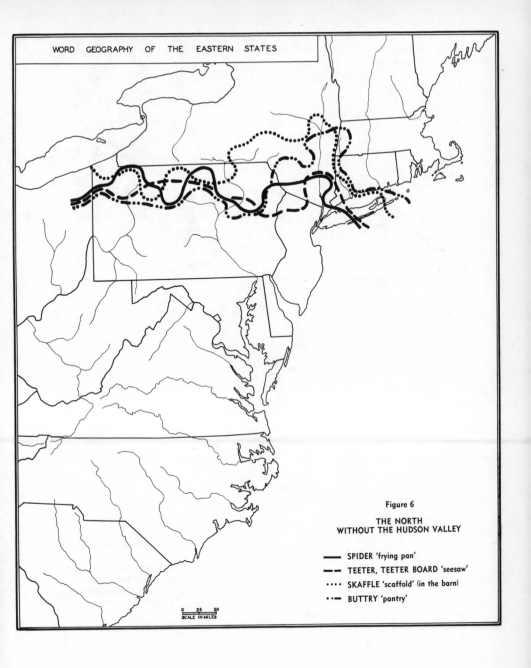

Figure 6

THE NORTH
WITHOUT THE HUDSON VALLEY

——— SPIDER 'frying pan'

— — TEETER, TEETER BOARD 'seesaw'

•••• SKAFFLE 'scaffold' (in the barn)

•—• BUTTRY 'pantry'

0   25   50
SCALE IN MILES

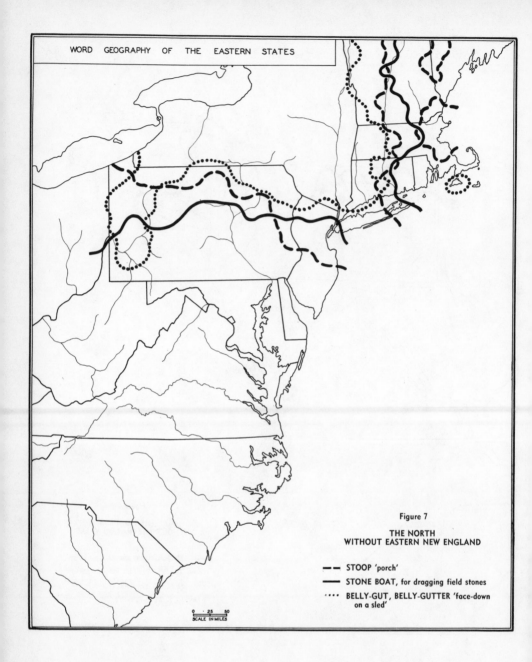

WORD GEOGRAPHY OF THE EASTERN STATES

Figure 7

THE NORTH
WITHOUT EASTERN NEW ENGLAND

— — STOOP 'porch'
—— STONE BOAT, for dragging field stones
···· BELLY-GUT, BELLY-GUTTER 'face-down
on a sled'

0   25   50
SCALE IN MILES

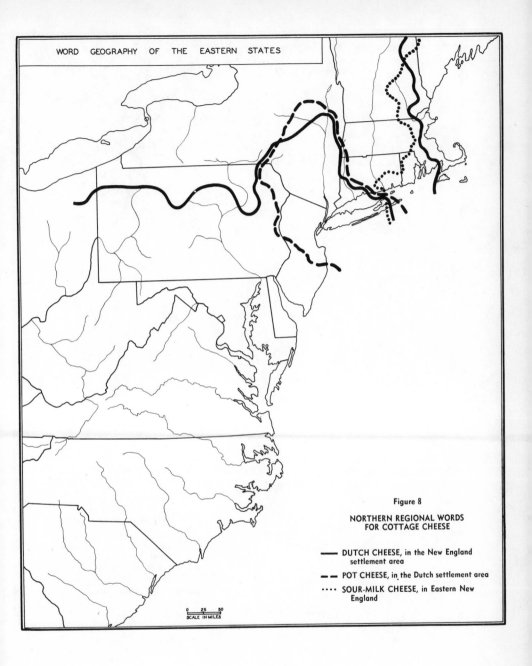

Figure 8

NORTHERN REGIONAL WORDS
FOR COTTAGE CHEESE

—— DUTCH CHEESE, in the New England
settlement area

– – POT CHEESE, in the Dutch settlement area

···· SOUR-MILK CHEESE, in Eastern New
England

0   25   50
SCALE IN MILES

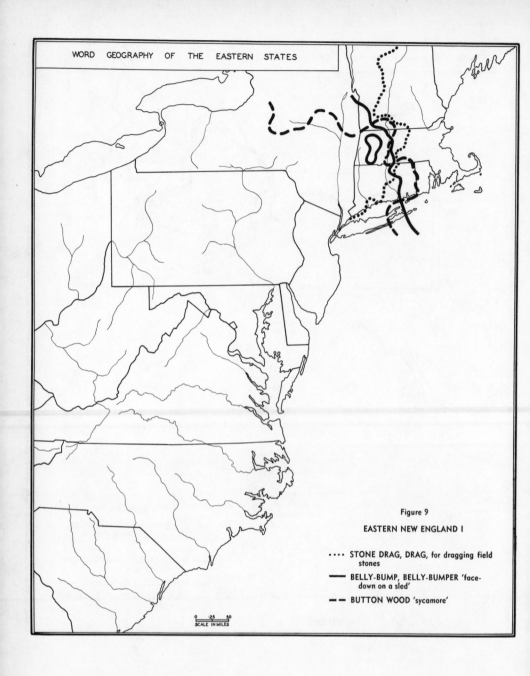

WORD GEOGRAPHY OF THE EASTERN STATES

Figure 9

EASTERN NEW ENGLAND I

•••• STONE DRAG, DRAG, for dragging field
stones

━━ BELLY-BUMP, BELLY-BUMPER 'face-
down on a sled'

－－ BUTTON WOOD 'sycamore'

0   25   50
SCALE IN MILES

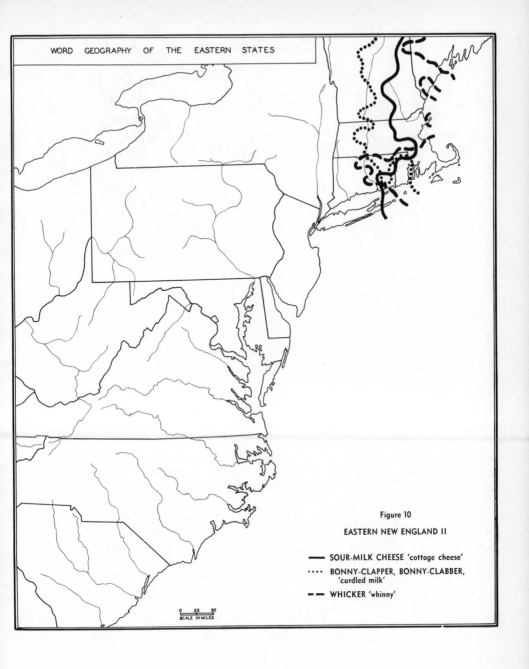

Figure 10

EASTERN NEW ENGLAND II

—— SOUR-MILK CHEESE 'cottage cheese'
•••• BONNY-CLAPPER, BONNY-CLABBER, 'curdled milk'
– – WHICKER 'whinny'

0   25   50
SCALE IN MILES

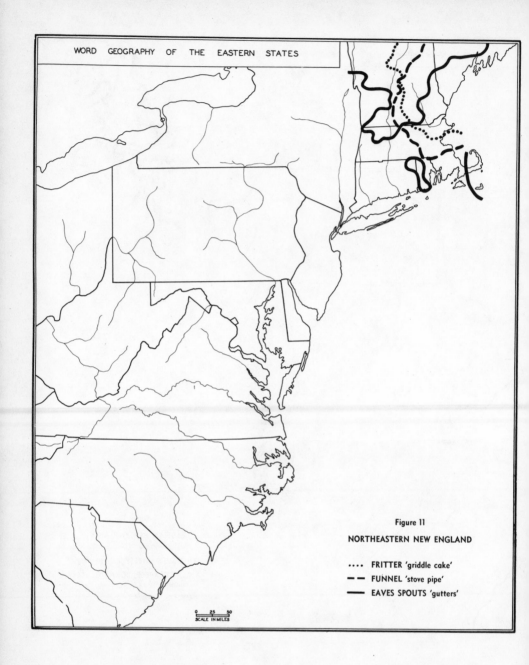

Figure 11

NORTHEASTERN NEW ENGLAND

···· FRITTER 'griddle cake'
– – FUNNEL 'stove pipe'
—— EAVES SPOUTS 'gutters'

0 25 50
SCALE IN MILES

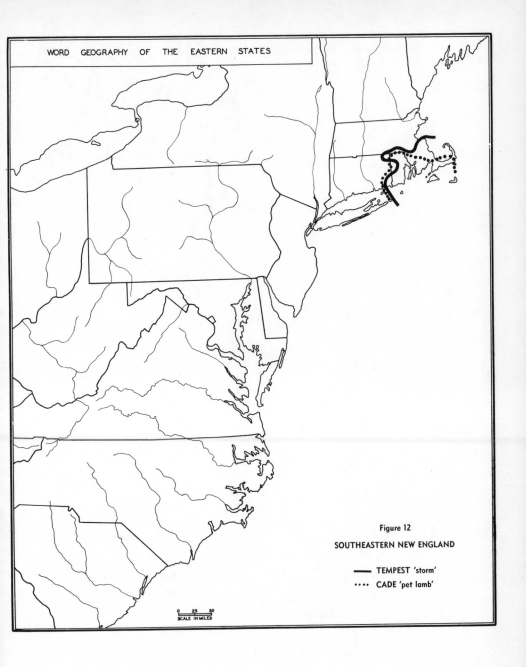

Figure 12

SOUTHEASTERN NEW ENGLAND

—— TEMPEST 'storm'
•••• CADE 'pet lamb'

0   25   50
SCALE IN MILES

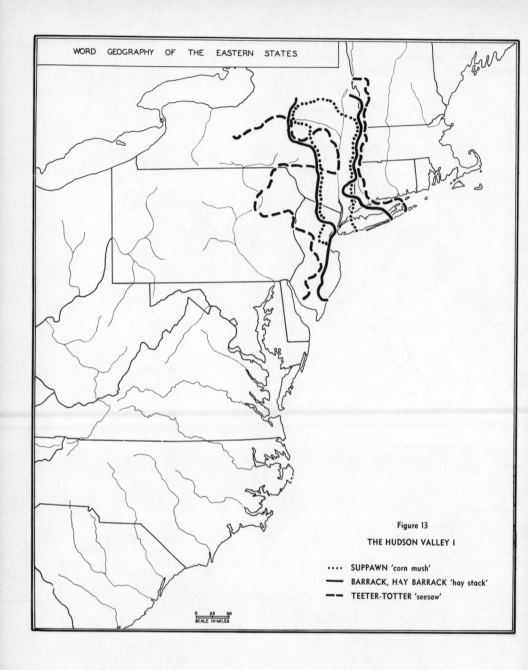

Figure 13

THE HUDSON VALLEY I

•••• SUPPAWN 'corn mush'

——— BARRACK, HAY BARRACK 'hay stack'

— — TEETER-TOTTER 'seesaw'

0   25   50
SCALE IN MILES

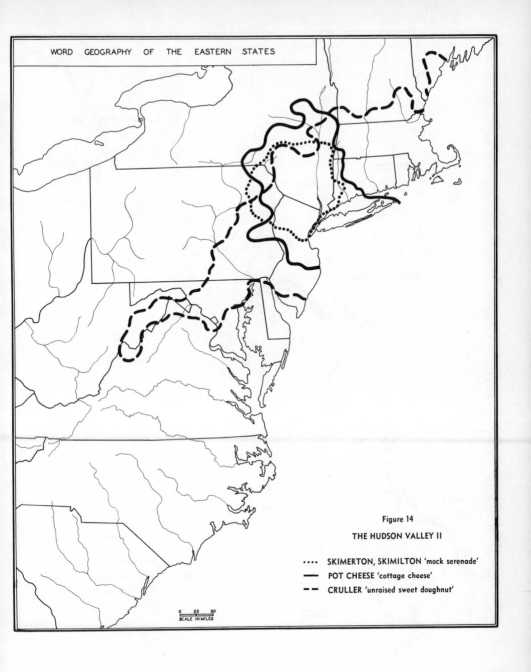

Figure 14

THE HUDSON VALLEY II

•••• SKIMERTON, SKIMILTON 'mock serenade'
—— POT CHEESE 'cottage cheese'
– – CRULLER 'unraised sweet doughnut'

0   25   50
SCALE IN MILES

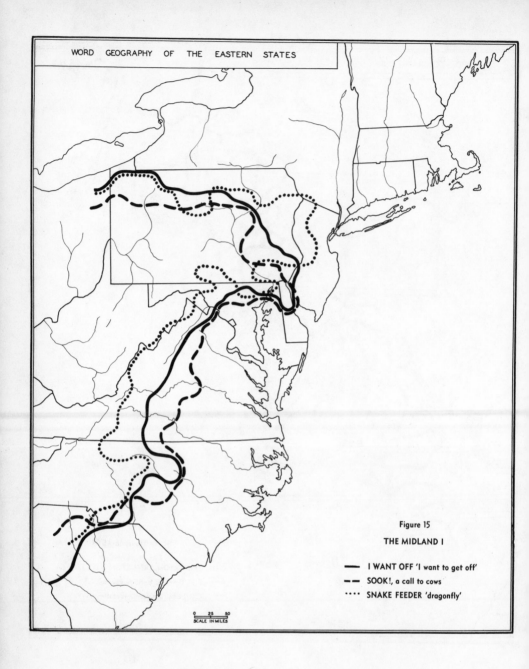

Figure 15

THE MIDLAND I

—— I WANT OFF 'I want to get off'
– – SOOK!, a call to cows
···· SNAKE FEEDER 'dragonfly'

0   25   50
SCALE IN MILES

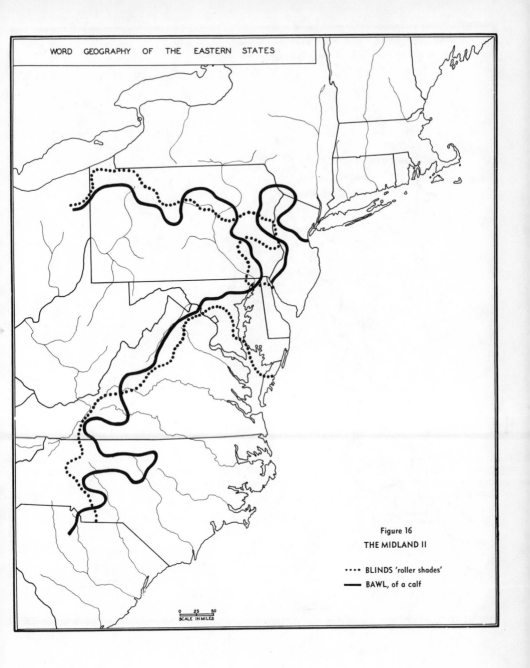

Figure 16
THE MIDLAND II

•••• BLINDS 'roller shades'
—— BAWL, of a calf

0   25   50
SCALE IN MILES

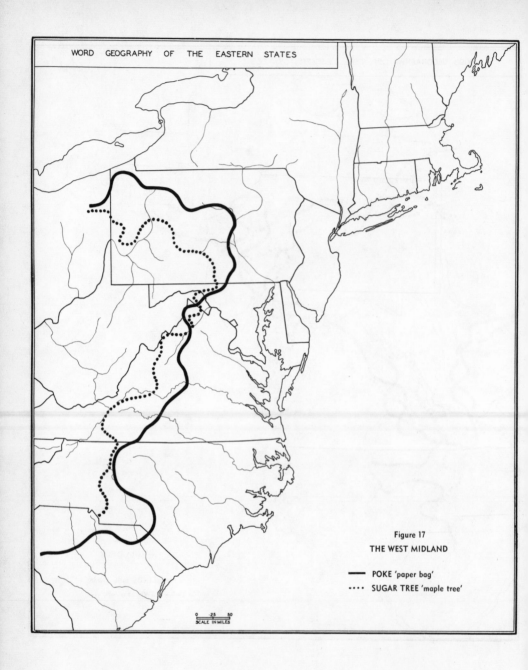

Figure 17

THE WEST MIDLAND

—— POKE 'paper bag'

···· SUGAR TREE 'maple tree'

0   25   50
SCALE IN MILES

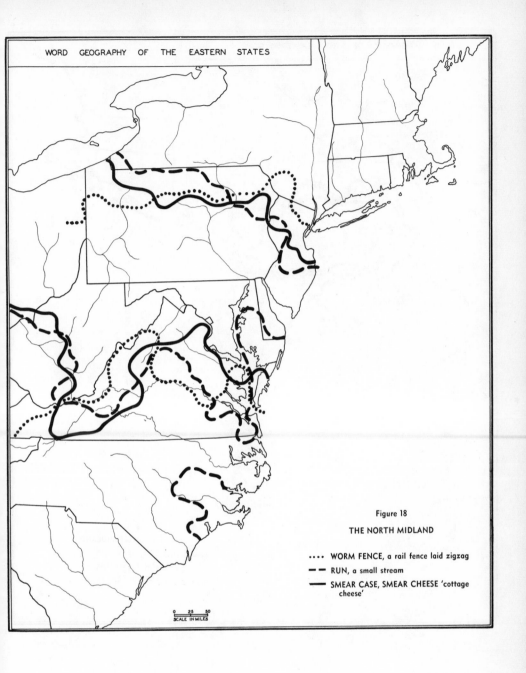

Figure 18

THE NORTH MIDLAND

···· WORM FENCE, a rail fence laid zigzag

– – RUN, a small stream

—— SMEAR CASE, SMEAR CHEESE 'cottage cheese'

0   25   50
SCALE IN MILES

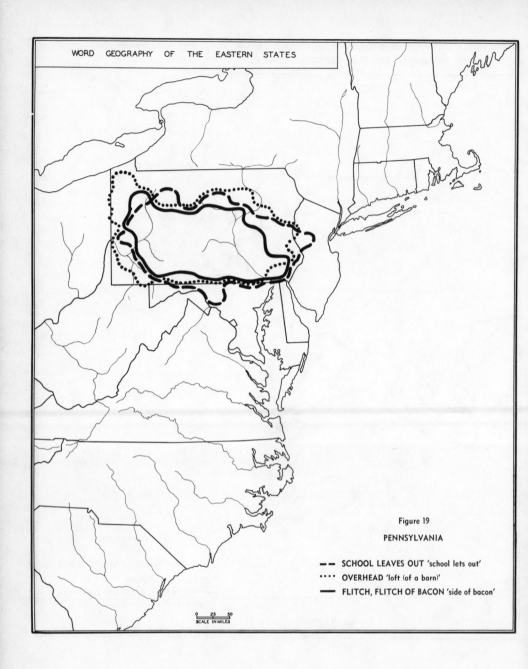

Figure 19

PENNSYLVANIA

– – SCHOOL LEAVES OUT 'school lets out'

•••• OVERHEAD 'loft (of a barn)'

—— FLITCH, FLITCH OF BACON 'side of bacon'

0   25   50
SCALE IN MILES

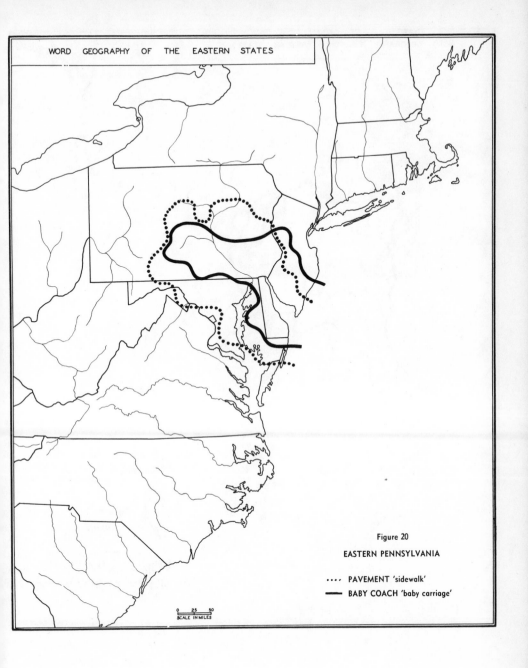

WORD GEOGRAPHY OF THE EASTERN STATES

Figure 20

EASTERN PENNSYLVANIA

···· PAVEMENT 'sidewalk'
—— BABY COACH 'baby carriage'

0   25   50
SCALE IN MILES

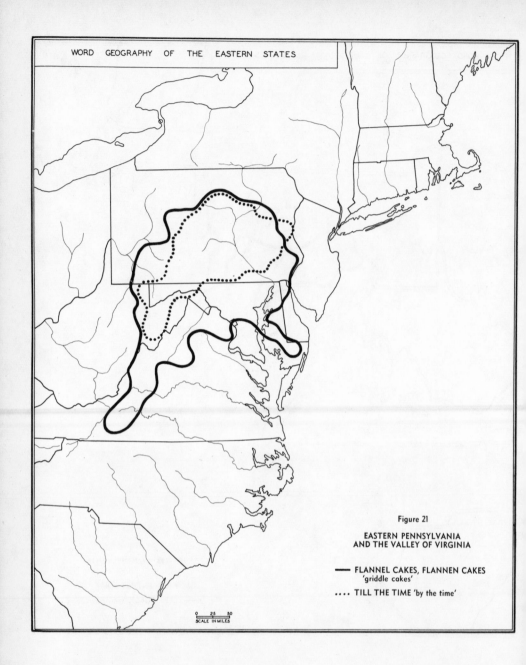

Figure 21

EASTERN PENNSYLVANIA
AND THE VALLEY OF VIRGINIA

—— FLANNEL CAKES, FLANNEN CAKES
'griddle cakes'

.... TILL THE TIME 'by the time'

0   25   50
SCALE IN MILES

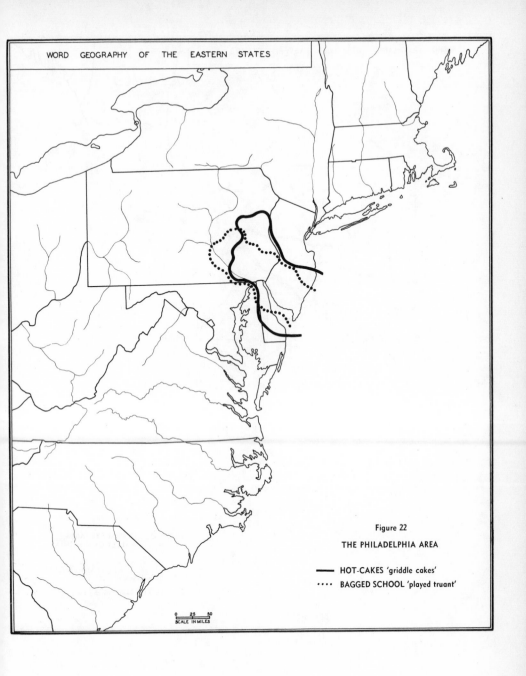

Figure 22

THE PHILADELPHIA AREA

—— HOT-CAKES 'griddle cakes'
•••• BAGGED SCHOOL 'played truant'

0   25   50
SCALE IN MILES

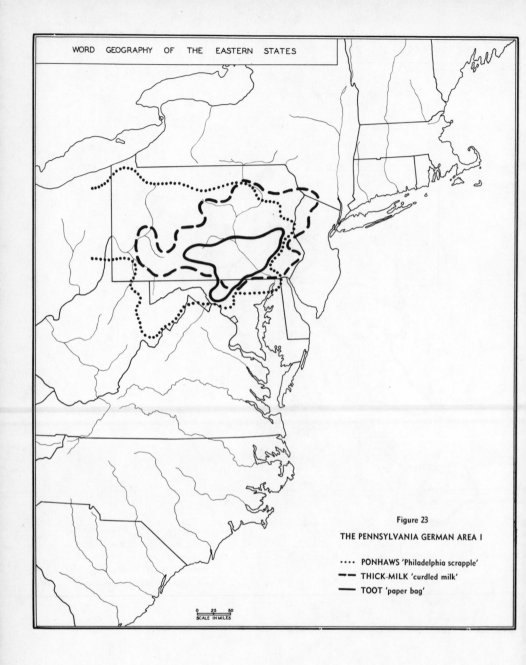

Figure 23

THE PENNSYLVANIA GERMAN AREA I

···· PONHAWS 'Philadelphia scrapple'

— — THICK-MILK 'curdled milk'

—— TOOT 'paper bag'

0   25   50
SCALE IN MILES

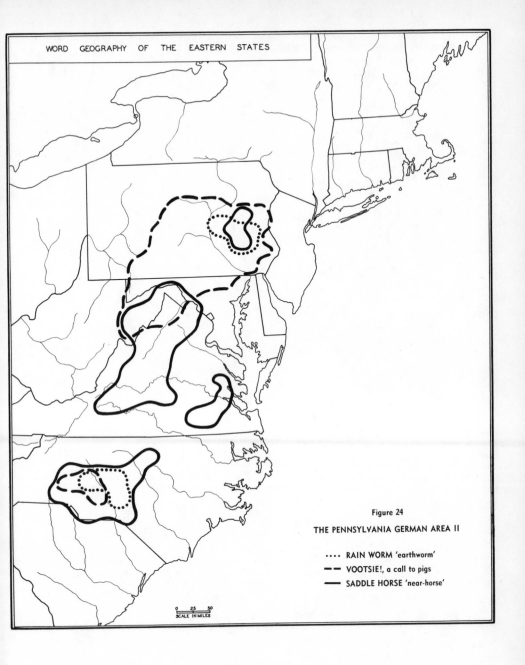

Figure 24

THE PENNSYLVANIA GERMAN AREA II

···· RAIN WORM 'earthworm'
— — VOOTSIE!, a call to pigs
—— SADDLE HORSE 'near-horse'

0   25   50
SCALE IN MILES

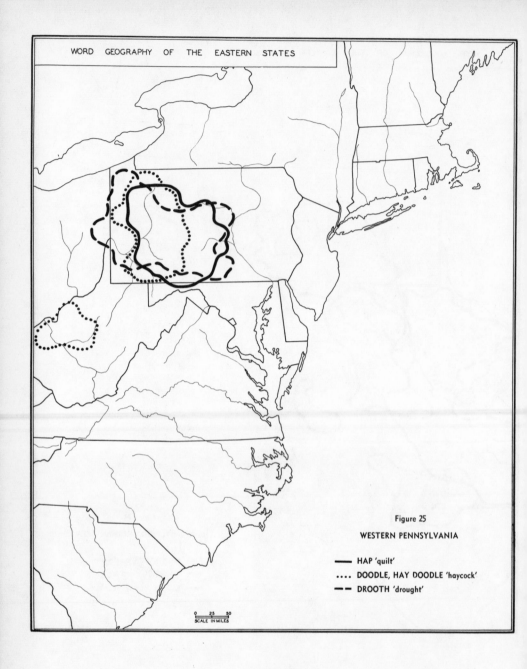

WORD GEOGRAPHY OF THE EASTERN STATES

Figure 25

WESTERN PENNSYLVANIA

—— HAP 'quilt'
.... DOODLE, HAY DOODLE 'haycock'
– – DROOTH 'drought'

0   25   50
SCALE IN MILES

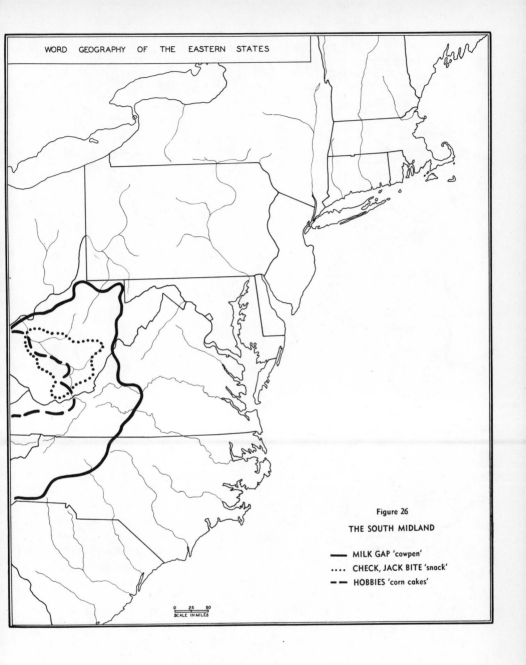

Figure 26

THE SOUTH MIDLAND

—— MILK GAP 'cowpen'
.... CHECK, JACK BITE 'snack'
– – HOBBIES 'corn cakes'

0   25   50
SCALE IN MILES

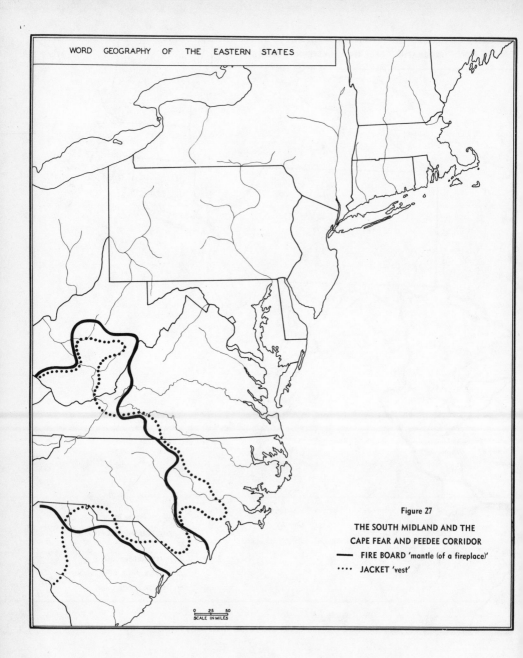

Figure 27

THE SOUTH MIDLAND AND THE
CAPE FEAR AND PEEDEE CORRIDOR

—— FIRE BOARD 'mantle (of a fireplace)'

···· JACKET 'vest'

0   25   50
SCALE IN MILES

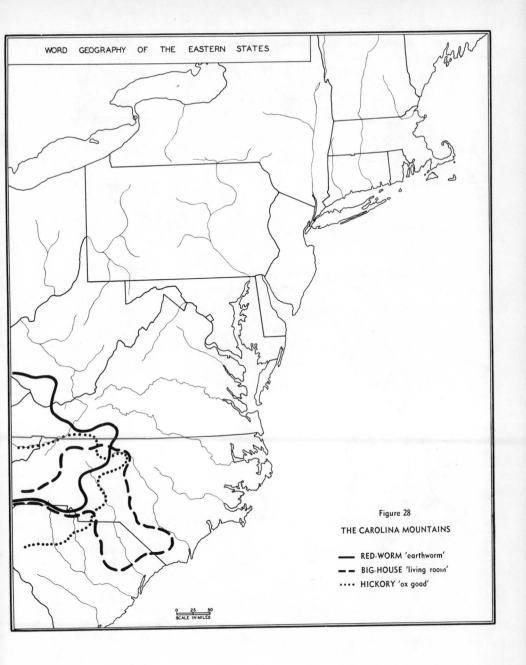

Figure 28

THE CAROLINA MOUNTAINS

—— RED-WORM 'earthworm'
– – BIG-HOUSE 'living room'
•••• HICKORY 'ox goad'

0   25   50
SCALE IN MILES

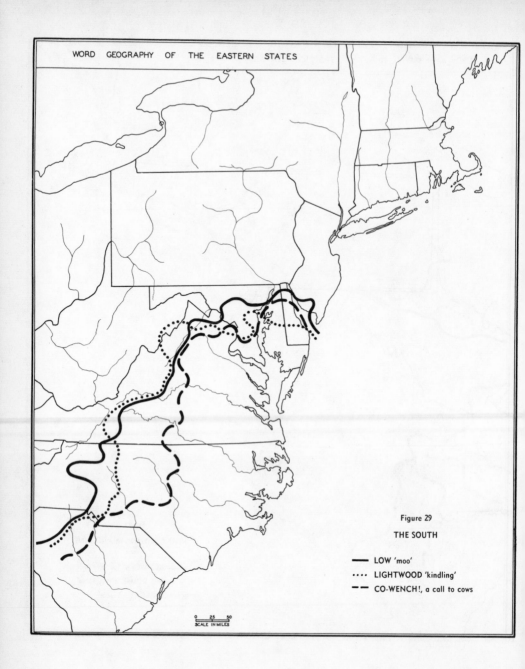

Figure 29

THE SOUTH

—— LOW 'moo'

···· LIGHTWOOD 'kindling'

— — CO-WENCH!, a call to cows

0   25   50
SCALE IN MILES

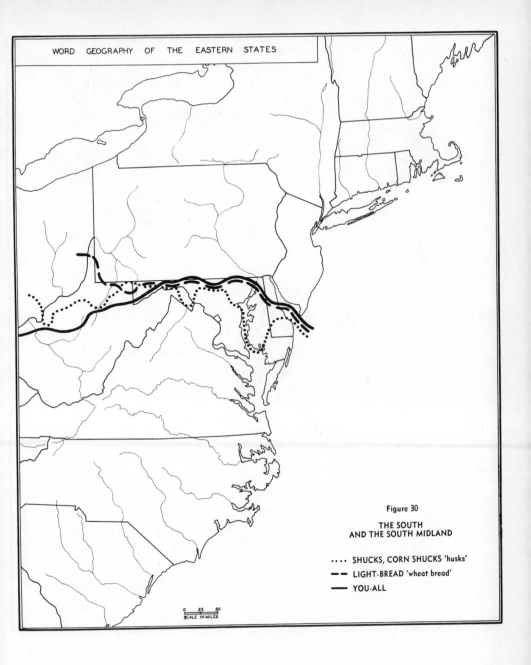

Figure 30

**THE SOUTH
AND THE SOUTH MIDLAND**

···· SHUCKS, CORN SHUCKS 'husks'

—— LIGHT-BREAD 'wheat bread'

—— YOU-ALL

0   25   50
SCALE IN MILES

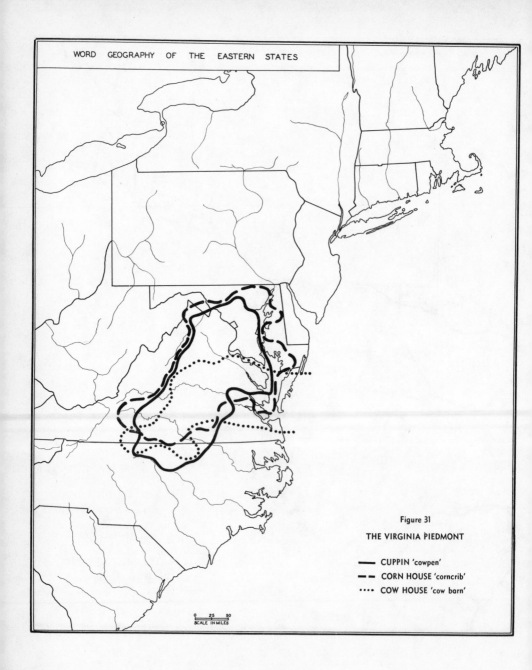

Figure 31

THE VIRGINIA PIEDMONT

——— CUPPIN 'cowpen'
– – – CORN HOUSE 'corncrib'
····· COW HOUSE 'cow barn'

0   25   50
SCALE IN MILES

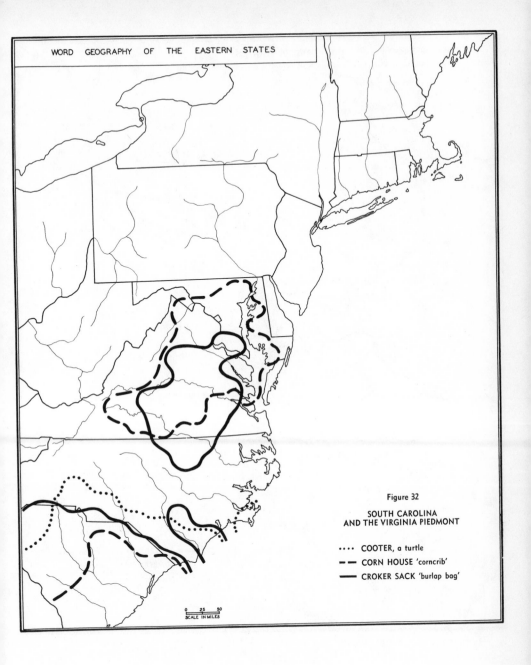

Figure 32

SOUTH CAROLINA
AND THE VIRGINIA PIEDMONT

•••• COOTER, a turtle
– – CORN HOUSE 'corncrib'
—— CROKER SACK 'burlap bag'

0   25   50
SCALE IN MILES

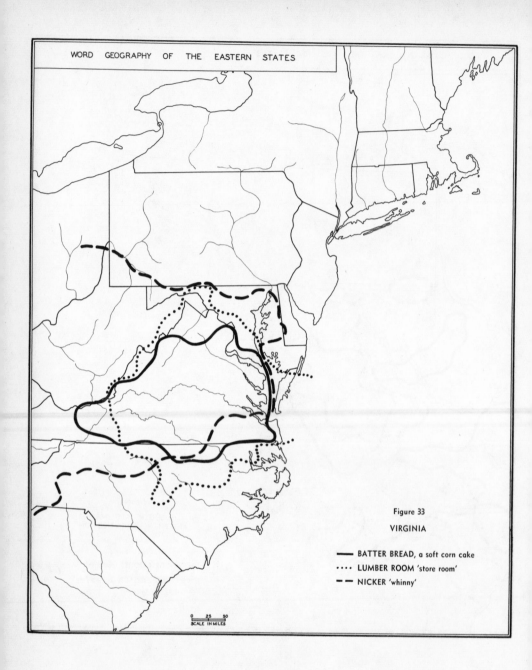

Figure 33

VIRGINIA

━━━ BATTER BREAD, a soft corn cake
•••• LUMBER ROOM 'store room'
━ ━ NICKER 'whinny'

0   25   50
SCALE IN MILES

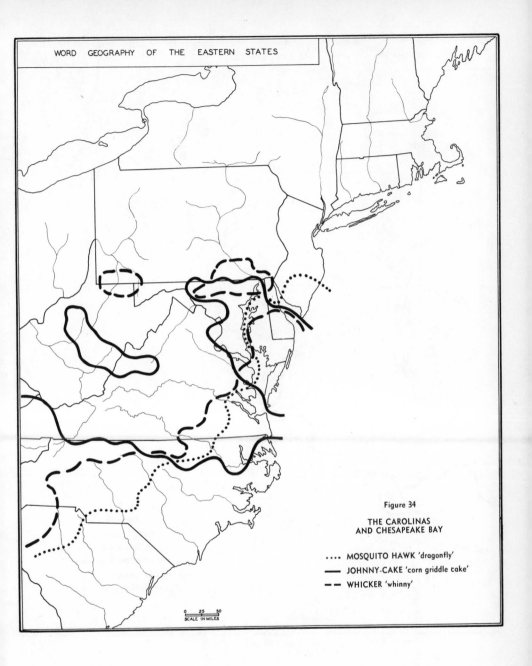

Figure 34

THE CAROLINAS
AND CHESAPEAKE BAY

···· MOSQUITO HAWK 'dragonfly'
——— JOHNNY-CAKE 'corn griddle cake'
– – – WHICKER 'whinny'

0   25   50
SCALE IN MILES

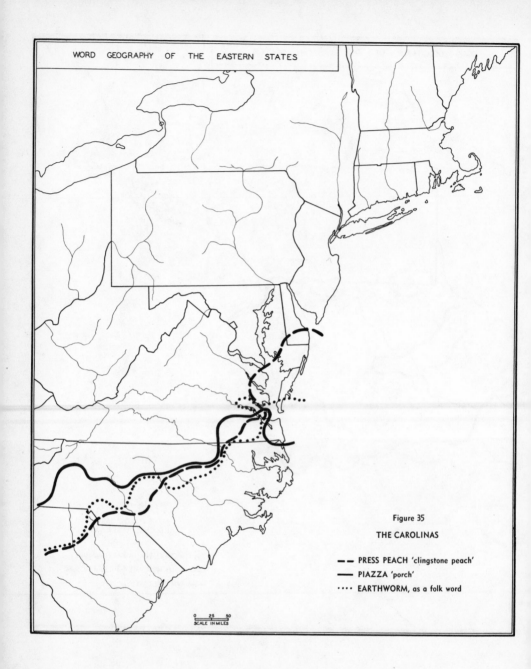

Figure 35

THE CAROLINAS

– – PRESS PEACH 'clingstone peach'
—— PIAZZA 'porch'
.... EARTHWORM, as a folk word

0   25   50
SCALE IN MILES

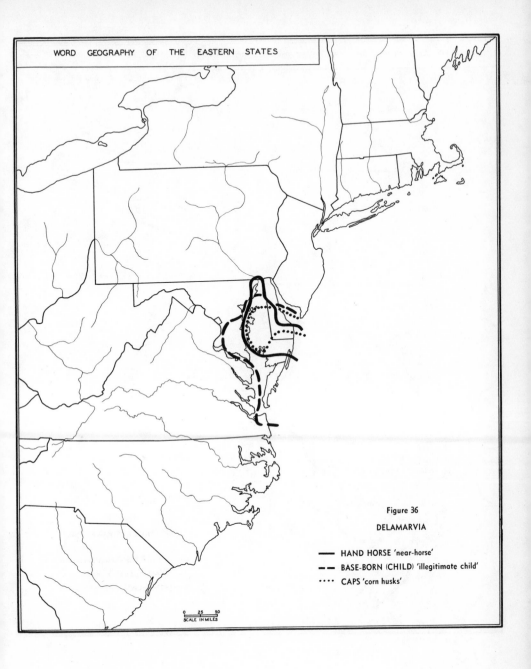

Figure 36

DELAMARVIA

——— HAND HORSE 'near-horse'

– – – BASE-BORN (CHILD) 'illegitimate child'

···· CAPS 'corn husks'

0   25   50
SCALE IN MILES

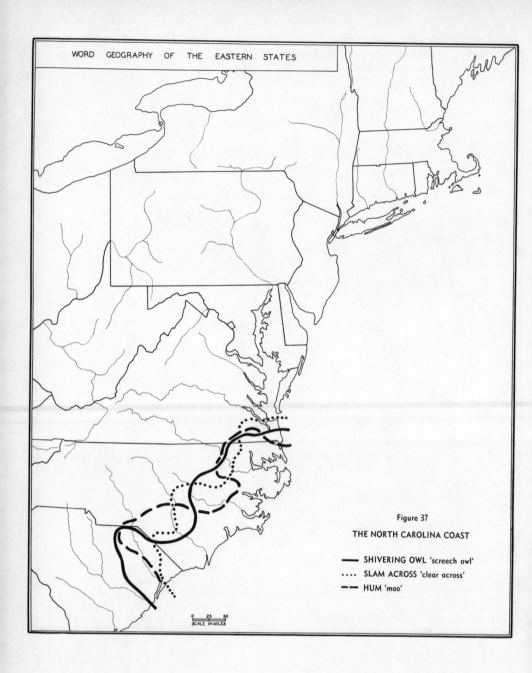

Figure 37

THE NORTH CAROLINA COAST

—— SHIVERING OWL 'screech owl'
···· SLAM ACROSS 'clear across'
–– HUM 'moo'

0   25   50
SCALE IN MILES

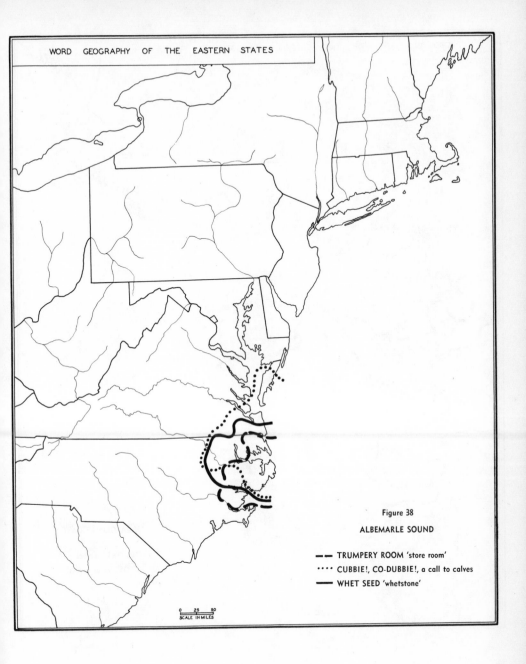

Figure 38

ALBEMARLE SOUND

– – TRUMPERY ROOM 'store room'

•••• CUBBIE!, CO-DUBBIE!, a call to calves

—— WHET SEED 'whetstone'

0   25   50
SCALE IN MILES

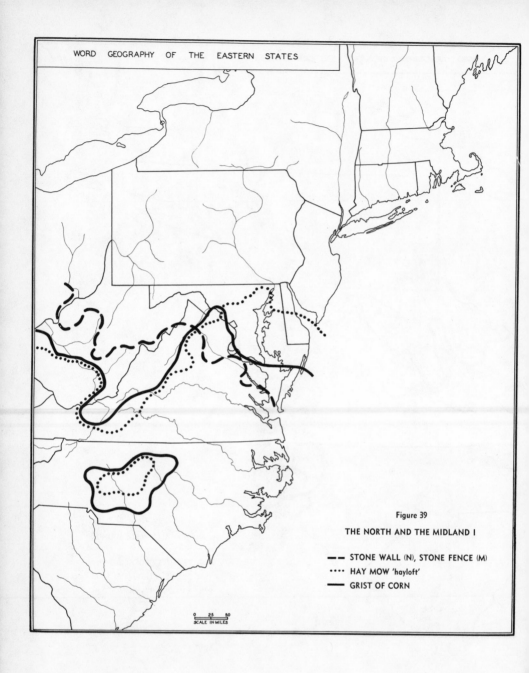

Figure 39

THE NORTH AND THE MIDLAND I

– – STONE WALL (N), STONE FENCE (M)
•••• HAY MOW 'hayloft'
— GRIST OF CORN

0 25 50
SCALE IN MILES

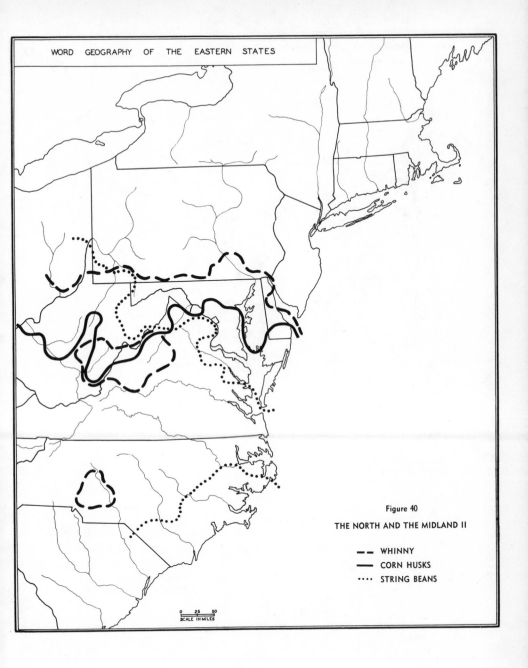

Figure 40

THE NORTH AND THE MIDLAND II

－－ WHINNY
— CORN HUSKS
···· STRING BEANS

0   25   50
SCALE IN MILES

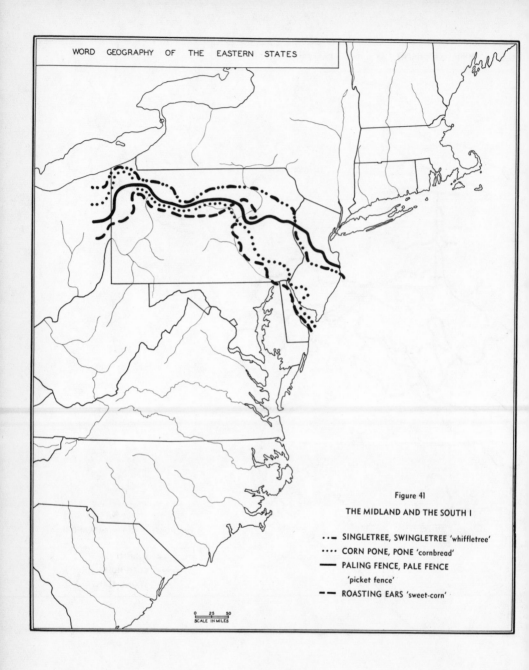

Figure 41

THE MIDLAND AND THE SOUTH I

··— SINGLETREE, SWINGLETREE 'whiffletree'
···· CORN PONE, PONE 'cornbread'
—— PALING FENCE, PALE FENCE
       'picket fence'
— — ROASTING EARS 'sweet-corn'

0   25   50
SCALE IN MILES

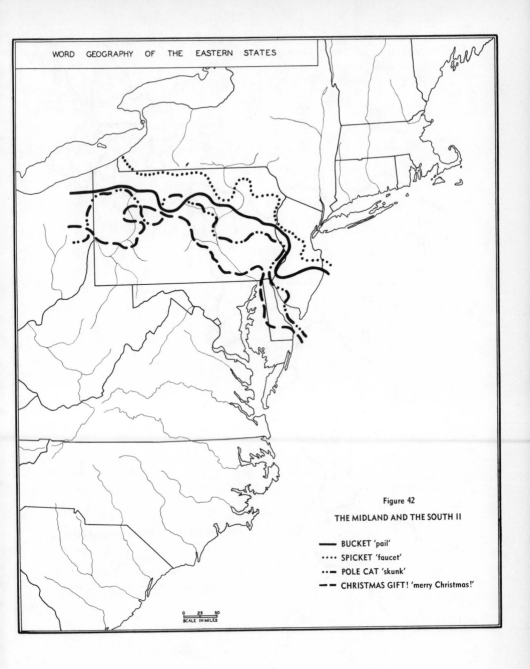

WORD GEOGRAPHY OF THE EASTERN STATES

Figure 42

THE MIDLAND AND THE SOUTH II

———— BUCKET 'pail'
•••• SPICKET 'faucet'
•••— POLE CAT 'skunk'
— — CHRISTMAS GIFT! 'merry Christmas!'

0   25   50
SCALE IN MILES

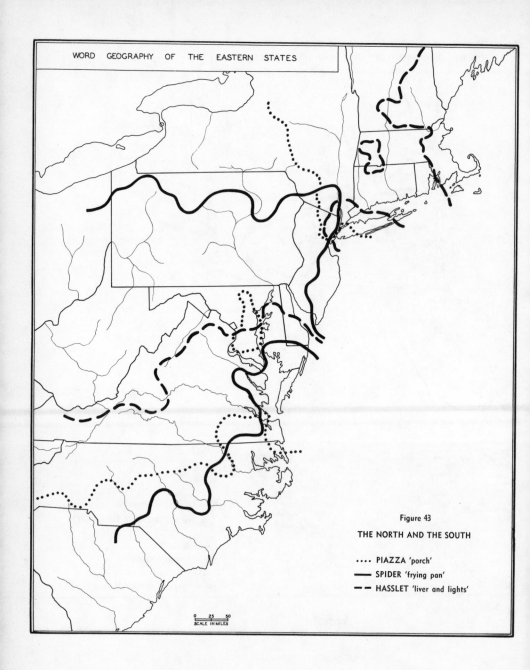

Figure 43

THE NORTH AND THE SOUTH

···· PIAZZA 'porch'
——— SPIDER 'frying pan'
— — HASSLET 'liver and lights'

0   25   50
SCALE IN MILES

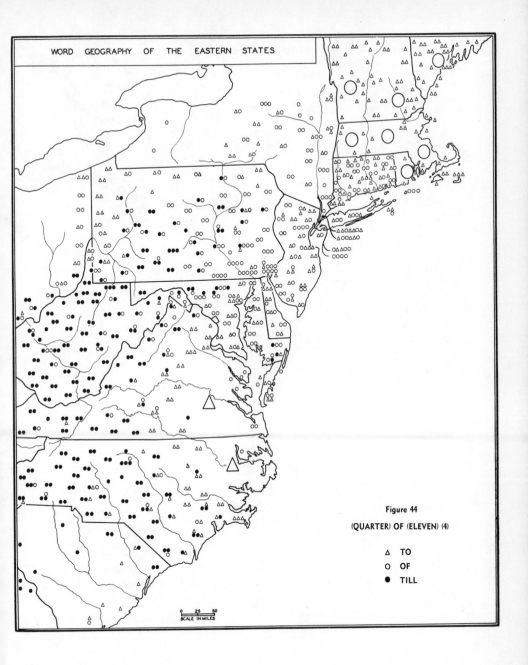

Figure 44

(QUARTER) OF (ELEVEN) (4)

△ TO
○ OF
● TILL

0   25   50
SCALE IN MILES

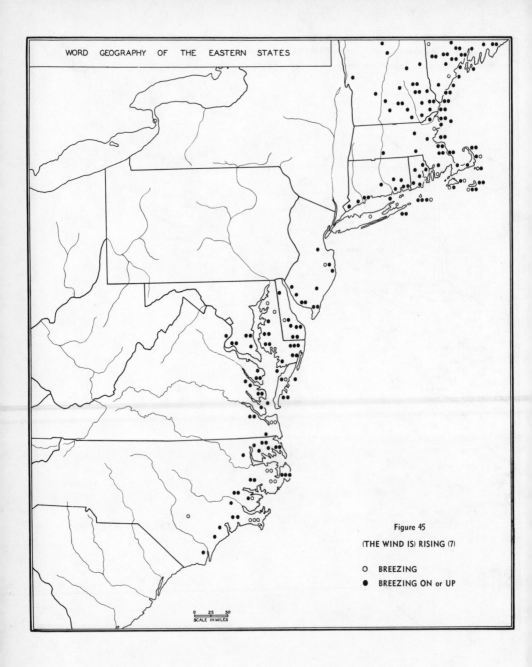

Figure 45

(THE WIND IS) RISING (7)

O   BREEZING

●   BREEZING ON or UP

0   25   50
SCALE IN MILES

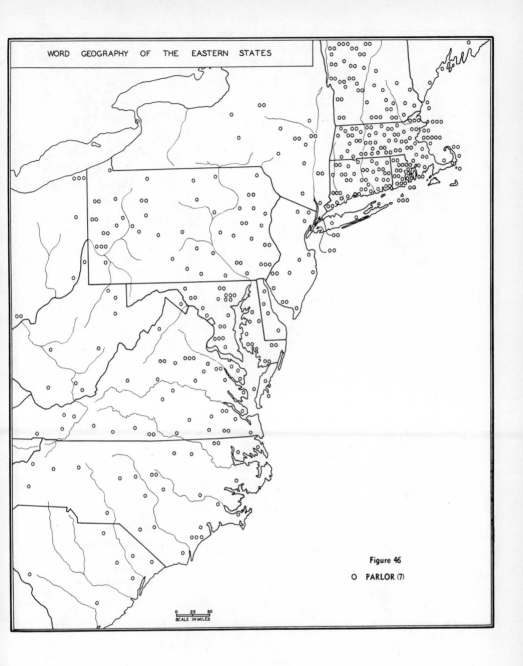

Figure 46

O PARLOR (7)

0   25   50
SCALE IN MILES

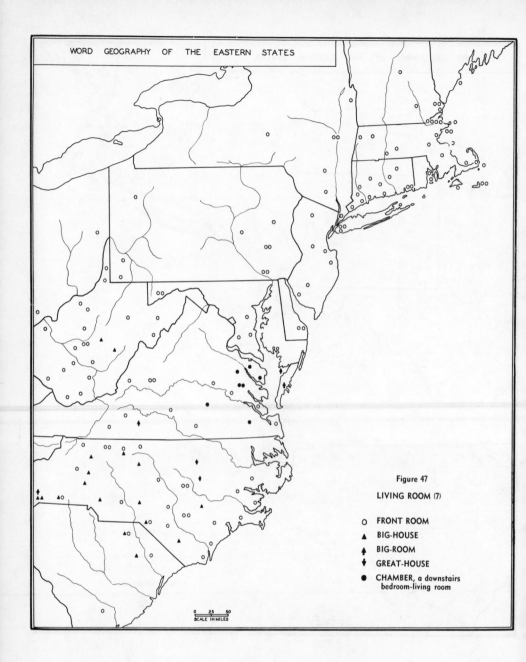

Figure 47

LIVING ROOM (7)

○ FRONT ROOM

▲ BIG-HOUSE

♠ BIG-ROOM

♣ GREAT-HOUSE

● CHAMBER, a downstairs
   bedroom-living room

0   25   50
SCALE IN MILES

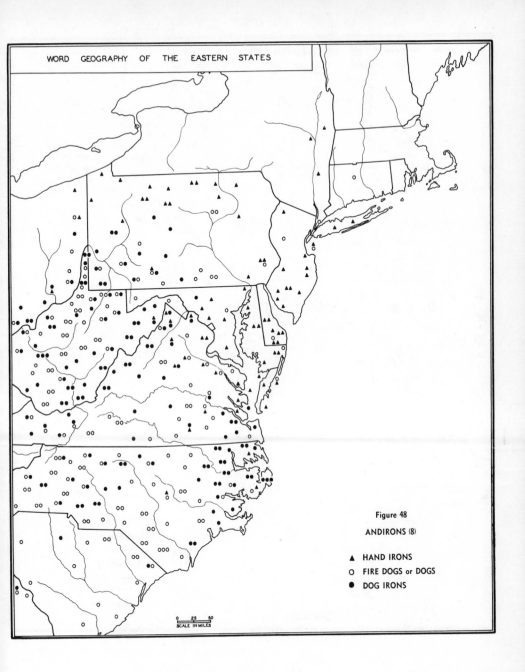

Figure 48

ANDIRONS (8)

▲ HAND IRONS

○ FIRE DOGS or DOGS

● DOG IRONS

0   25   50
SCALE IN MILES

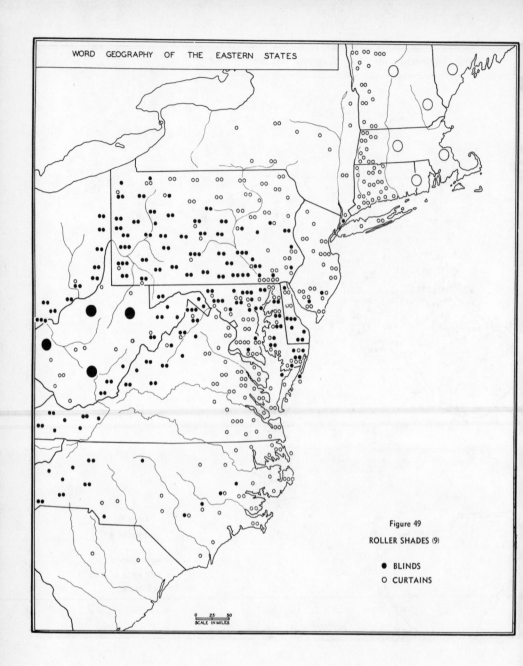

Figure 49

ROLLER SHADES (9)

● BLINDS

O CURTAINS

0 25 50
SCALE IN MILES

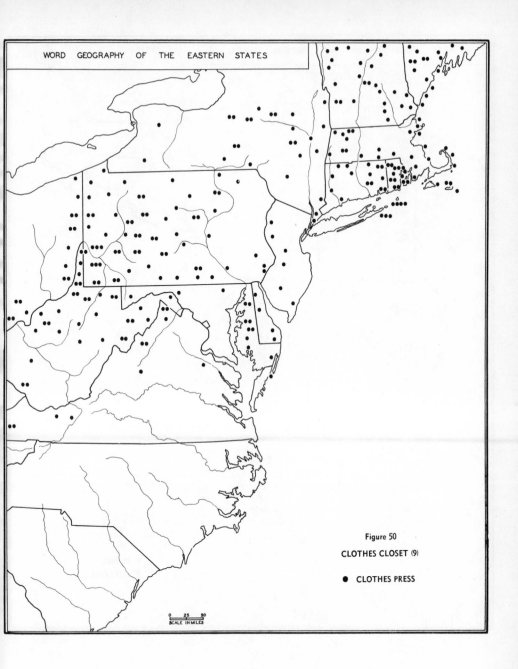

Figure 50

CLOTHES CLOSET (9)

● **CLOTHES PRESS**

0   25   50
SCALE IN MILES

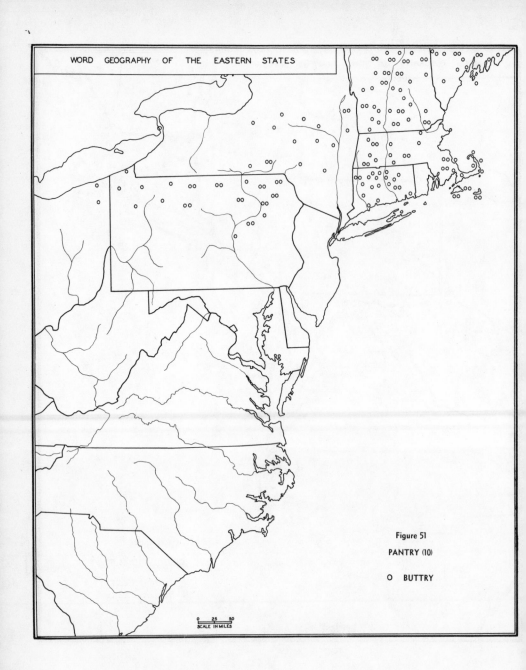

Figure 51

PANTRY (10)

O BUTTRY

0   25   50
SCALE IN MILES

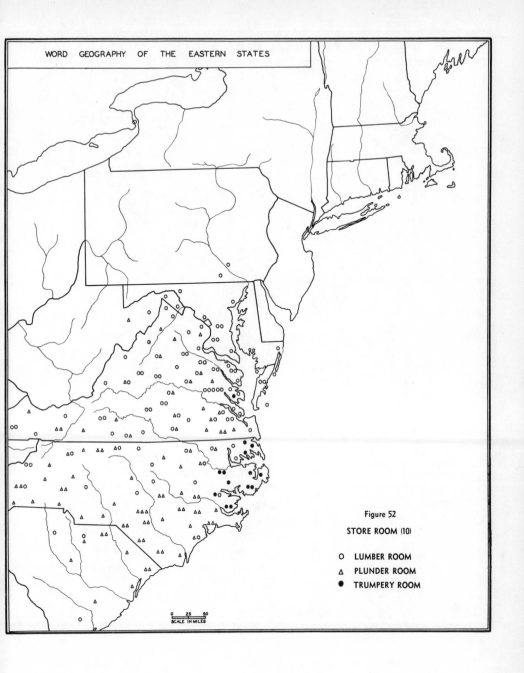

Figure 52

STORE ROOM (10)

O LUMBER ROOM
△ PLUNDER ROOM
● TRUMPERY ROOM

0   25   50
SCALE IN MILES

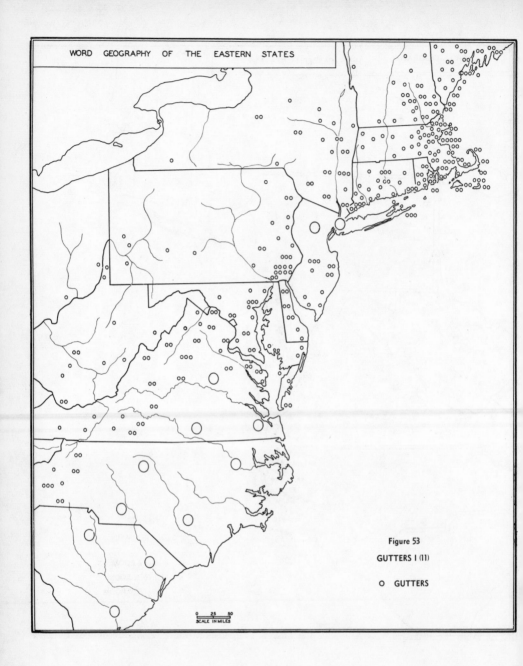

Figure 53

GUTTERS I (11)

O GUTTERS

0   25   50
SCALE IN MILES

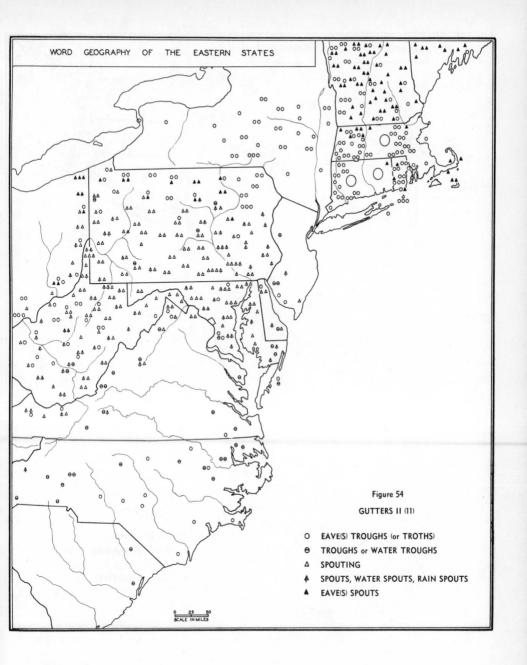

WORD GEOGRAPHY OF THE EASTERN STATES

Figure 54

GUTTERS II (11)

O   EAVE(S) TROUGHS (or TROTHS)
⊖   TROUGHS or WATER TROUGHS
△   SPOUTING
⚶   SPOUTS, WATER SPOUTS, RAIN SPOUTS
▲   EAVE(S) SPOUTS

0   25   50
SCALE IN MILES

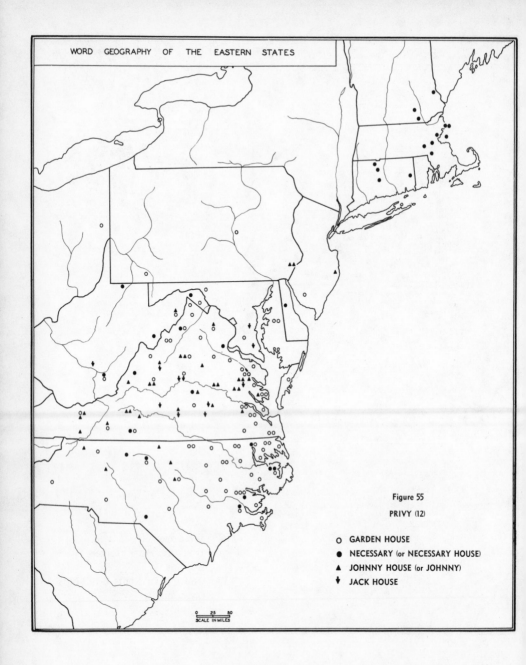

WORD GEOGRAPHY OF THE EASTERN STATES

Figure 55

PRIVY (12)

○ GARDEN HOUSE
● NECESSARY (or NECESSARY HOUSE)
▲ JOHNNY HOUSE (or JOHNNY)
↓ JACK HOUSE

0   25   50
SCALE IN MILES

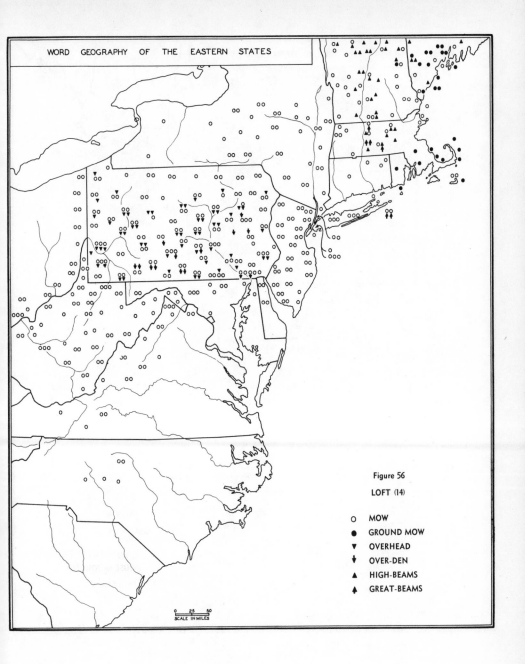

Figure 56

LOFT (14)

○ MOW
● GROUND MOW
▼ OVERHEAD
↓ OVER-DEN
▲ HIGH-BEAMS
♠ GREAT-BEAMS

0   25   50
SCALE IN MILES

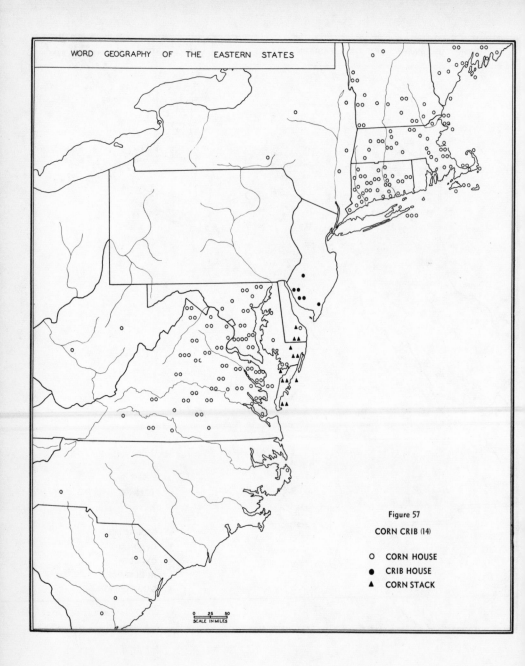

Figure 57

CORN CRIB (14)

○   CORN HOUSE
●   CRIB HOUSE
▲   CORN STACK

0   25   50
SCALE IN MILES

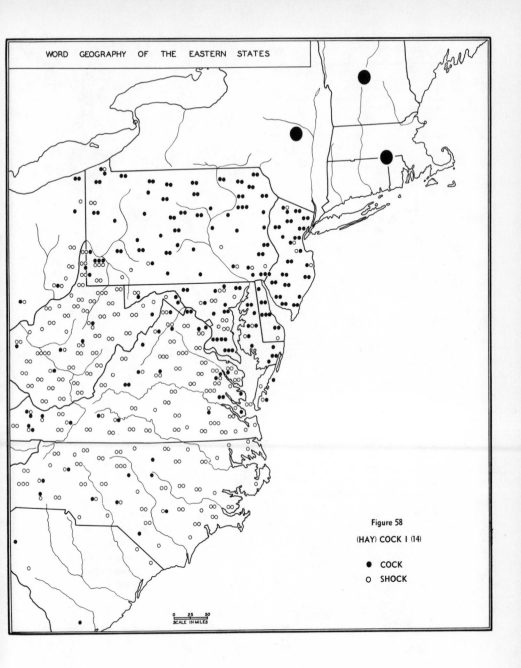

Figure 58

(HAY) COCK I (14)

● COCK

○ SHOCK

0   25   50
SCALE IN MILES

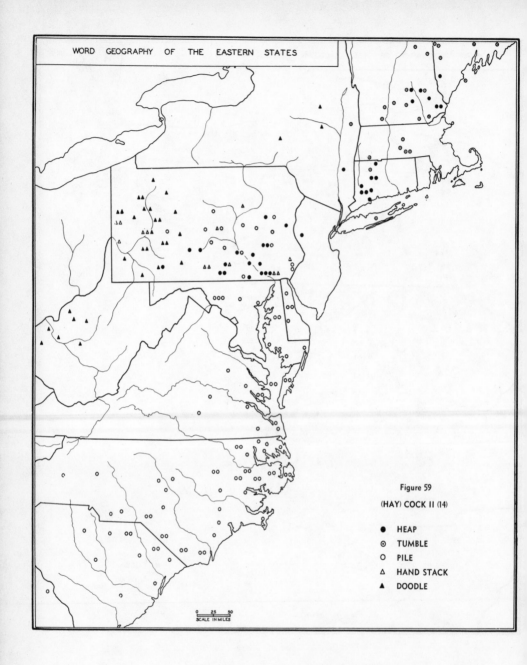

WORD GEOGRAPHY OF THE EASTERN STATES

Figure 59

(HAY) COCK II (14)

● HEAP
⊙ TUMBLE
○ PILE
△ HAND STACK
▲ DOODLE

0 25 50
SCALE IN MILES

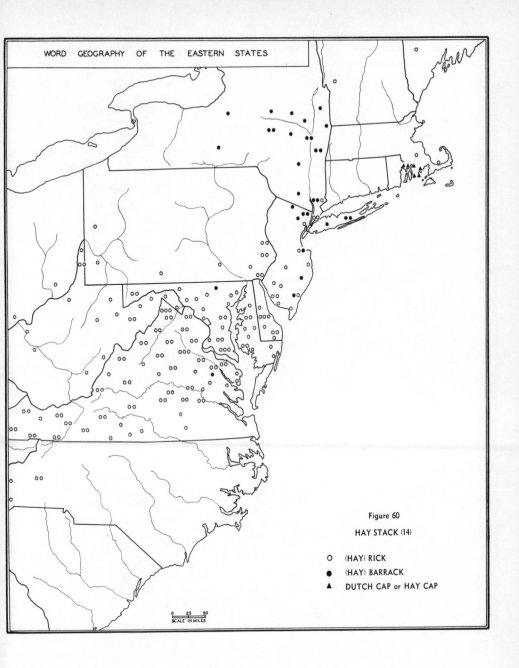

WORD GEOGRAPHY OF THE EASTERN STATES

Figure 60

HAY STACK (14)

O   (HAY) RICK

●   (HAY) BARRACK

▲   DUTCH CAP or HAY CAP

0   25   50
SCALE IN MILES

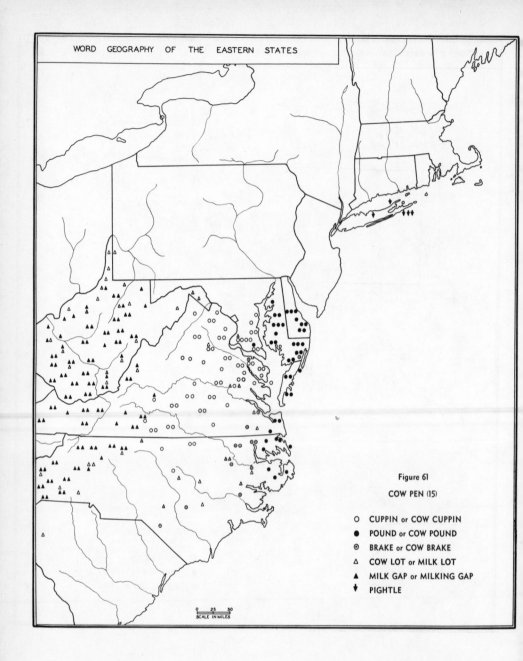

Figure 61

COW PEN (15)

○ CUPPIN or COW CUPPIN
● POUND or COW POUND
⊙ BRAKE or COW BRAKE
△ COW LOT or MILK LOT
▲ MILK GAP or MILKING GAP
↓ PIGHTLE

0   25   50
SCALE IN MILES

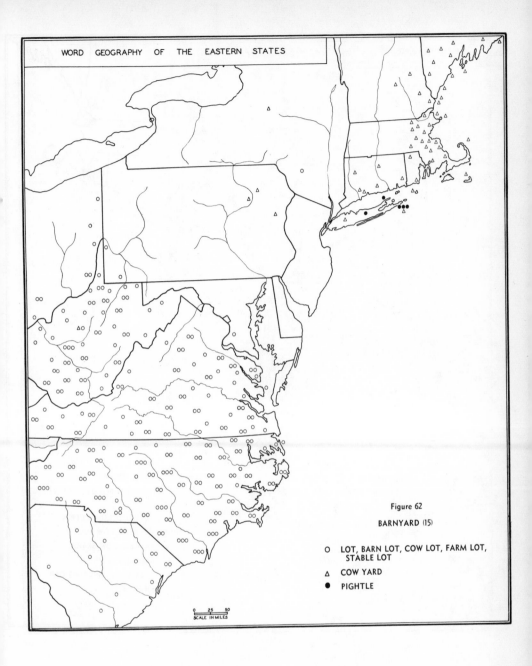

WORD GEOGRAPHY OF THE EASTERN STATES

Figure 62

BARNYARD (15)

O   LOT, BARN LOT, COW LOT, FARM LOT,
    STABLE LOT
△   COW YARD
●   PIGHTLE

0   25   50
SCALE IN MILES

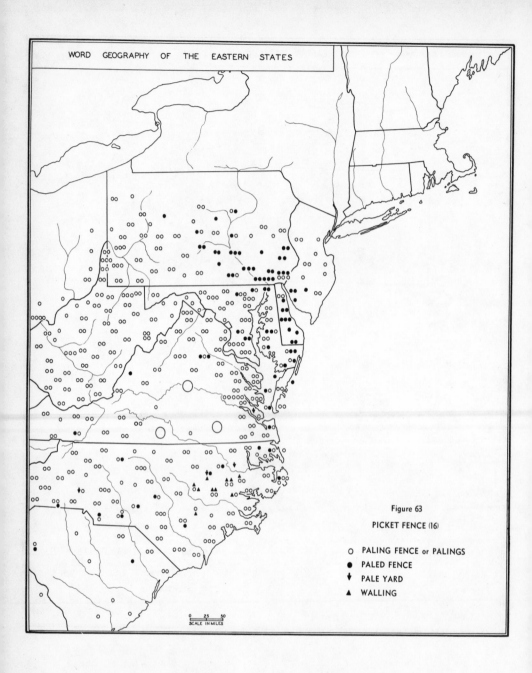

Figure 63

PICKET FENCE (16)

○ PALING FENCE or PALINGS
● PALED FENCE
↓ PALE YARD
▲ WALLING

0   25   50
SCALE IN MILES

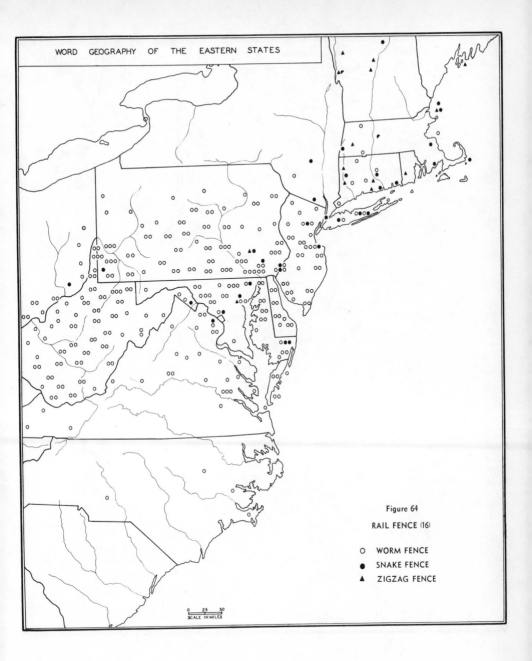

Figure 64

RAIL FENCE (16)

○   WORM FENCE
●   SNAKE FENCE
▲   ZIGZAG FENCE

0   25   50
SCALE IN MILES

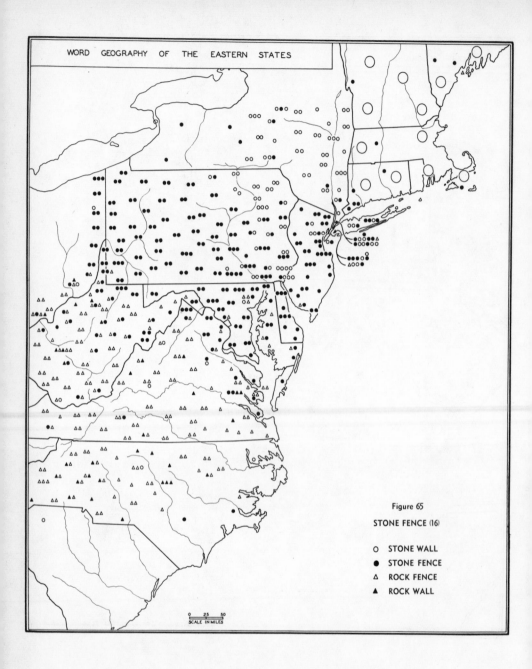

Figure 65

STONE FENCE (16)

○ STONE WALL
● STONE FENCE
△ ROCK FENCE
▲ ROCK WALL

0   25   50
SCALE IN MILES

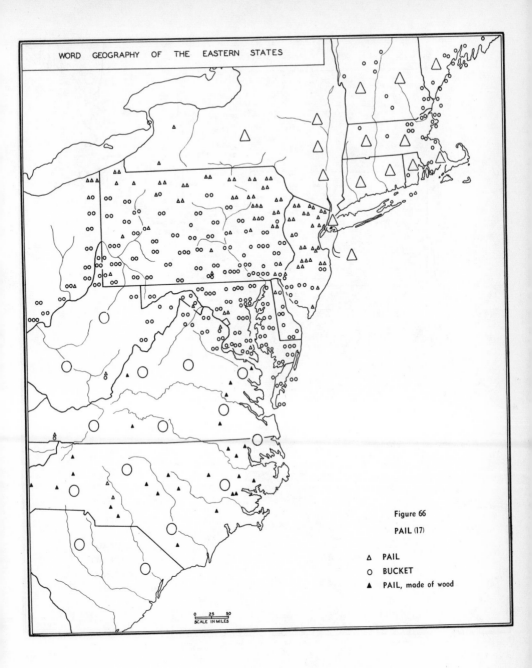

Figure 66

PAIL (17)

△ PAIL
○ BUCKET
▲ PAIL, made of wood

0   25   50
SCALE IN MILES

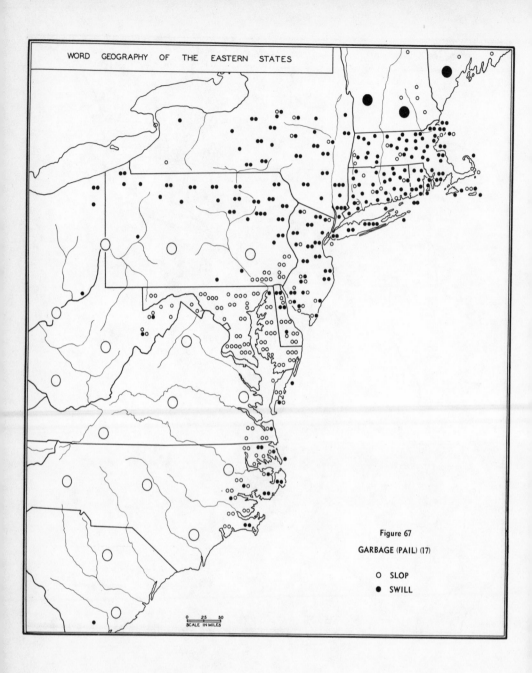

Figure 67

GARBAGE (PAIL) (17)

○ SLOP
● SWILL

0   25   50
SCALE IN MILES

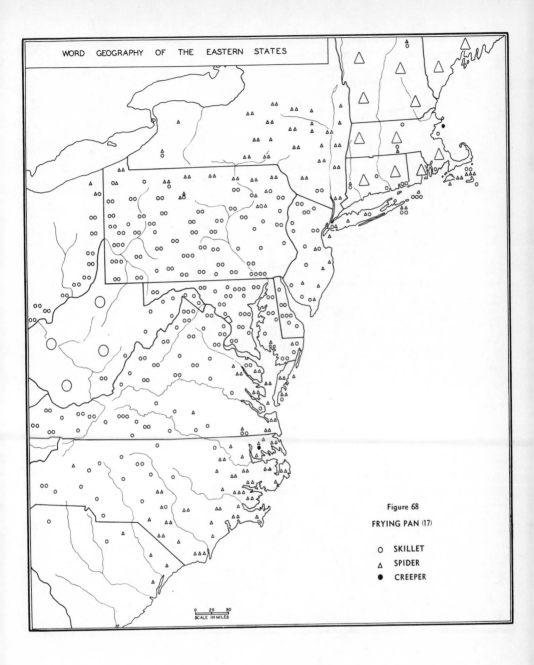

Figure 68

FRYING PAN (17)

○ SKILLET
△ SPIDER
● CREEPER

0   25   50
SCALE IN MILES

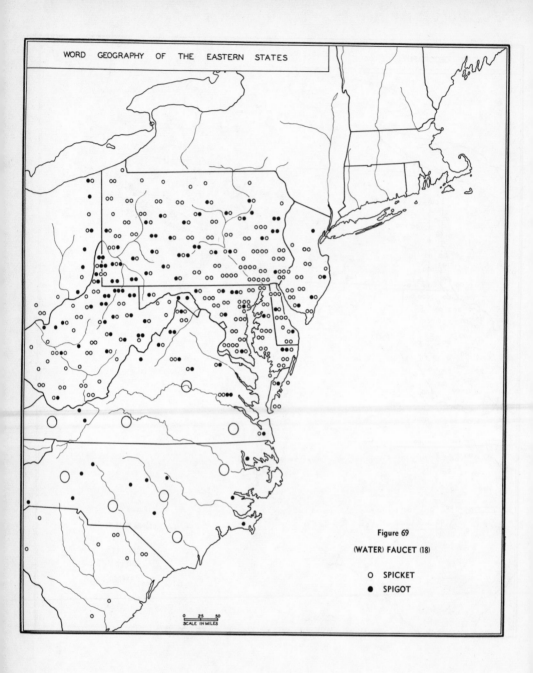

Figure 69

(WATER) FAUCET (18)

O   SPICKET

●   SPIGOT

0   25   50
SCALE IN MILES

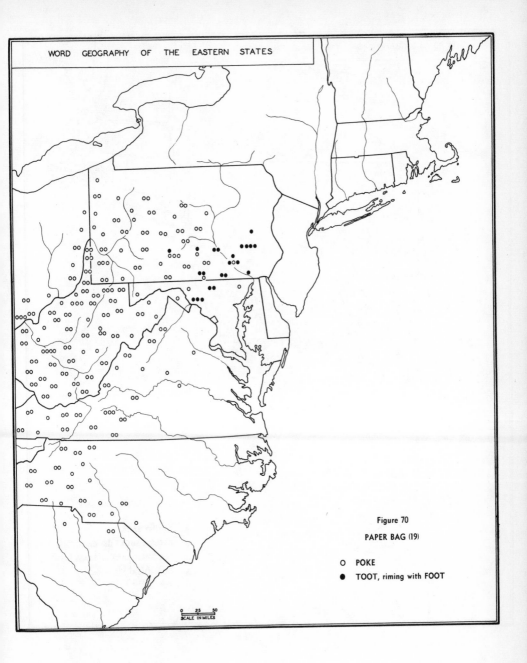

Figure 70

PAPER BAG (19)

O POKE
● TOOT, riming with FOOT

0   25   50
SCALE IN MILES

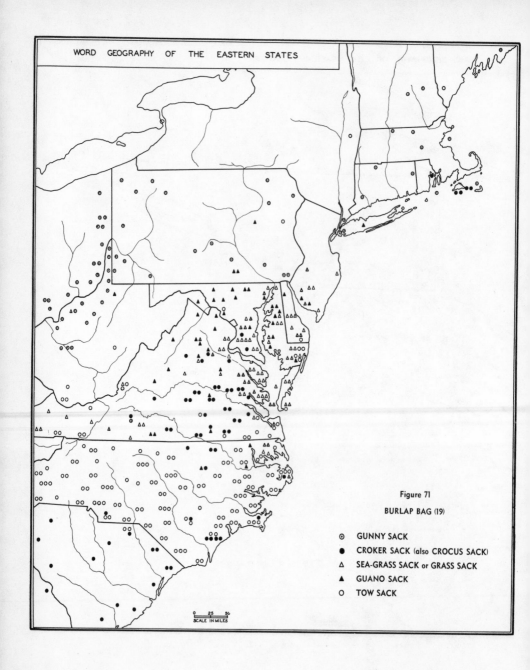

Figure 71

BURLAP BAG (19)

⊙ GUNNY SACK

● CROKER SACK (also CROCUS SACK)

△ SEA-GRASS SACK or GRASS SACK

▲ GUANO SACK

○ TOW SACK

0   25   50
SCALE IN MILES

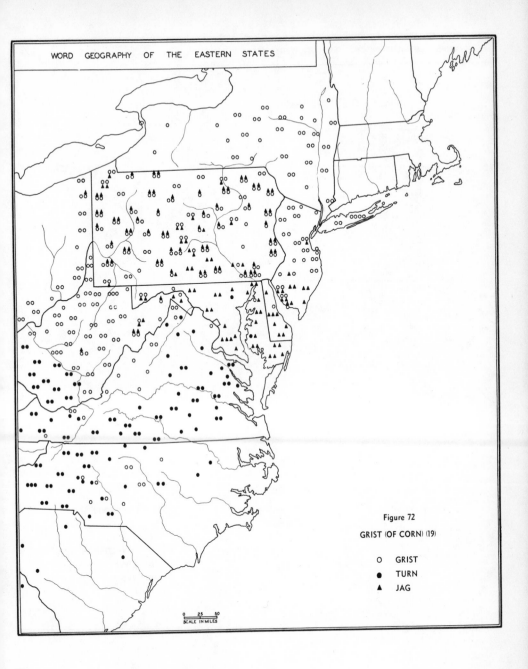

Figure 72

GRIST (OF CORN) (19)

O GRIST

● TURN

▲ JAG

0   25   50
SCALE IN MILES

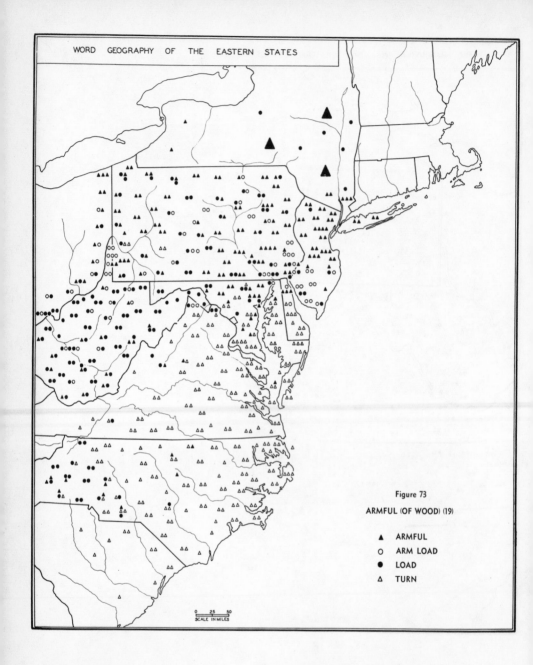

Figure 73

ARMFUL (OF WOOD) (19)

▲ ARMFUL
○ ARM LOAD
● LOAD
△ TURN

0   25   50
SCALE IN MILES

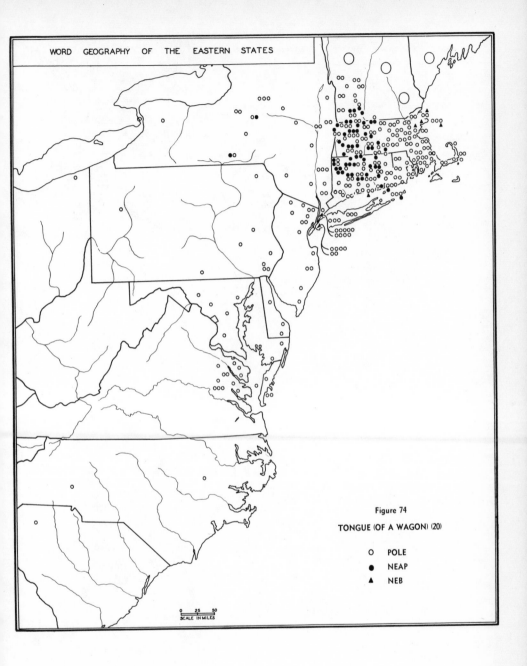

Figure 74

TONGUE (OF A WAGON) (20)

○   POLE

●   NEAP

▲   NEB

0 25   50
SCALE IN MILES

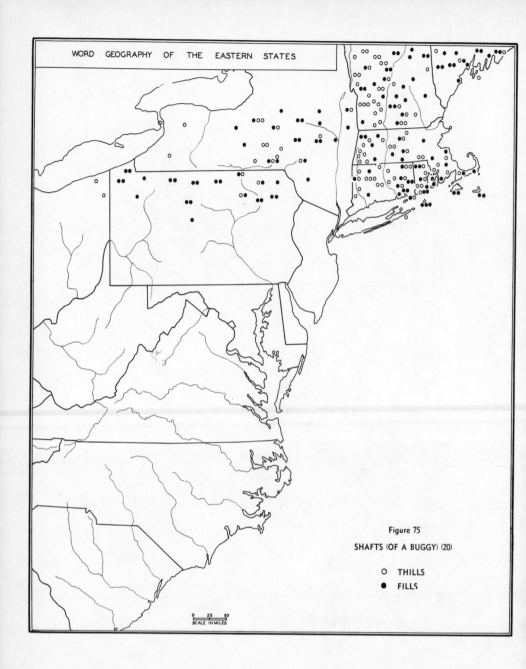

Figure 75

SHAFTS (OF A BUGGY) (20)

O   THILLS
●   FILLS

0   25   50
SCALE IN MILES

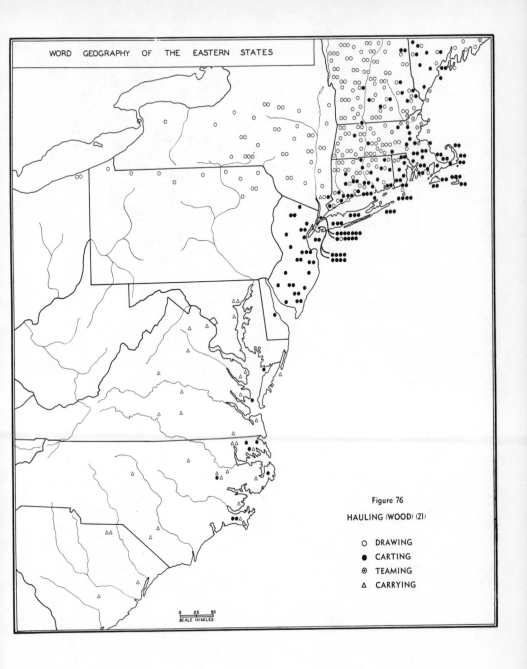

Figure 76

HAULING (WOOD) (21)

○ DRAWING
● CARTING
⊙ TEAMING
△ CARRYING

0   25   50
SCALE IN MILES

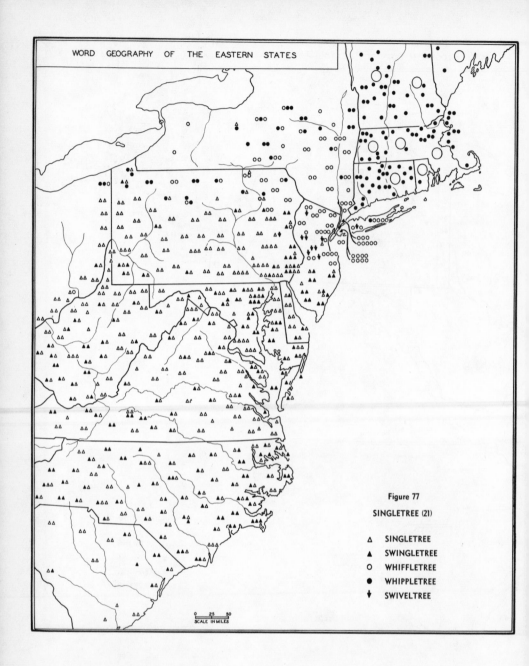

Figure 77

SINGLETREE (21)

△ SINGLETREE
▲ SWINGLETREE
○ WHIFFLETREE
● WHIPPLETREE
↓ SWIVELTREE

0   25   50
SCALE IN MILES

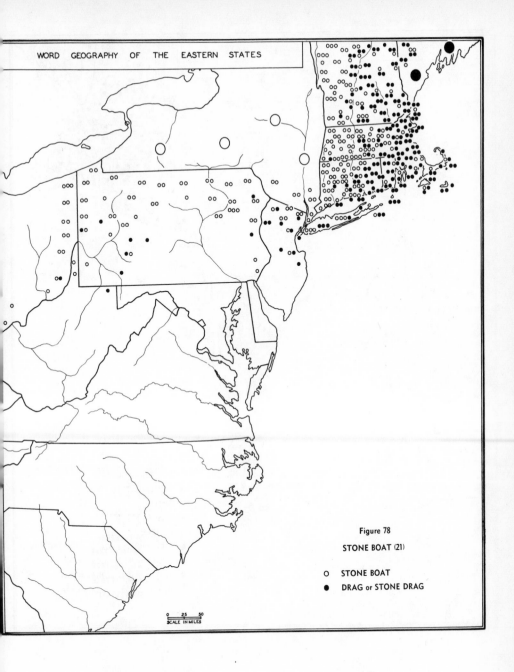

Figure 78

STONE BOAT (21)

○   STONE BOAT

●   DRAG or STONE DRAG

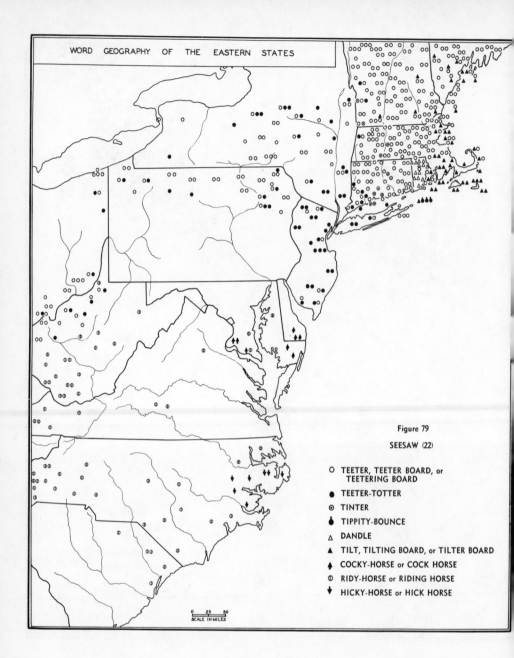

Figure 79

SEESAW (22)

○ TEETER, TEETER BOARD, or
   TEETERING BOARD
● TEETER-TOTTER
◉ TINTER
🌢 TIPPITY-BOUNCE
△ DANDLE
▲ TILT, TILTING BOARD, or TILTER BOARD
♠ COCKY-HORSE or COCK HORSE
◍ RIDY-HORSE or RIDING HORSE
↓ HICKY-HORSE or HICK HORSE

0   25   50
SCALE IN MILES

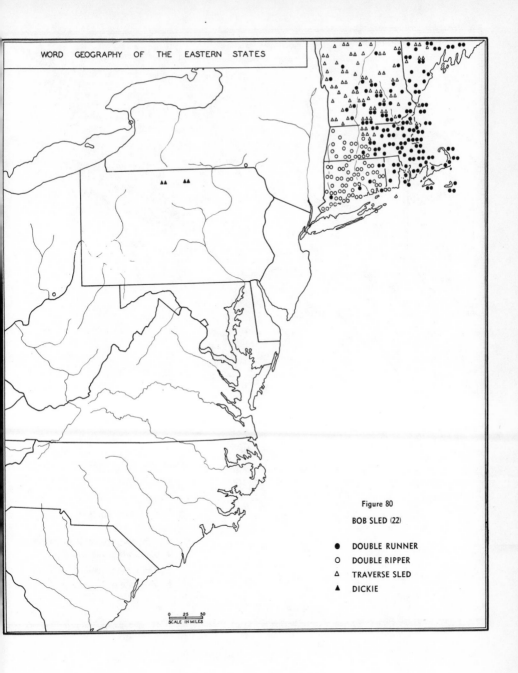

Figure 80

BOB SLED (22)

● DOUBLE RUNNER
○ DOUBLE RIPPER
△ TRAVERSE SLED
▲ DICKIE

0   25   50
SCALE IN MILES

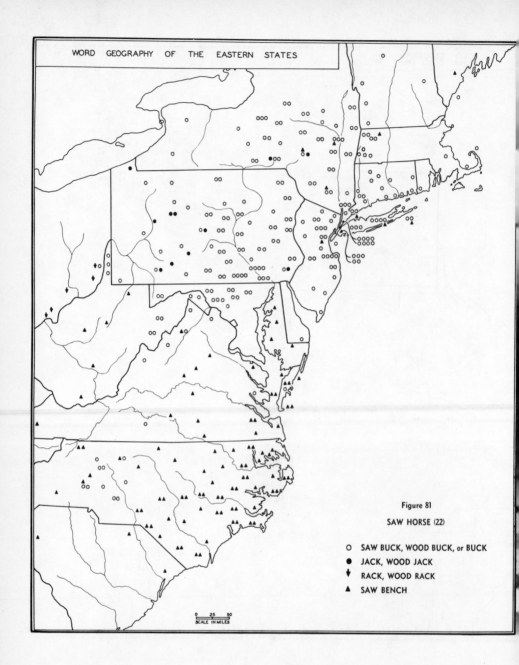

Figure 81

SAW HORSE (22)

O SAW BUCK, WOOD BUCK, or BUCK
● JACK, WOOD JACK
↓ RACK, WOOD RACK
▲ SAW BENCH

0   25   50
SCALE IN MILES

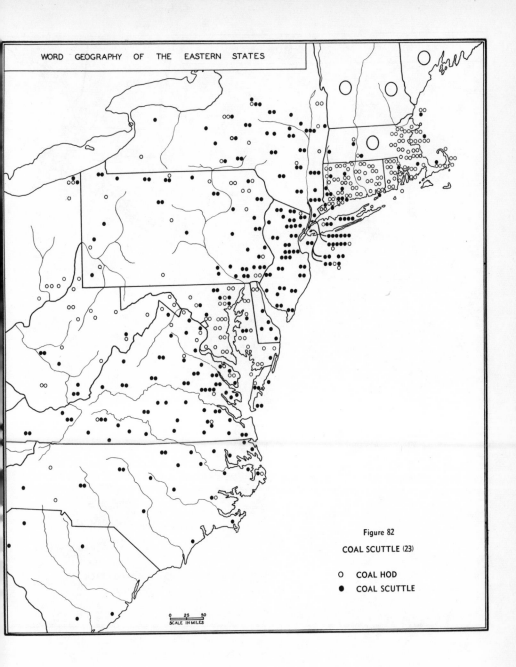

Figure 82

COAL SCUTTLE (23)

O   COAL HOD

●   COAL SCUTTLE

0   25   50
SCALE IN MILES

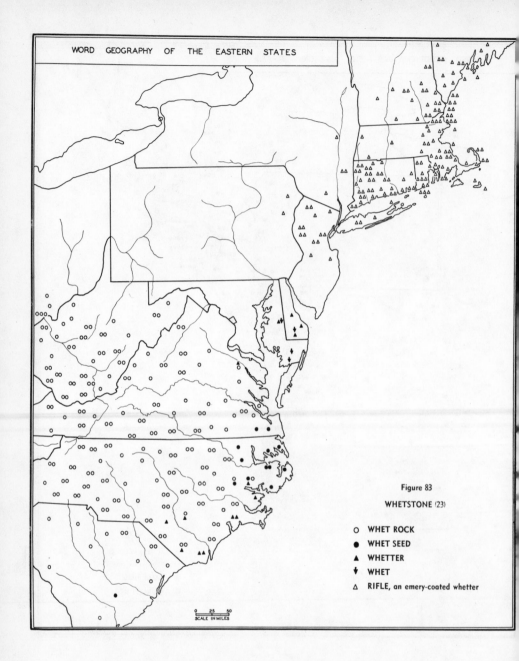

WORD GEOGRAPHY OF THE EASTERN STATES

Figure 83

WHETSTONE (23)

O   WHET ROCK
●   WHET SEED
▲   WHETTER
♦   WHET
△   RIFLE, an emery-coated whetter

0   25   50
SCALE IN MILES

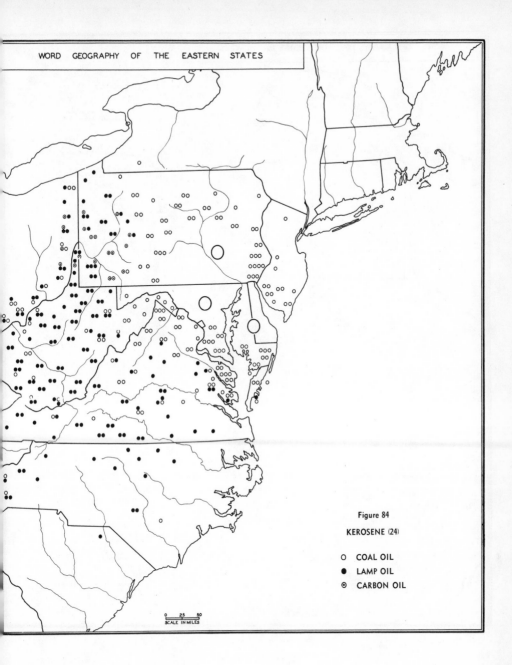

Figure 84

KEROSENE (24)

○ COAL OIL

● LAMP OIL

◉ CARBON OIL

0   25   50
SCALE IN MILES

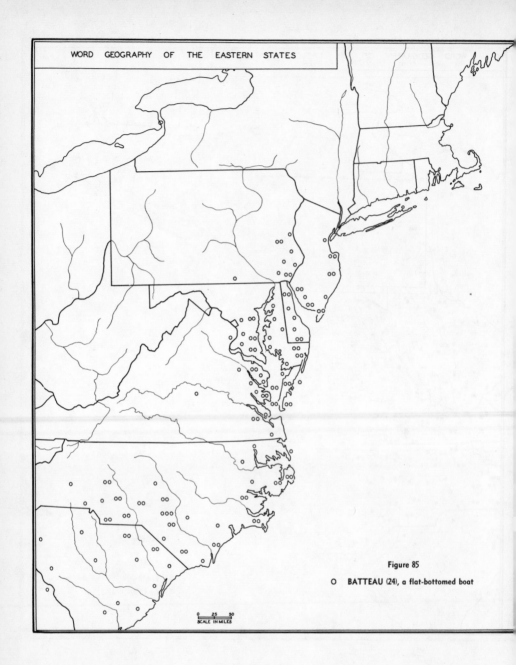

Figure 85

O   **BATTEAU** (24), a flat-bottomed boat

0   25   50
SCALE IN MILES

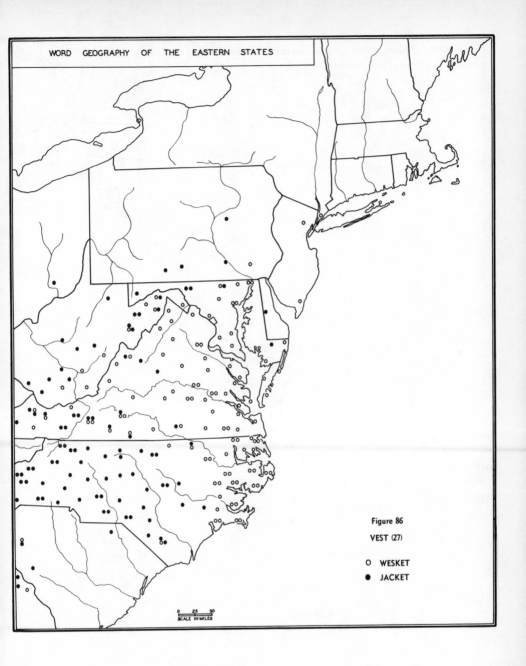

WORD GEOGRAPHY OF THE EASTERN STATES

Figure 86

VEST (27)

O WESKET

● JACKET

0   25   50
SCALE IN MILES

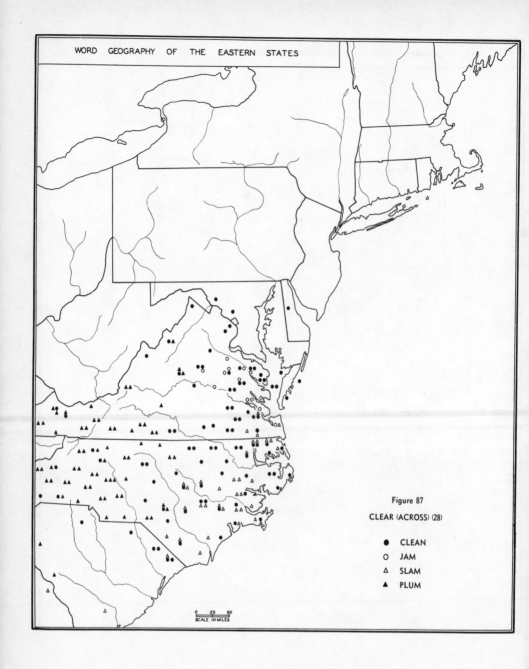

WORD GEOGRAPHY OF THE EASTERN STATES

Figure 87

CLEAR (ACROSS) (28)

● CLEAN
○ JAM
△ SLAM
▲ PLUM

0 25 50
SCALE IN MILES

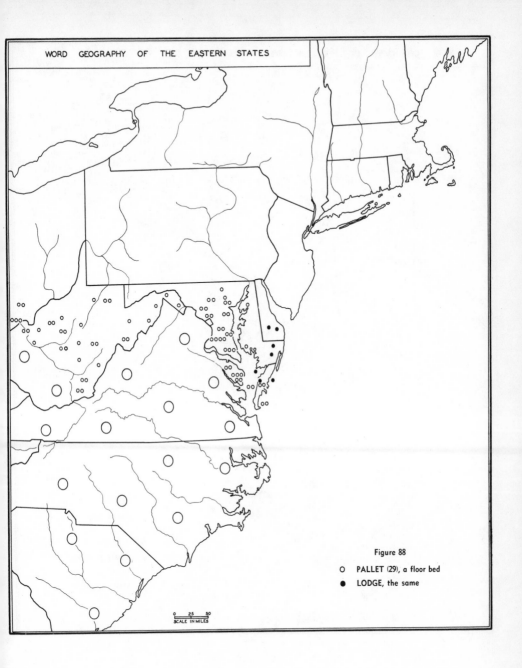

Figure 88

O   PALLET (29), a floor bed

●   LODGE, the same

0   25   50
SCALE IN MILES

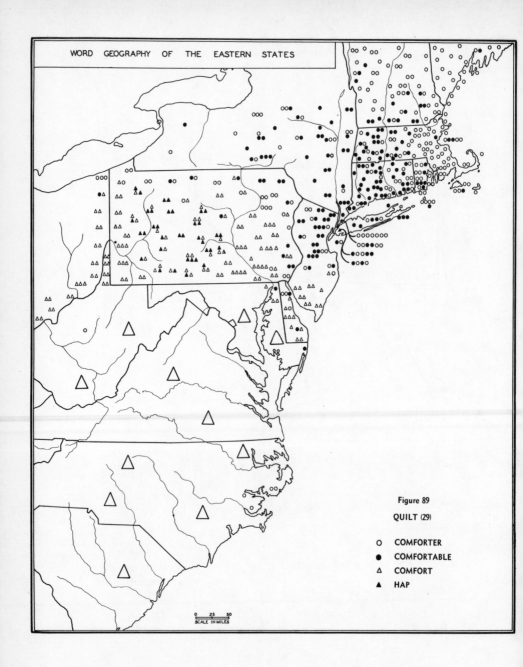

WORD GEOGRAPHY OF THE EASTERN STATES

Figure 89

QUILT (29)

○ COMFORTER
● COMFORTABLE
△ COMFORT
▲ HAP

0   25   50
SCALE IN MILES

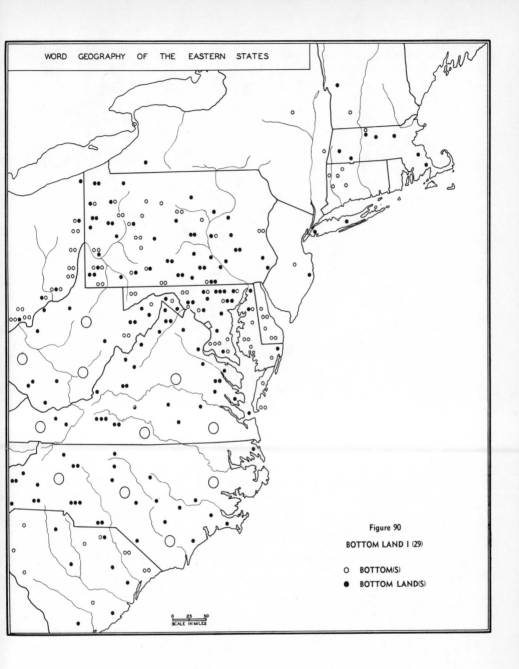

Figure 90

BOTTOM LAND I (29)

○   BOTTOM(S)

●   BOTTOM LAND(S)

0   25   50
SCALE IN MILES

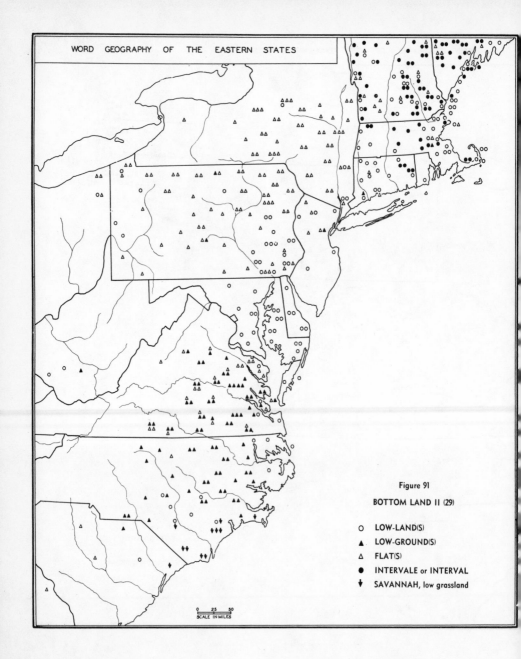

WORD GEOGRAPHY OF THE EASTERN STATES

Figure 91

BOTTOM LAND II (29)

○ LOW-LAND(S)
▲ LOW-GROUND(S)
△ FLAT(S)
● INTERVALE or INTERVAL
↓ SAVANNAH, low grassland

0   25   50
SCALE IN MILES

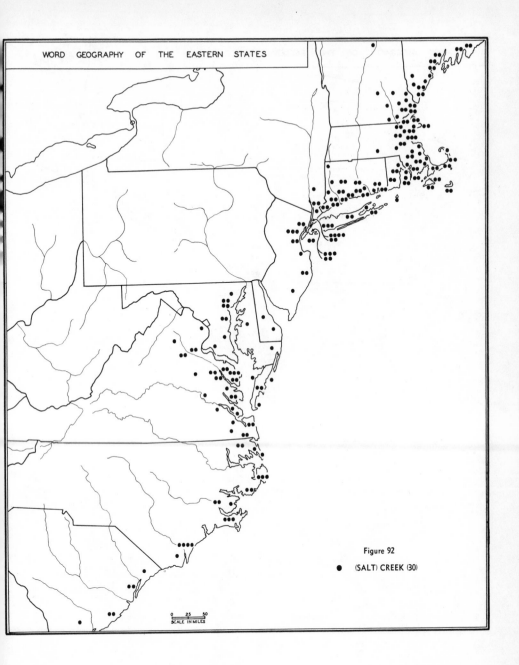

WORD GEOGRAPHY OF THE EASTERN STATES

Figure 92

● (SALT) CREEK (30)

0   25   50
SCALE IN MILES

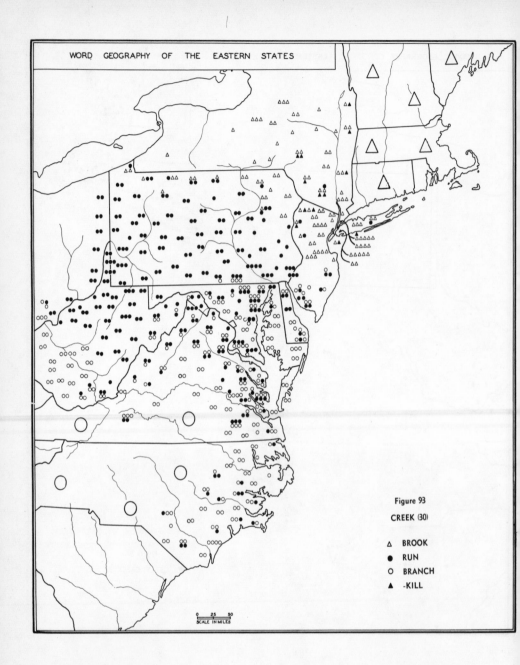

WORD GEOGRAPHY OF THE EASTERN STATES

Figure 93

CREEK (30)

△ BROOK
● RUN
○ BRANCH
▲ -KILL

0   25   50
SCALE IN MILES

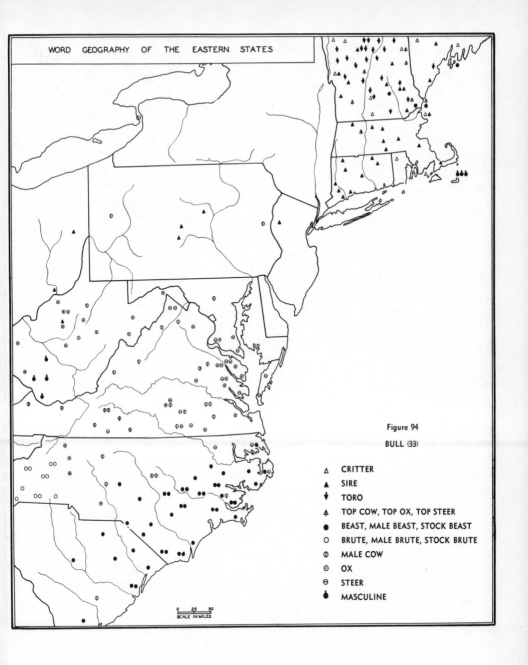

Figure 94

BULL (33)

△ CRITTER
▲ SIRE
↓ TORO
↟ TOP COW, TOP OX, TOP STEER
● BEAST, MALE BEAST, STOCK BEAST
○ BRUTE, MALE BRUTE, STOCK BRUTE
◐ MALE COW
⊙ OX
⊖ STEER
◓ MASCULINE

0   25   50
SCALE IN MILES

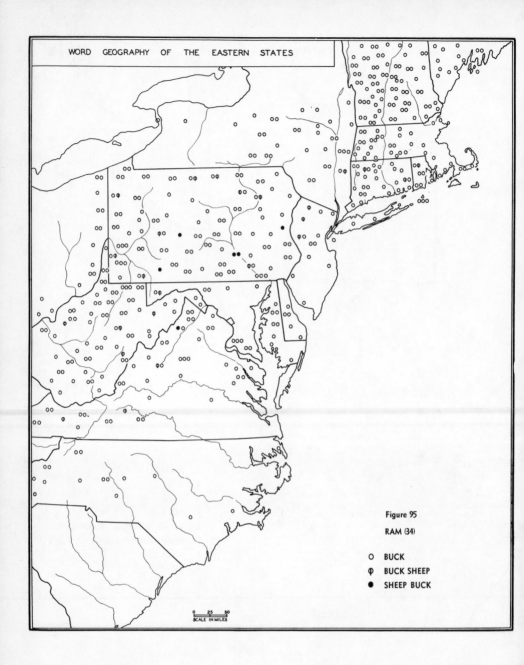

WORD GEOGRAPHY OF THE EASTERN STATES

Figure 95

RAM (34)

○ BUCK
φ BUCK SHEEP
● SHEEP BUCK

0   25   50
SCALE IN MILES

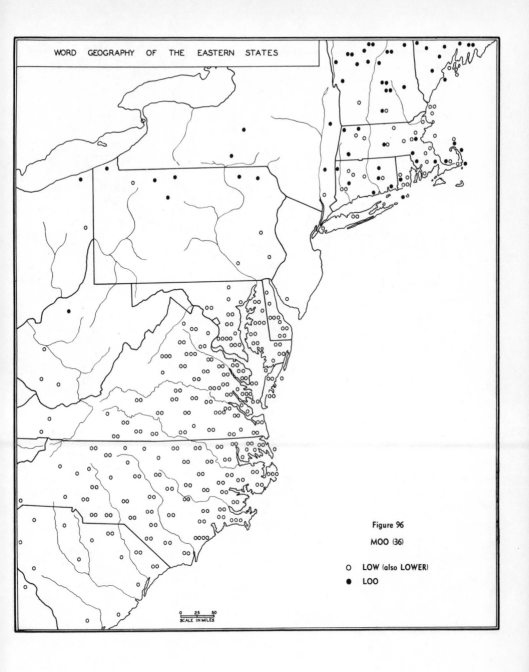

WORD GEOGRAPHY OF THE EASTERN STATES

Figure 96

MOO (36)

O   LOW (also LOWER)

●   LOO

0   25   50
SCALE IN MILES

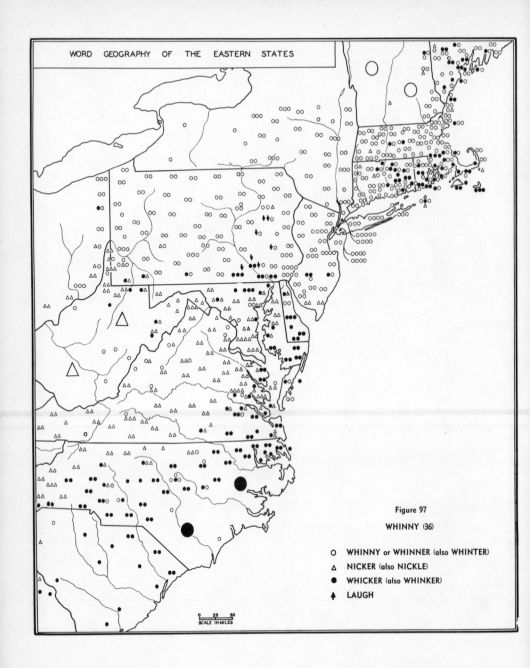

WORD GEOGRAPHY OF THE EASTERN STATES

Figure 97

WHINNY (36)

○ WHINNY or WHINNER (also WHINTER)
△ NICKER (also NICKLE)
● WHICKER (also WHINKER)
♠ LAUGH

0   25   50
SCALE IN MILES

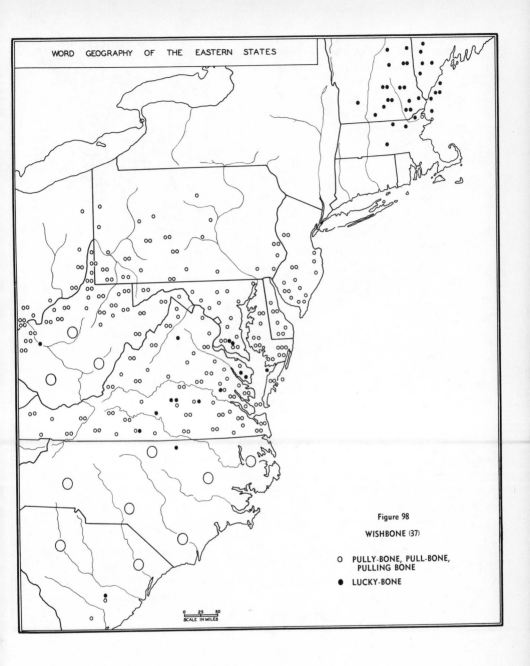

WORD GEOGRAPHY OF THE EASTERN STATES

Figure 98

WISHBONE (37)

○ PULLY-BONE, PULL-BONE,
PULLING BONE
● LUCKY-BONE

SCALE IN MILES
0   25   50

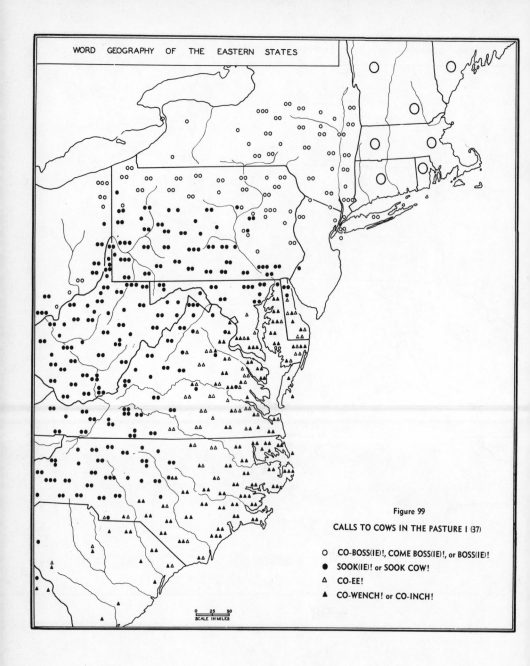

WORD GEOGRAPHY OF THE EASTERN STATES

Figure 99

CALLS TO COWS IN THE PASTURE I (37)

O   CO-BOSS(IE)!, COME BOSS(IE)!, or BOSS(IE)!

●   SOOK(IE)! or SOOK COW!

△   CO-EE!

▲   CO-WENCH! or CO-INCH!

SCALE IN MILES
0   25   50

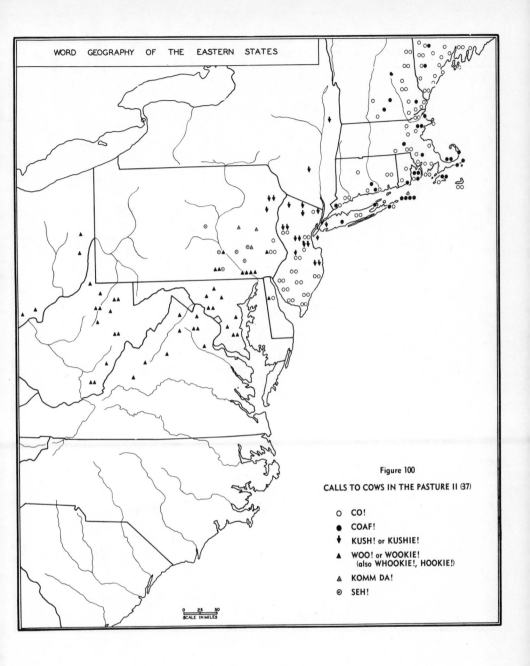

Figure 100

CALLS TO COWS IN THE PASTURE II (37)

○   CO!

●   COAF!

↓   KUSH! or KUSHIE!

▲   WOO! or WOOKIE!
    (also WHOOKIE!, HOOKIE!)

△   KOMM DA!

⊙   SEH!

0   25   50
SCALE IN MILES

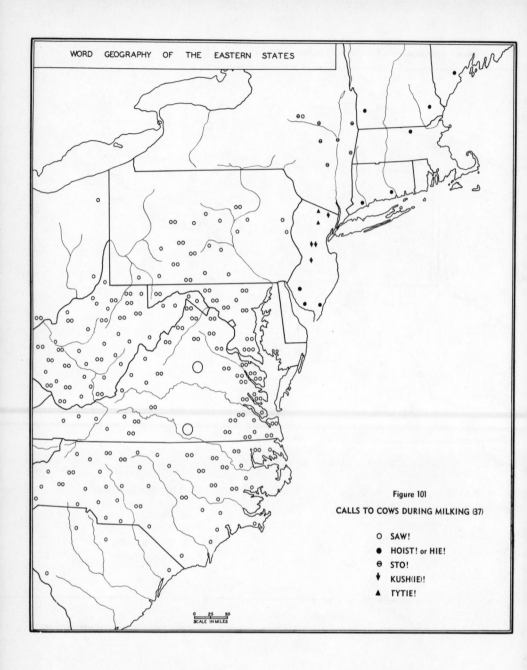

Figure 101

CALLS TO COWS DURING MILKING (37)

O SAW!

● HOIST! or HIE!

Θ STO!

↓ KUSH(IE)!

▲ TYTIE!

0   25   50
SCALE IN MILES

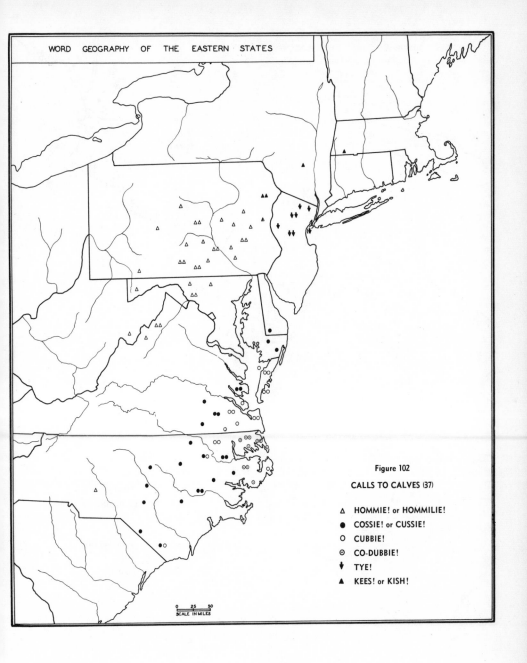

Figure 102

CALLS TO CALVES (37)

△ HOMMIE! or HOMMILIE!

● COSSIE! or CUSSIE!

○ CUBBIE!

⊙ CO-DUBBIE!

↓ TYE!

▲ KEES! or KISH!

0   25   50
SCALE IN MILES

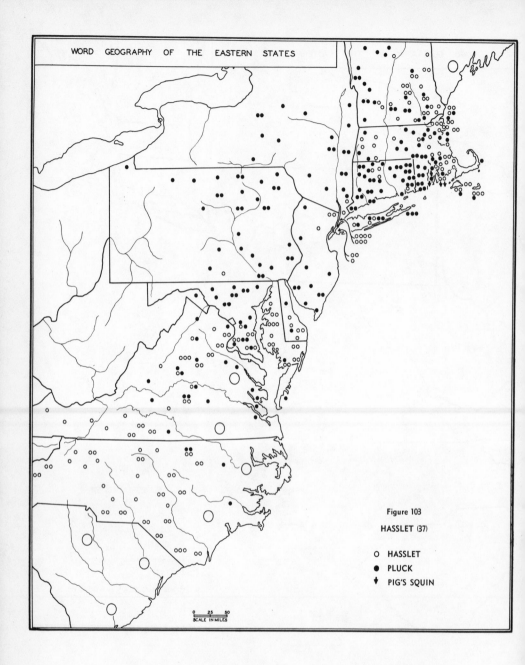

Figure 103

HASSLET (37)

○ HASSLET
● PLUCK
↓ PIG'S SQUIN

0   25   50
SCALE IN MILES

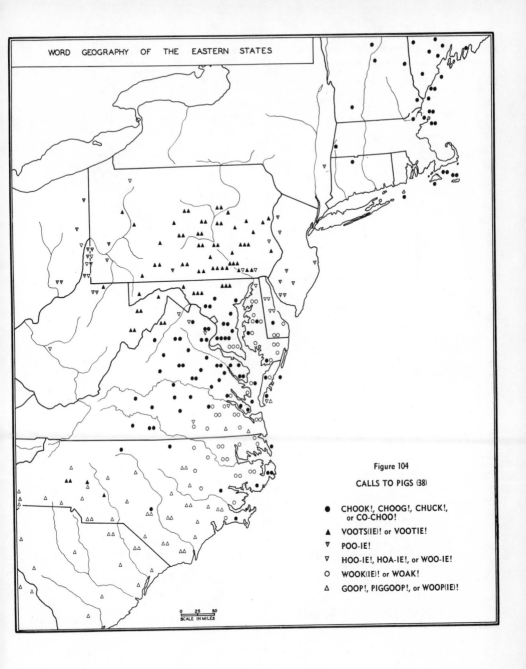

Figure 104

CALLS TO PIGS (38)

●   CHOOK!, CHOOG!, CHUCK!, or CO-CHOO!

▲   VOOTS(IE)! or VOOTIE!

▽   POO-IE!

▽   HOO-IE!, HOA-IE!, or WOO-IE!

○   WOOK(IE)! or WOAK!

△   GOOP!, PIGGOOP!, or WOOP(IE)!

0 25 50
SCALE IN MILES

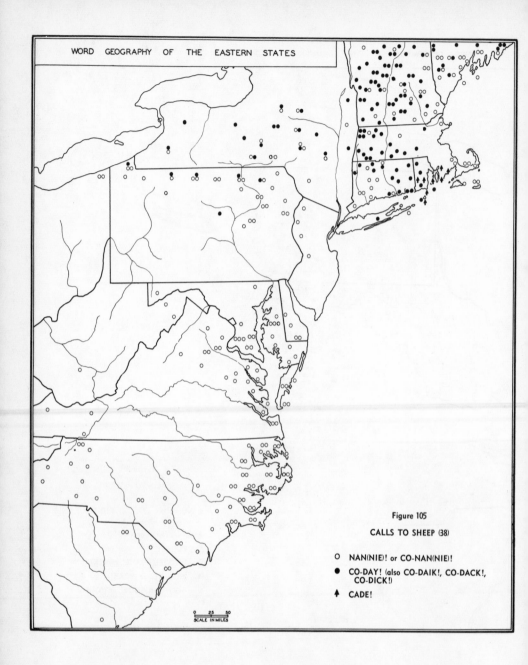

WORD GEOGRAPHY OF THE EASTERN STATES

Figure 105

CALLS TO SHEEP (38)

O NAN(NIE)! or CO-NAN(NIE)!
● CO-DAY! (also CO-DAIK!, CO-DACK!,
    CO-DICK!)
♠ CADE!

0   25   50
SCALE IN MILES

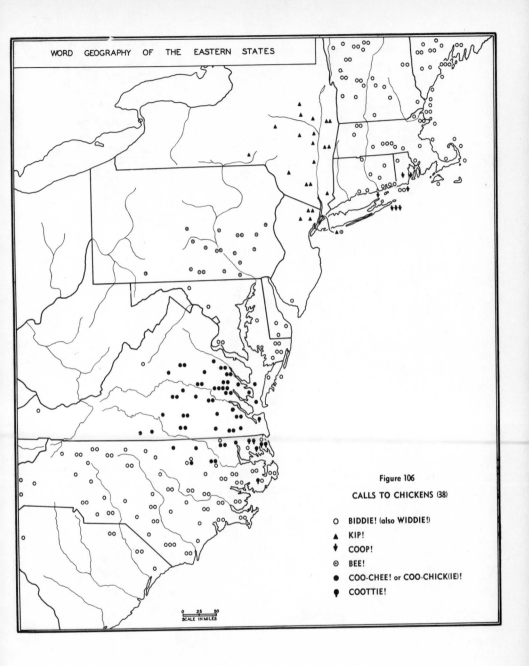

WORD GEOGRAPHY OF THE EASTERN STATES

Figure 106

CALLS TO CHICKENS (38)

O   BIDDIE! (also WIDDIE!)

▲   KIP!

✚   COOP!

⊙   BEE!

●   COO-CHEE! or COO-CHICK(IE)!

♀   COOTTIE!

0   25   50
SCALE IN MILES

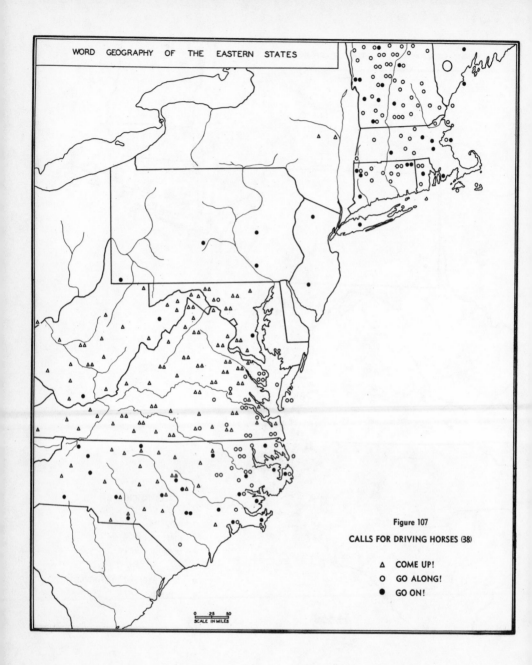

Figure 107

CALLS FOR DRIVING HORSES (38)

△ COME UP!

O GO ALONG!

● GO ON!

0   25   50
SCALE IN MILES

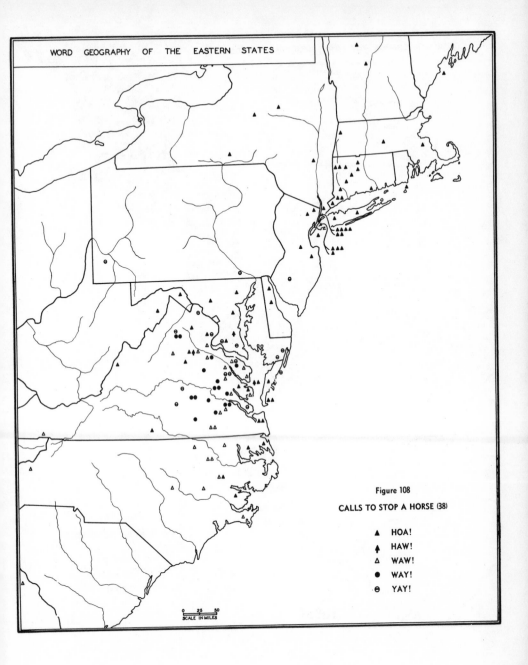

WORD GEOGRAPHY OF THE EASTERN STATES

Figure 108

CALLS TO STOP A HORSE (38)

▲ HOA!

⬆ HAW!

△ WAW!

● WAY!

θ YAY!

0 25 50
SCALE IN MILES

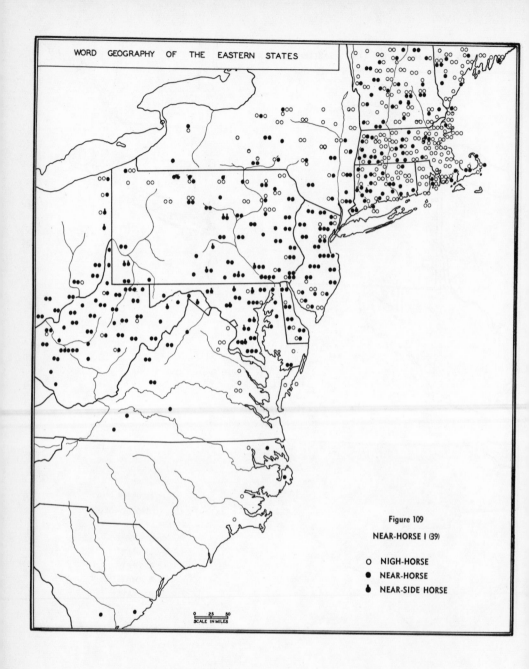

Figure 109

NEAR-HORSE I (39)

O   NIGH-HORSE

●   NEAR-HORSE

◖   NEAR-SIDE HORSE

0 25 50
SCALE IN MILES

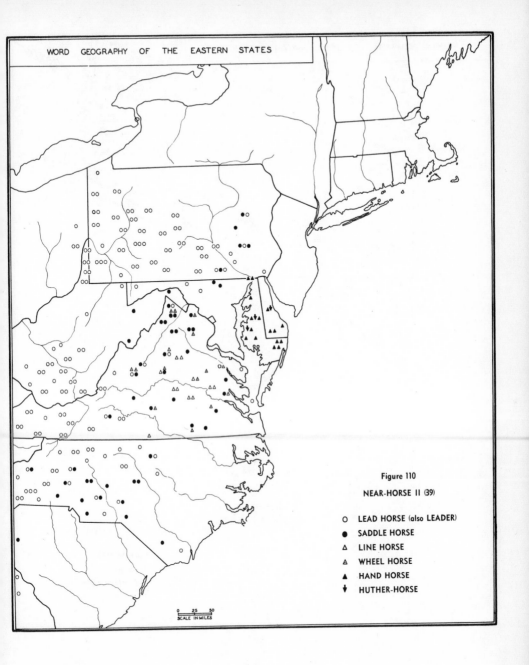

WORD GEOGRAPHY OF THE EASTERN STATES

Figure 110

NEAR-HORSE II (39)

O   LEAD HORSE (also LEADER)
●   SADDLE HORSE
△   LINE HORSE
▲   WHEEL HORSE
▲   HAND HORSE
↓   HUTHER-HORSE

0   25   50
SCALE IN MILES

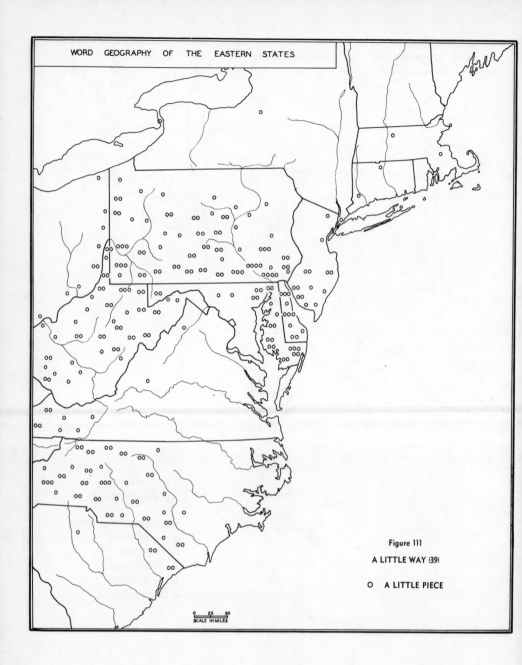

Figure 111

A LITTLE WAY (39)

O   A LITTLE PIECE

SCALE IN MILES
0   25   50

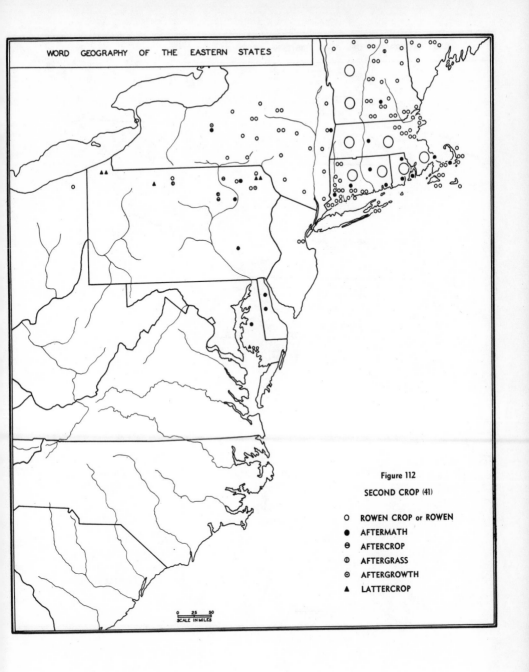

Figure 112

SECOND CROP (41)

○ ROWEN CROP or ROWEN
● AFTERMATH
⊖ AFTERCROP
⦶ AFTERGRASS
⊙ AFTERGROWTH
▲ LATTERCROP

0   25   50
SCALE IN MILES

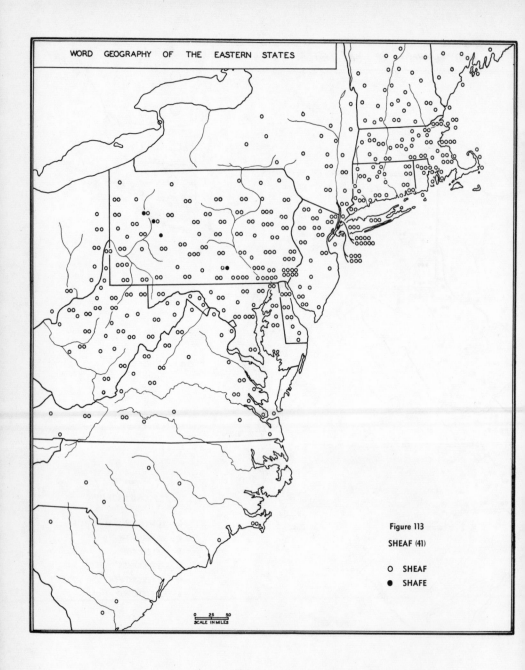

Figure 113

SHEAF (41)

O SHEAF
● SHAFE

0   25   50
SCALE IN MILES

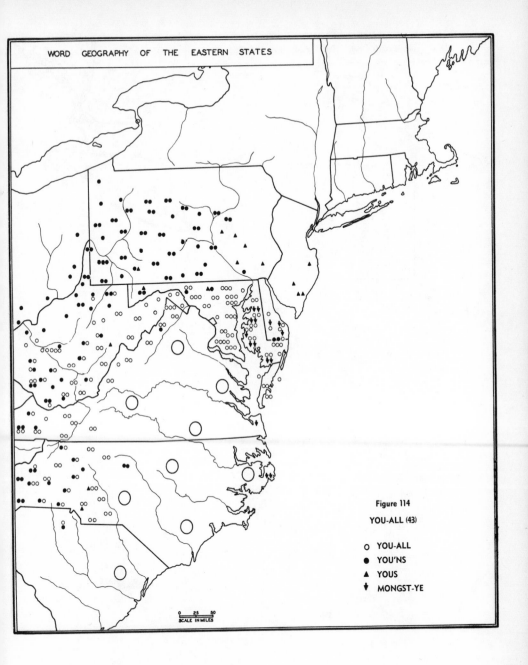

WORD GEOGRAPHY OF THE EASTERN STATES

Figure 114

YOU-ALL (43)

○ YOU-ALL
● YOU'NS
▲ YOUS
↓ MONGST-YE

0 25 50
SCALE IN MILES

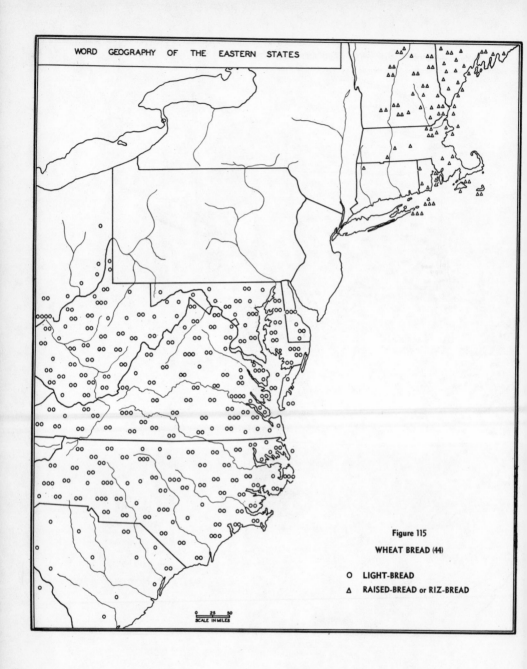

Figure 115

WHEAT BREAD (44)

O   LIGHT-BREAD

△   RAISED-BREAD or RIZ-BREAD

0   25   50
SCALE IN MILES

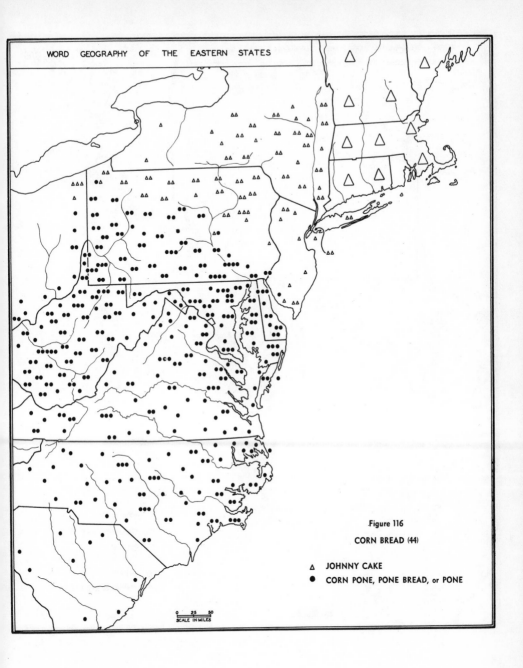

Figure 116

CORN BREAD (44)

△ JOHNNY CAKE

● CORN PONE, PONE BREAD, or PONE

0   25   50
SCALE IN MILES

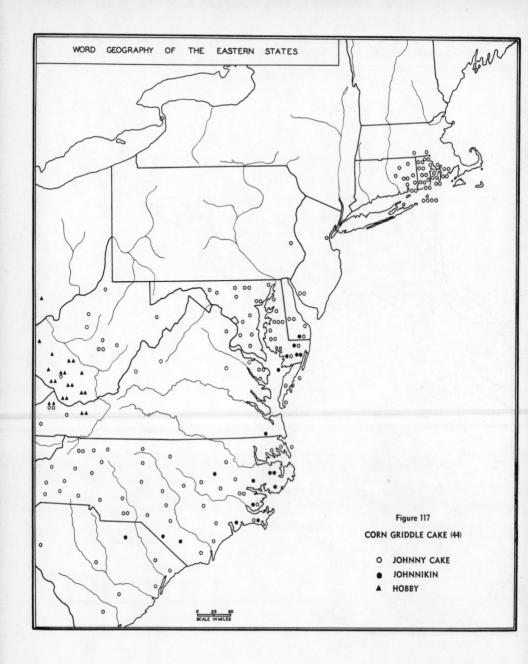

Figure 117

CORN GRIDDLE CAKE (44)

O   JOHNNY CAKE

●   JOHNNIKIN

▲   HOBBY

0   25   50
SCALE IN MILES

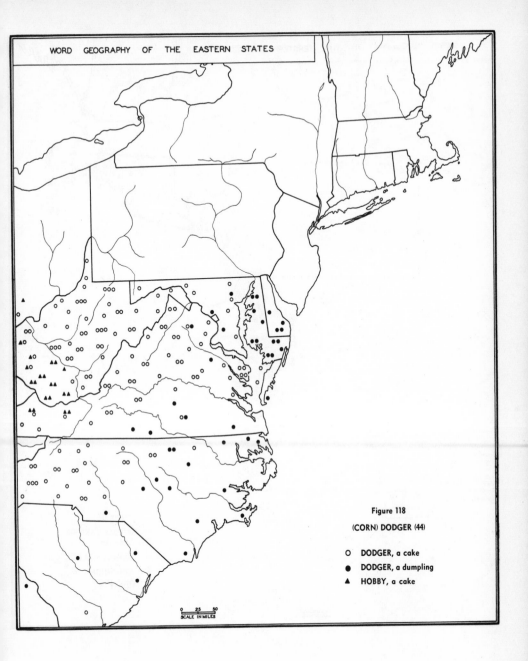

Figure 118

(CORN) DODGER (44)

O   DODGER, a cake
●   DODGER, a dumpling
▲   HOBBY, a cake

0   25   50
SCALE IN MILES

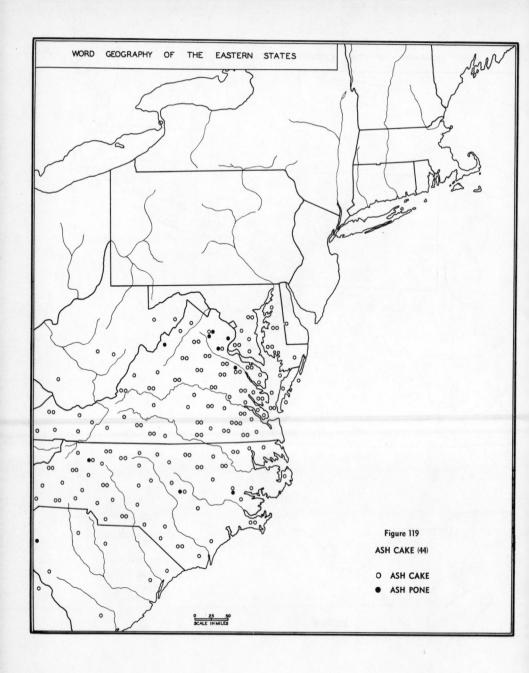

Figure 119

ASH CAKE (44)

O   ASH CAKE
●   ASH PONE

0   25   50
SCALE IN MILES

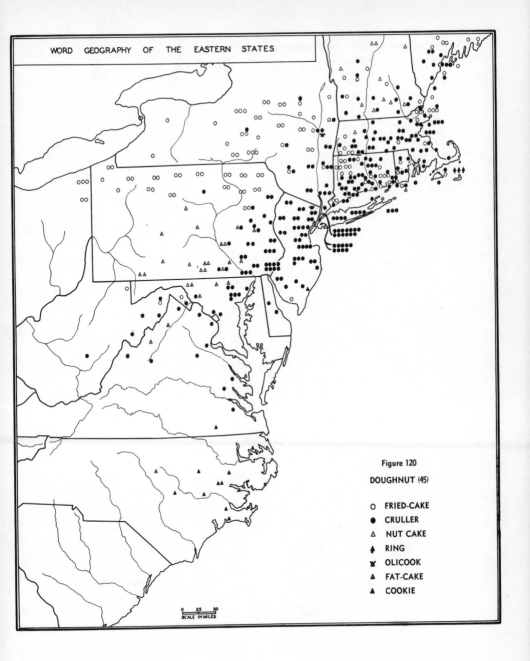

Figure 120

DOUGHNUT (45)

O   FRIED-CAKE
●   CRULLER
△   NUT CAKE
♠   RING
✺   OLICOOK
▲   FAT-CAKE
▲   COOKIE

0   25   50
SCALE IN MILES

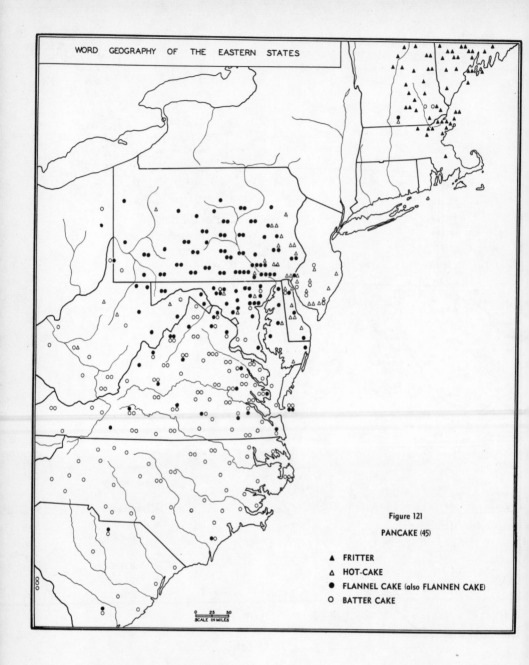

WORD GEOGRAPHY OF THE EASTERN STATES

Figure 121

PANCAKE (45)

▲ FRITTER

△ HOT-CAKE

● FLANNEL CAKE (also FLANNEN CAKE)

○ BATTER CAKE

0   25   50
SCALE IN MILES

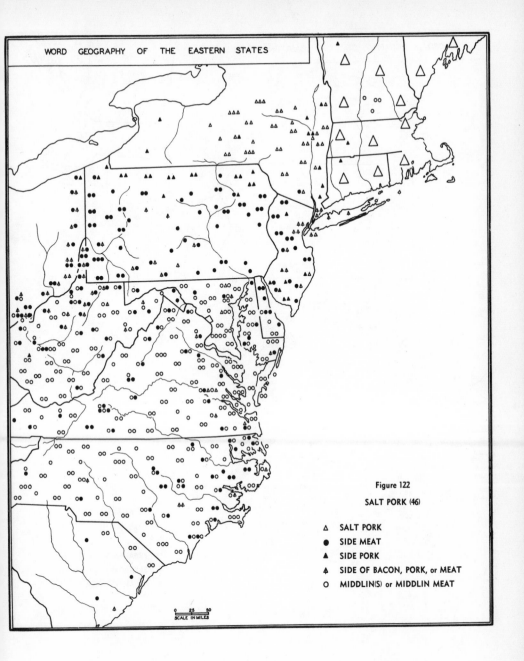

WORD GEOGRAPHY OF THE EASTERN STATES

Figure 122

SALT PORK (46)

△ SALT PORK
● SIDE MEAT
▲ SIDE PORK
⚶ SIDE OF BACON, PORK, or MEAT
○ MIDDLIN(S) or MIDDLIN MEAT

0   25   50
SCALE IN MILES

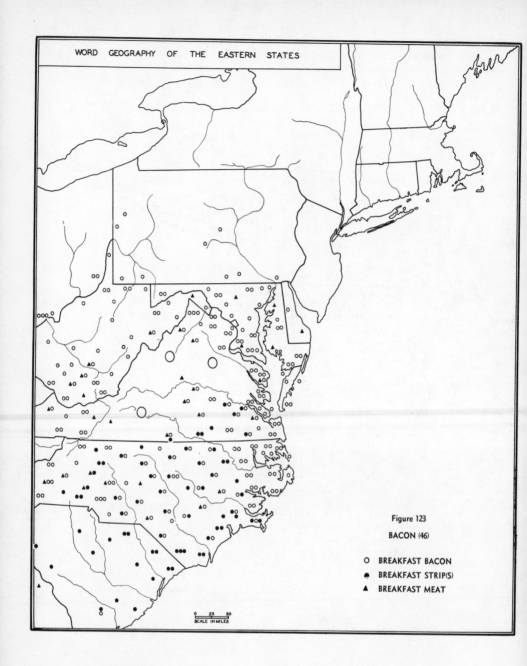

WORD GEOGRAPHY OF THE EASTERN STATES

Figure 123

BACON (46)

O BREAKFAST BACON

● BREAKFAST STRIP(S)

▲ BREAKFAST MEAT

0   25   50
SCALE IN MILES

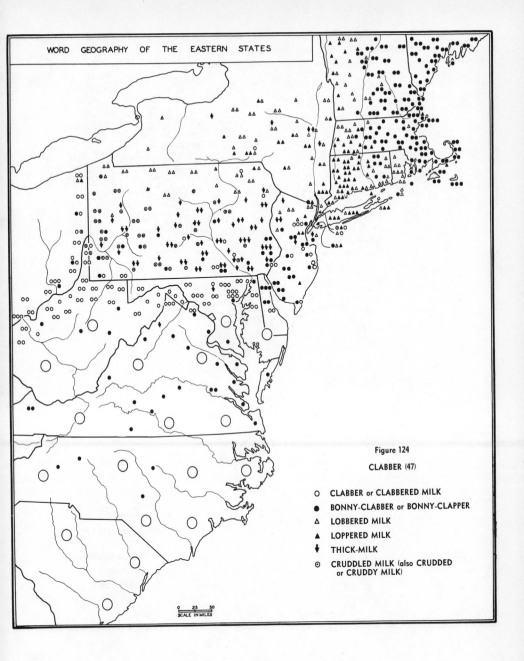

Figure 124

CLABBER (47)

○ CLABBER or CLABBERED MILK
● BONNY-CLABBER or BONNY-CLAPPER
△ LOBBERED MILK
▲ LOPPERED MILK
↓ THICK-MILK
⊙ CRUDDLED MILK (also CRUDDED or CRUDDY MILK)

0   25   50
SCALE IN MILES

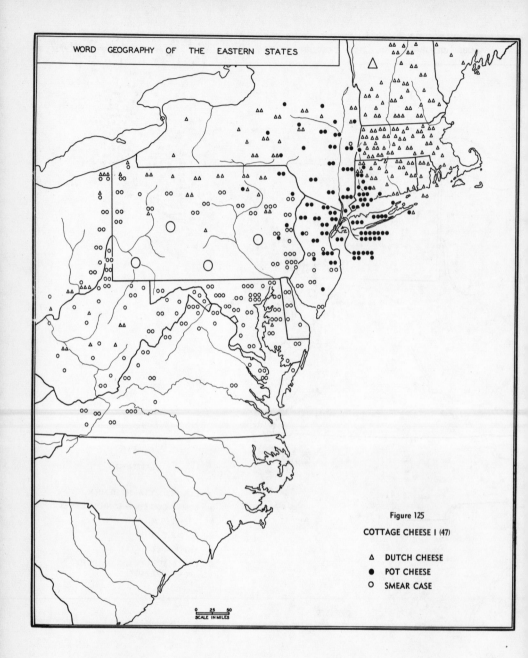

Figure 125

COTTAGE CHEESE I (47)

△ DUTCH CHEESE
● POT CHEESE
○ SMEAR CASE

0   25   50
SCALE IN MILES

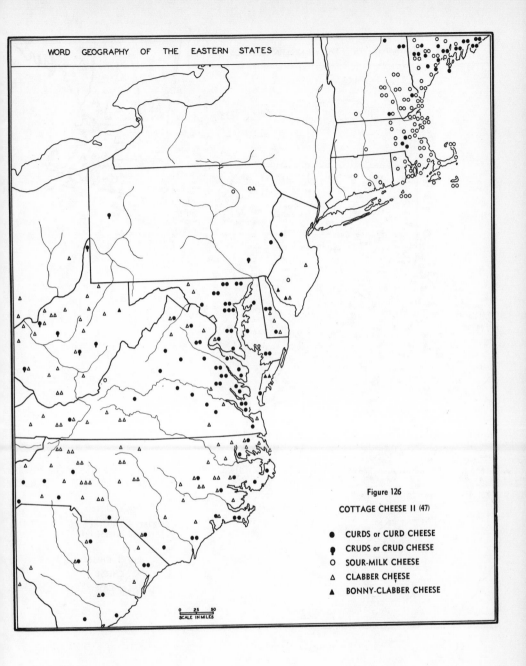

Figure 126

COTTAGE CHEESE II (47)

● CURDS or CURD CHEESE
♀ CRUDS or CRUD CHEESE
○ SOUR-MILK CHEESE
△ CLABBER CHEESE
▲ BONNY-CLABBER CHEESE

0   25   50
SCALE IN MILES

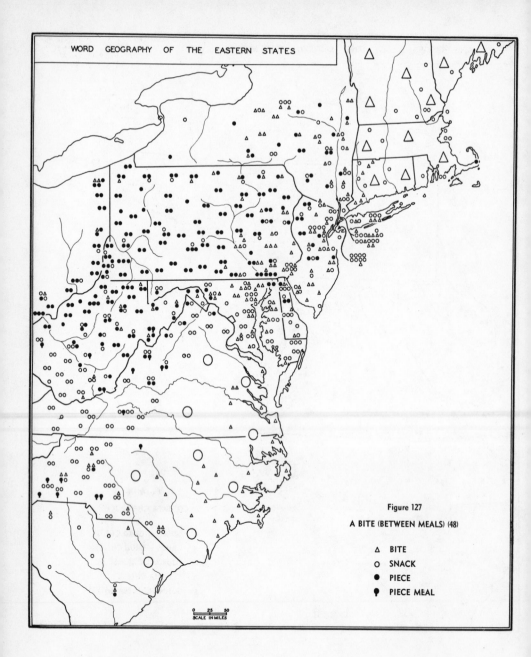

WORD GEOGRAPHY OF THE EASTERN STATES

Figure 127

A BITE (BETWEEN MEALS) (48)

△ BITE
○ SNACK
● PIECE
⬤ PIECE MEAL

0   25   50
SCALE IN MILES

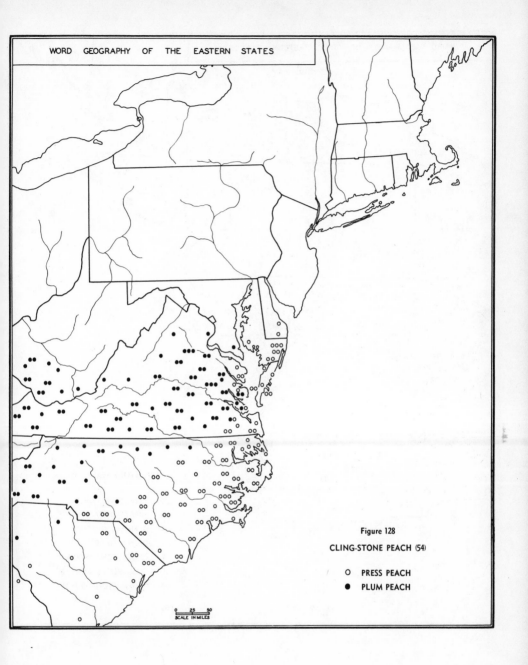

Figure 128

CLING-STONE PEACH (54)

O   PRESS PEACH
●   PLUM PEACH

0   25   50
SCALE IN MILES

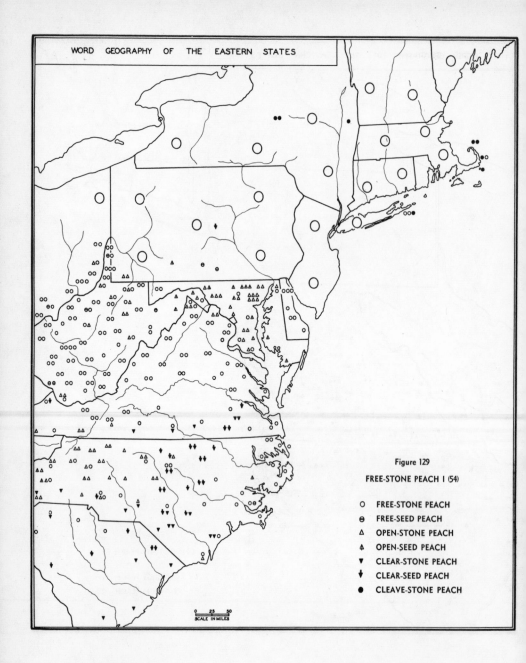

Figure 129

FREE-STONE PEACH I (54)

O FREE-STONE PEACH

θ FREE-SEED PEACH

△ OPEN-STONE PEACH

⬙ OPEN-SEED PEACH

▼ CLEAR-STONE PEACH

⬇ CLEAR-SEED PEACH

● CLEAVE-STONE PEACH

0   25   50
SCALE IN MILES

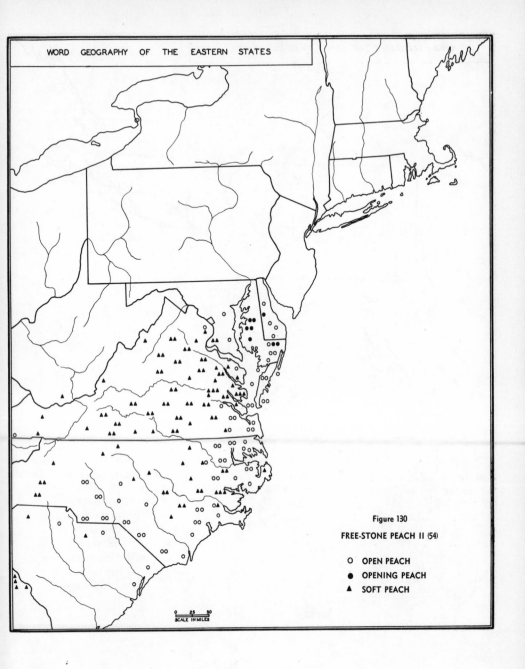

Figure 130

FREE-STONE PEACH II (54)

○ OPEN PEACH

● OPENING PEACH

▲ SOFT PEACH

0   25   50
SCALE IN MILES

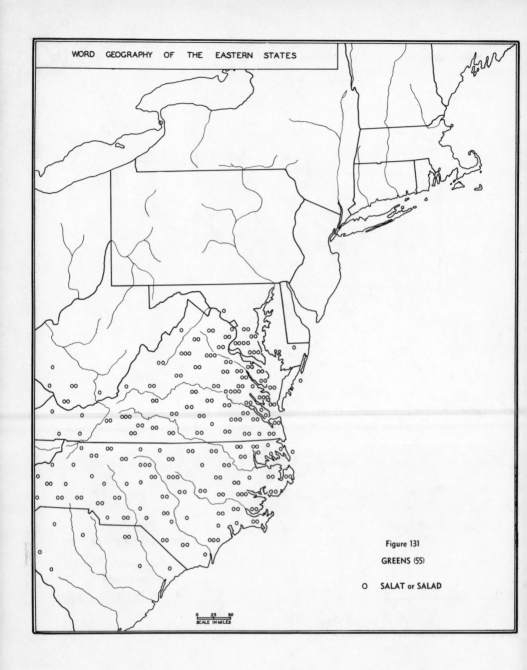

Figure 131

GREENS (55)

O   SALAT or SALAD

0   25   50
SCALE IN MILES

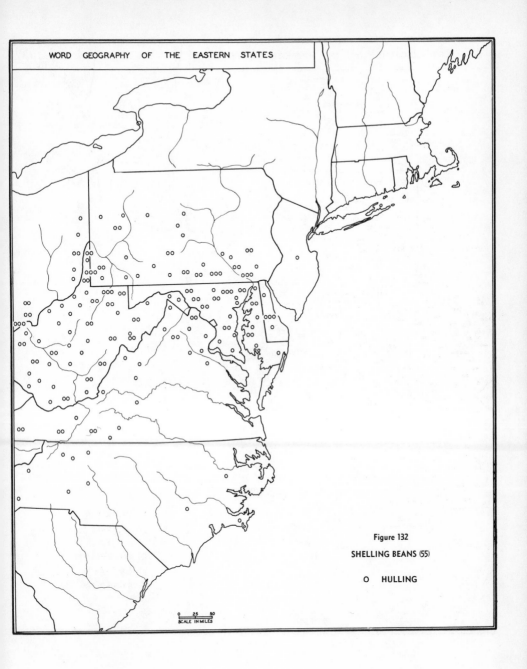

Figure 132

SHELLING BEANS (55)

O   HULLING

0   25   50
SCALE IN MILES

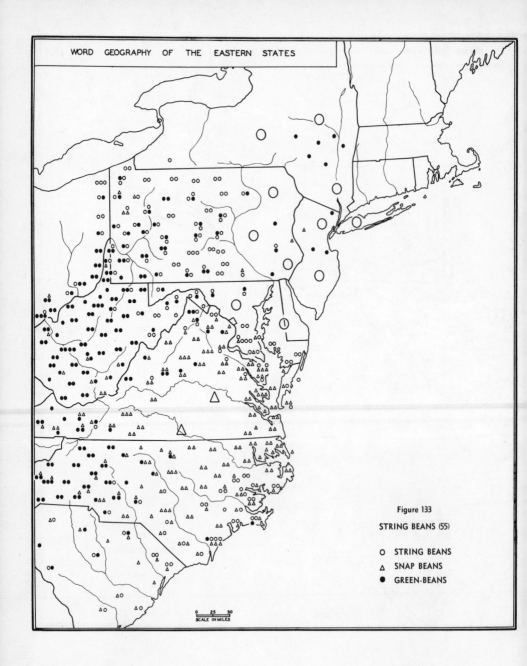

WORD GEOGRAPHY OF THE EASTERN STATES

Figure 133

STRING BEANS (55)

○ STRING BEANS

△ SNAP BEANS

● GREEN-BEANS

0   25   50
SCALE IN MILES

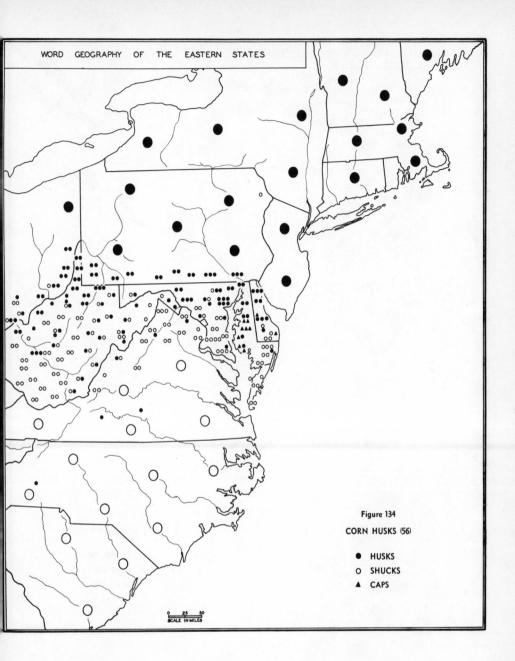

Figure 134

CORN HUSKS (56)

● HUSKS
○ SHUCKS
▲ CAPS

0   25   50
SCALE IN MILES

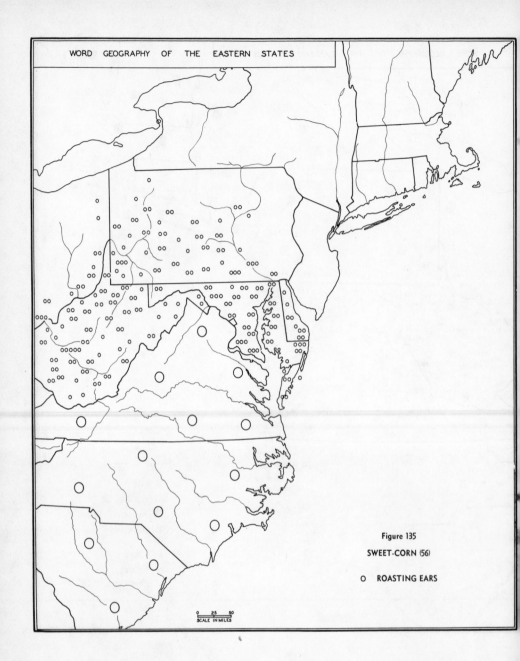

WORD GEOGRAPHY OF THE EASTERN STATES

Figure 135

SWEET-CORN (56)

O   ROASTING EARS

0   25   50
SCALE IN MILES

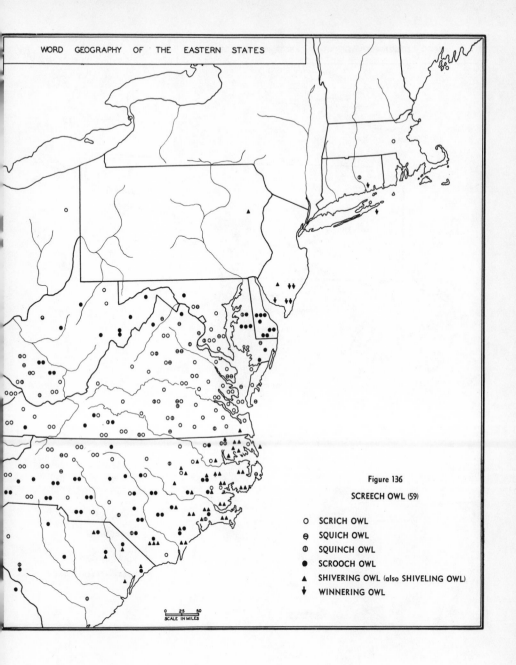

Figure 136

SCREECH OWL (59)

O   SCRICH OWL
⊖   SQUICH OWL
Φ   SQUINCH OWL
●   SCROOCH OWL
▲   SHIVERING OWL (also SHIVELING OWL)
↓   WINNERING OWL

0   25   50
SCALE IN MILES

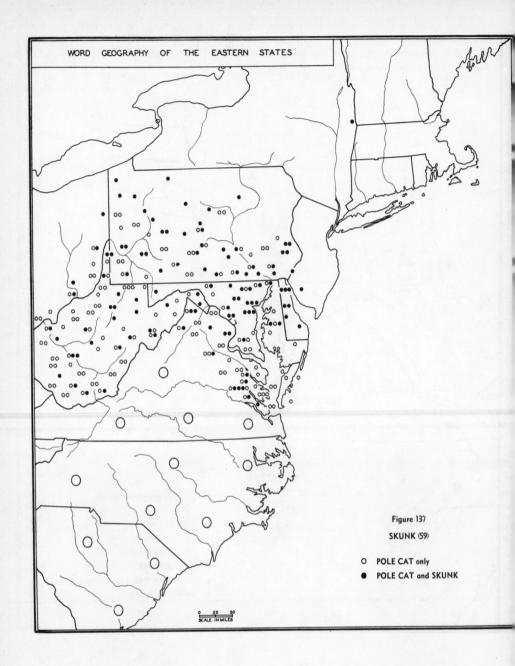

Figure 137

SKUNK (59)

○ POLE CAT only
● POLE CAT and SKUNK

0   25   50
SCALE IN MILES

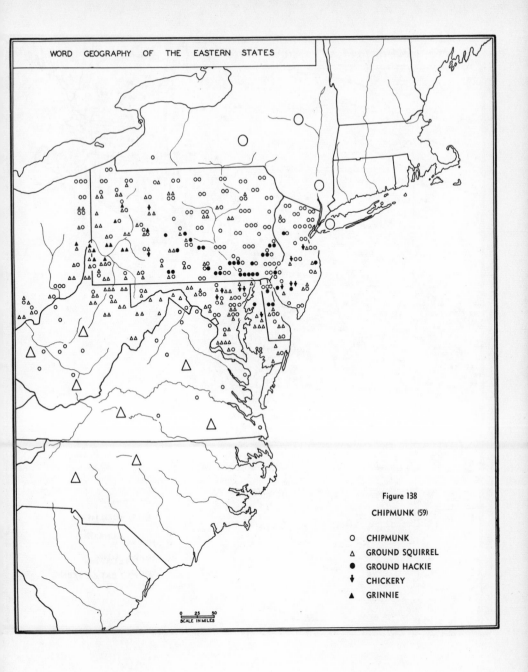

Figure 138

CHIPMUNK (59)

O CHIPMUNK

△ GROUND SQUIRREL

● GROUND HACKIE

↓ CHICKERY

▲ GRINNIE

0   25   50
SCALE IN MILES

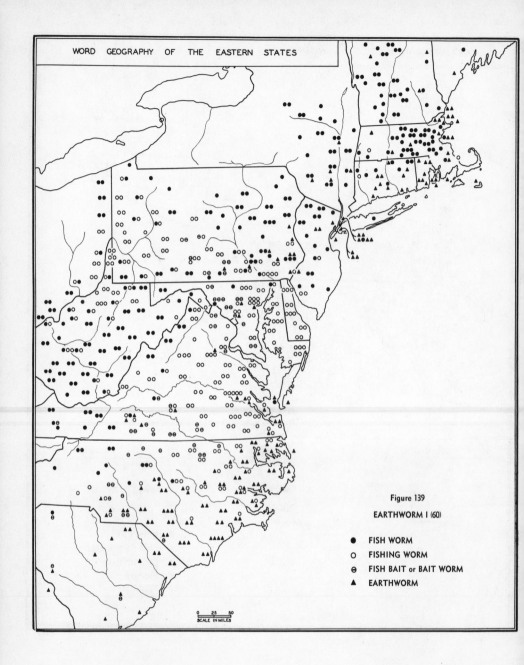

WORD GEOGRAPHY OF THE EASTERN STATES

Figure 139

EARTHWORM I (60)

● FISH WORM

○ FISHING WORM

⊖ FISH BAIT or BAIT WORM

▲ EARTHWORM

0 25 50
SCALE IN MILES

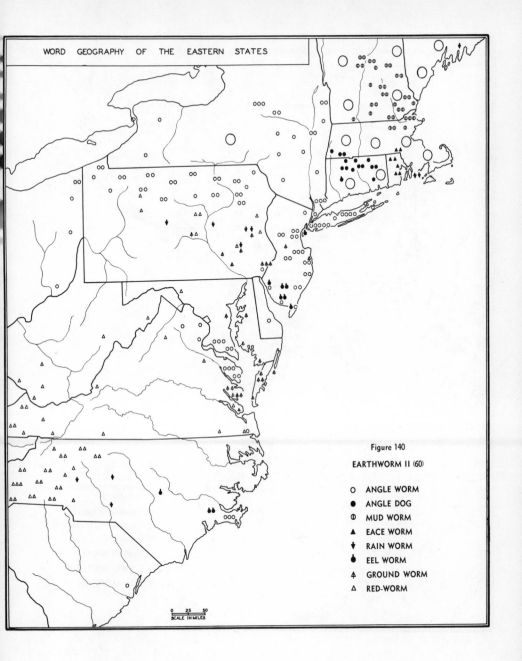

Figure 140

EARTHWORM II (60)

O   ANGLE WORM
●   ANGLE DOG
Φ   MUD WORM
▲   EACE WORM
✦   RAIN WORM
◖   EEL WORM
♣   GROUND WORM
△   RED-WORM

0   25   50
SCALE IN MILES

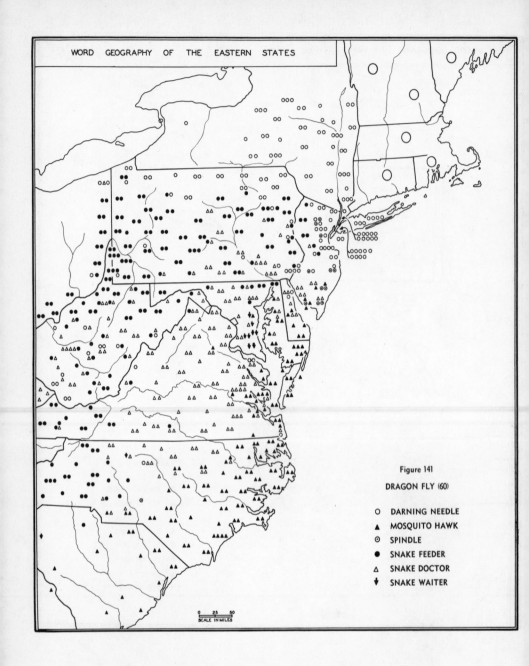

WORD GEOGRAPHY OF THE EASTERN STATES

Figure 141

DRAGON FLY (60)

O   DARNING NEEDLE
▲   MOSQUITO HAWK
⊙   SPINDLE
●   SNAKE FEEDER
△   SNAKE DOCTOR
▼   SNAKE WAITER

0   25   50
SCALE IN MILES

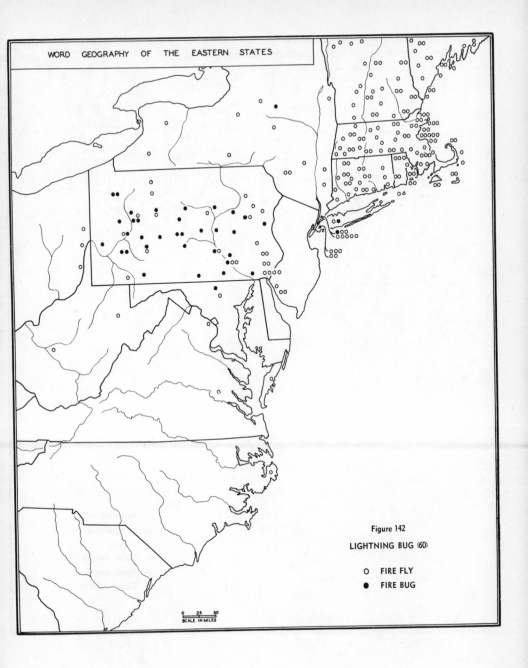

Figure 142

LIGHTNING BUG (60)

O   FIRE FLY

●   FIRE BUG

0   25   50
SCALE IN MILES

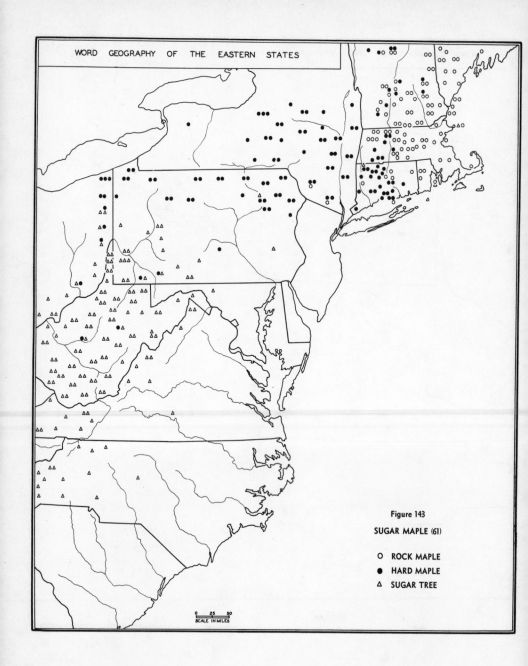

Figure 143

SUGAR MAPLE (61)

O ROCK MAPLE
● HARD MAPLE
△ SUGAR TREE

0   25   50
SCALE IN MILES

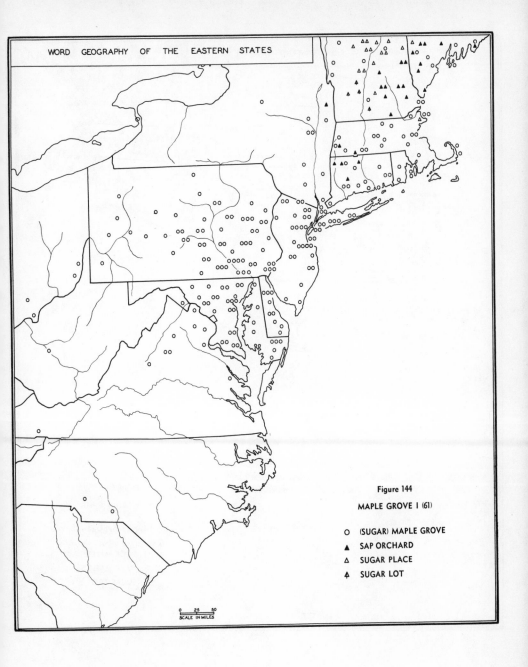

Figure 144

MAPLE GROVE I (61)

O   (SUGAR) MAPLE GROVE
▲   SAP ORCHARD
△   SUGAR PLACE
♠   SUGAR LOT

0   25   50
SCALE IN MILES

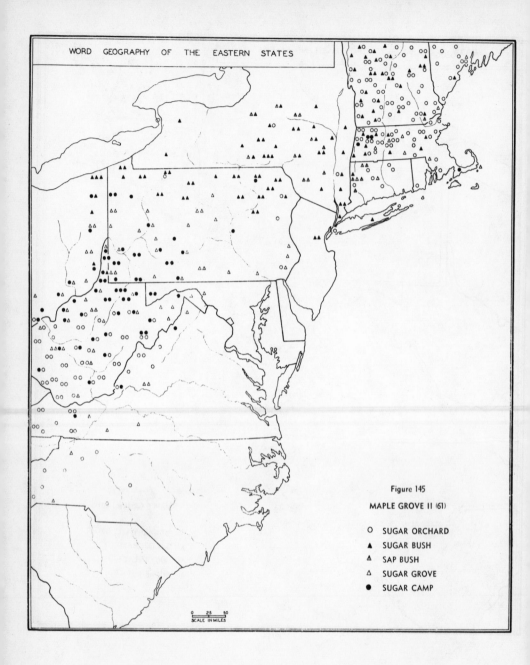

WORD GEOGRAPHY OF THE EASTERN STATES

Figure 145

MAPLE GROVE II (61)

O   SUGAR ORCHARD
▲   SUGAR BUSH
△   SAP BUSH
△   SUGAR GROVE
●   SUGAR CAMP

0   25   50
SCALE IN MILES

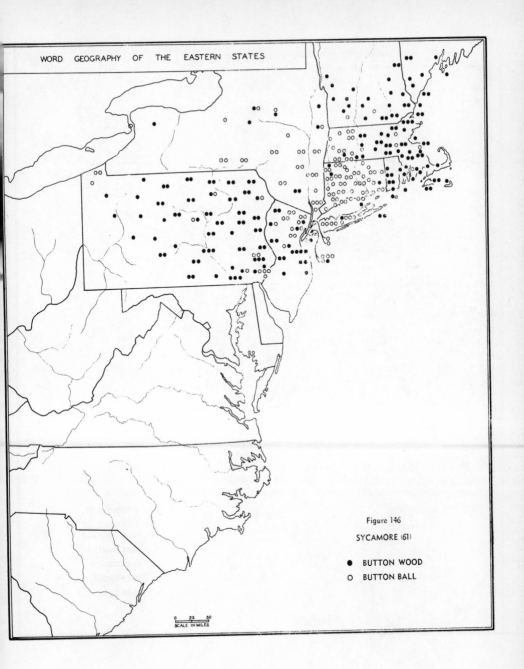

Figure 146

SYCAMORE (61)

● BUTTON WOOD
○ BUTTON BALL

0   25   50
SCALE IN MILES

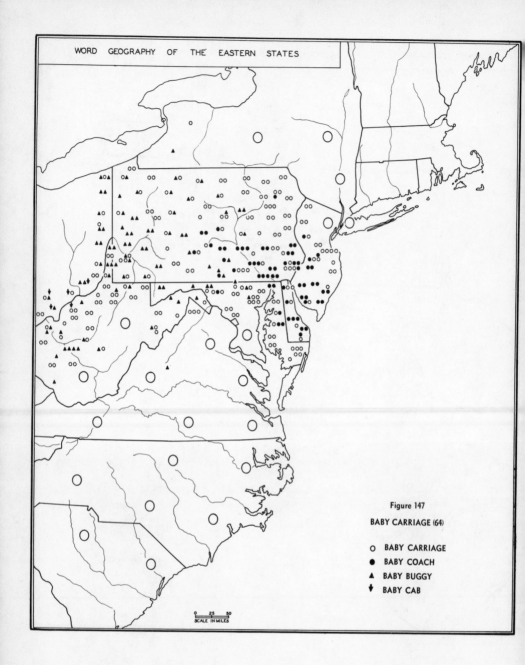

WORD GEOGRAPHY OF THE EASTERN STATES

Figure 147

BABY CARRIAGE (64)

○ BABY CARRIAGE
● BABY COACH
▲ BABY BUGGY
↓ BABY CAB

0 25 50
SCALE IN MILES

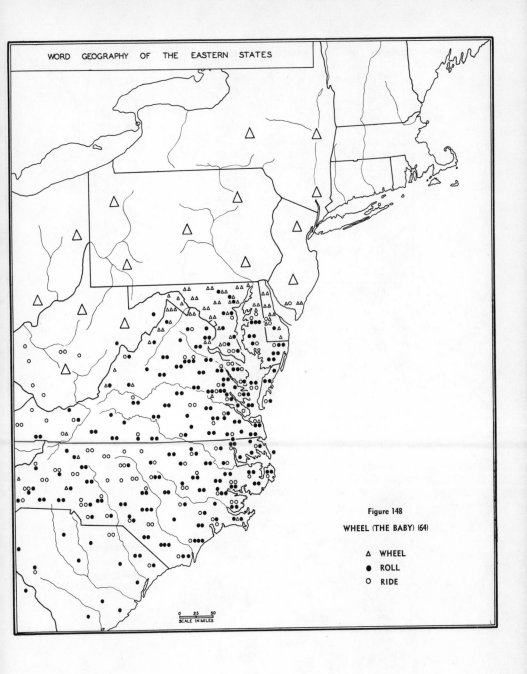

Figure 148

WHEEL (THE BABY) (64)

△   WHEEL
●   ROLL
○   RIDE

0   25   50
SCALE IN MILES

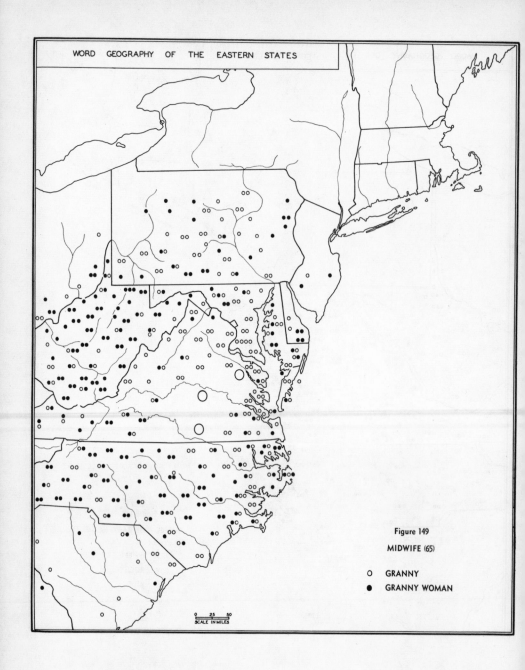

WORD GEOGRAPHY OF THE EASTERN STATES

Figure 149

MIDWIFE (65)

○ GRANNY

● GRANNY WOMAN

0   25   50
SCALE IN MILES

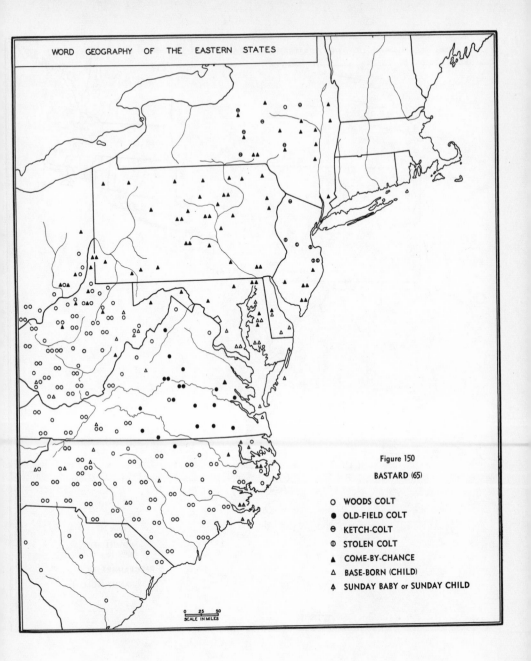

Figure 150

BASTARD (65)

○ WOODS COLT
● OLD-FIELD COLT
⊖ KETCH-COLT
⦶ STOLEN COLT
▲ COME-BY-CHANCE
△ BASE-BORN (CHILD)
⚐ SUNDAY BABY or SUNDAY CHILD

0   25   50
SCALE IN MILES

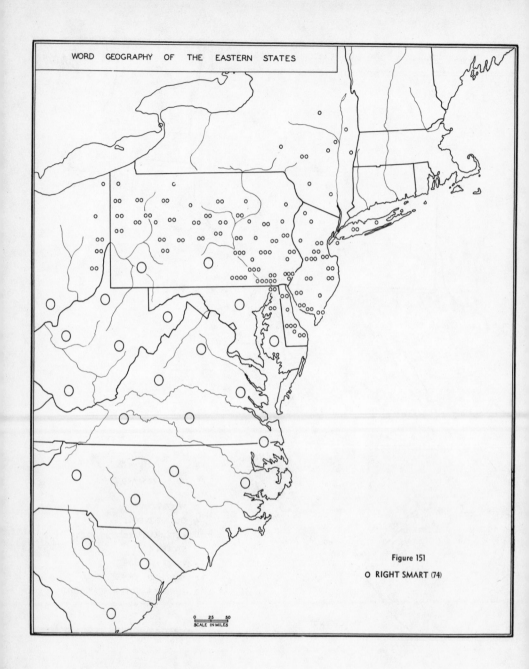

Figure 151

O RIGHT SMART (74)

0   25   50
SCALE IN MILES

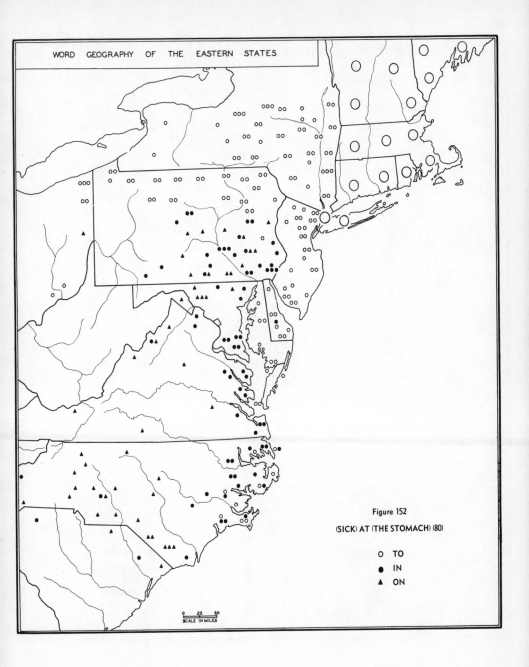

WORD GEOGRAPHY OF THE EASTERN STATES

Figure 152

(SICK) AT (THE STOMACH) (80)

○ TO
● IN
▲ ON

0   25   50
SCALE IN MILES

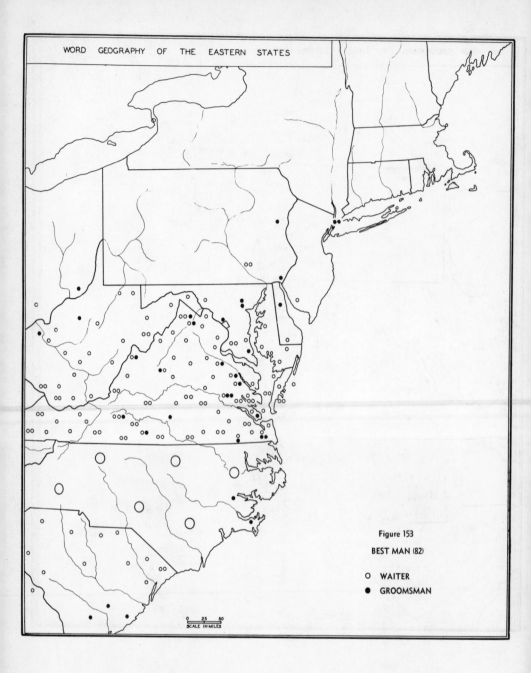

Figure 153

BEST MAN (82)

O WAITER
● GROOMSMAN

0   25   50
SCALE IN MILES

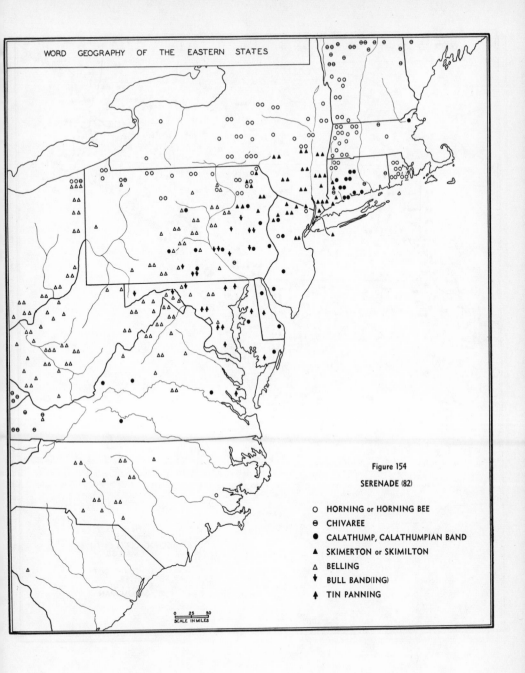

WORD GEOGRAPHY OF THE EASTERN STATES

Figure 154

SERENADE (82)

○ HORNING or HORNING BEE
⊖ CHIVAREE
● CALATHUMP, CALATHUMPIAN BAND
▲ SKIMERTON or SKIMILTON
△ BELLING
↓ BULL BAND(ING)
♦ TIN PANNING

0 25 50
SCALE IN MILES

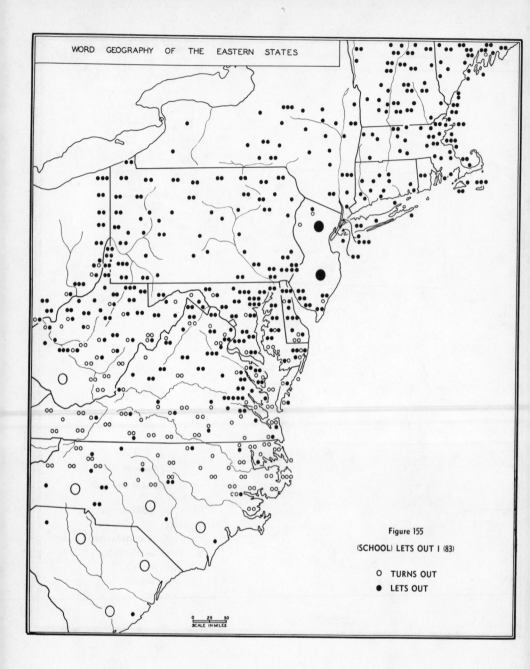

Figure 155

(SCHOOL) LETS OUT I (83)

○ TURNS OUT
● LETS OUT

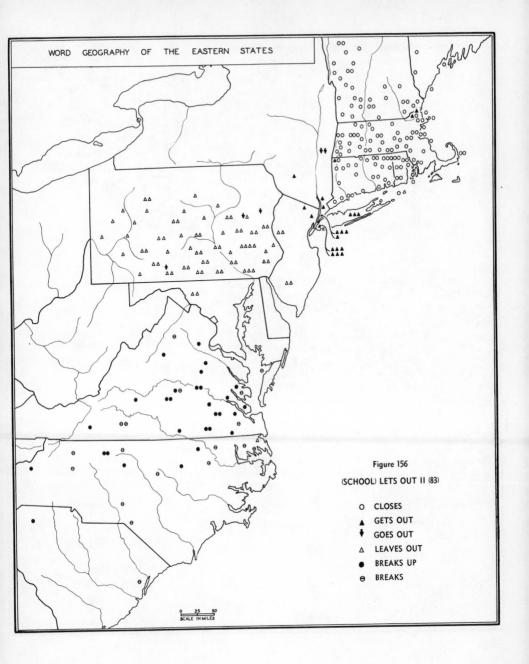

Figure 156

(SCHOOL) LETS OUT II (83)

O   CLOSES
▲   GETS OUT
↓   GOES OUT
△   LEAVES OUT
●   BREAKS UP
⊖   BREAKS

0   25   50
SCALE IN MILES

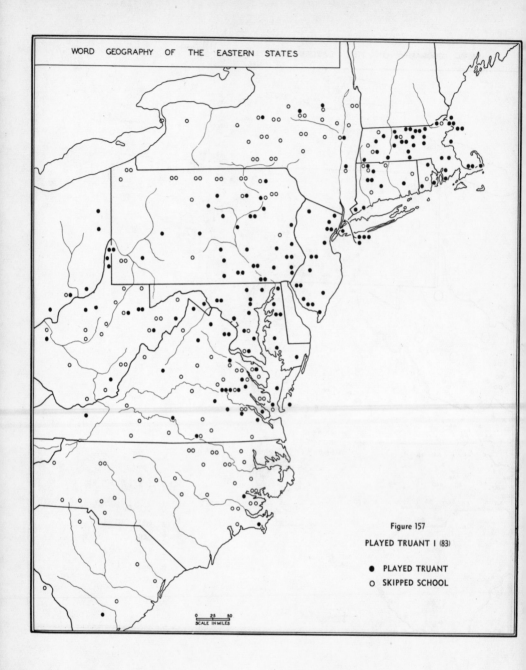

WORD GEOGRAPHY OF THE EASTERN STATES

Figure 157

PLAYED TRUANT I (83)

● PLAYED TRUANT
○ SKIPPED SCHOOL

0   25   50
SCALE IN MILES

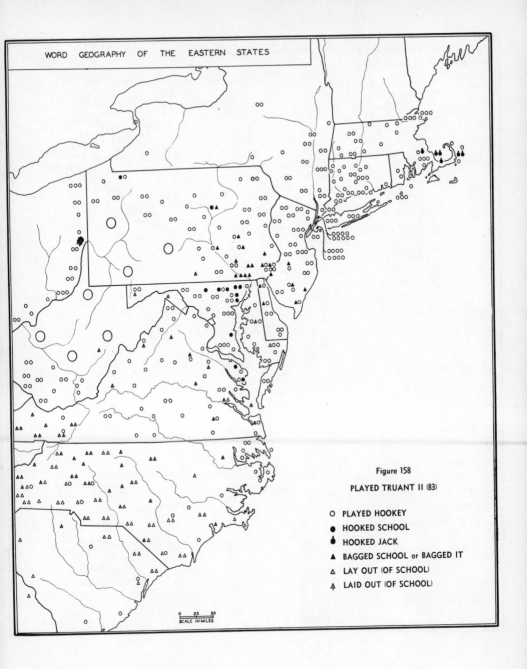

Figure 158

PLAYED TRUANT II (83)

○ PLAYED HOOKEY
● HOOKED SCHOOL
◖ HOOKED JACK
▲ BAGGED SCHOOL or BAGGED IT
△ LAY OUT (OF SCHOOL)
⚑ LAID OUT (OF SCHOOL)

0   25   50
SCALE IN MILES

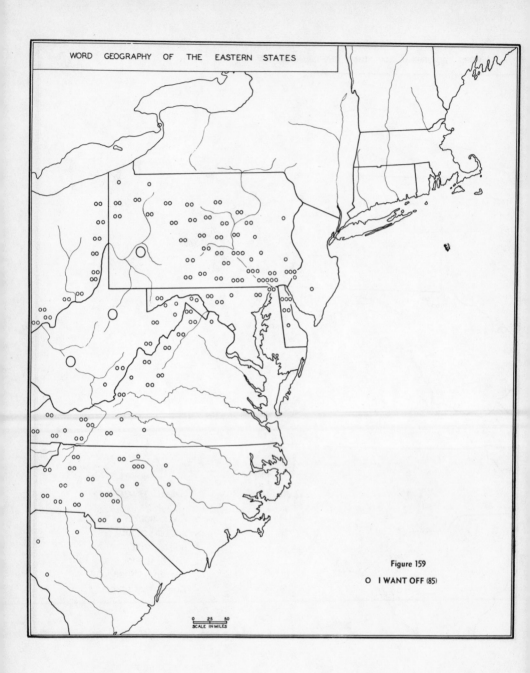

WORD GEOGRAPHY OF THE EASTERN STATES

Figure 159

O I WANT OFF (85)

0   25   50
SCALE IN MILES

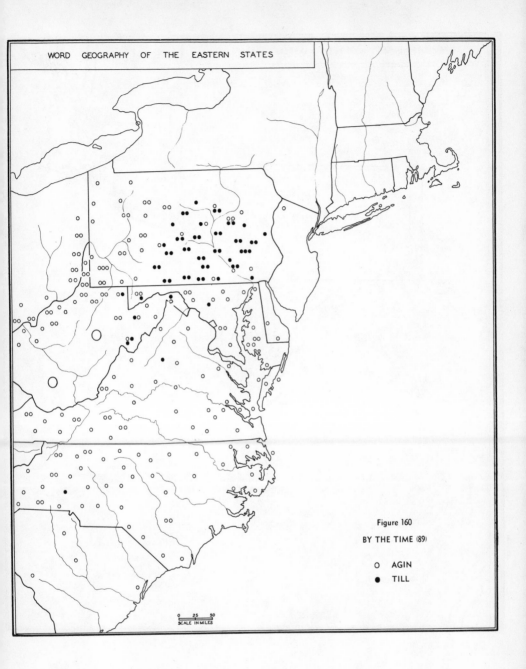

Figure 160

BY THE TIME (89)

○ AGIN

● TILL

0   25   50
SCALE IN MILES

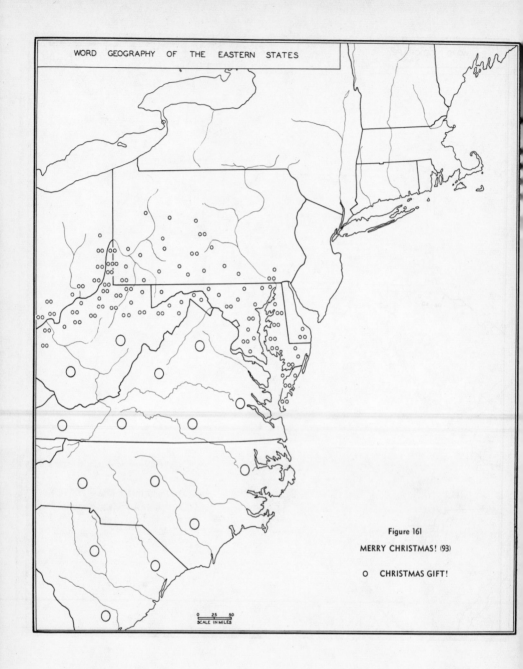

Figure 161

MERRY CHRISTMAS! (93)

O   CHRISTMAS GIFT!

0   25   50
SCALE IN MILES

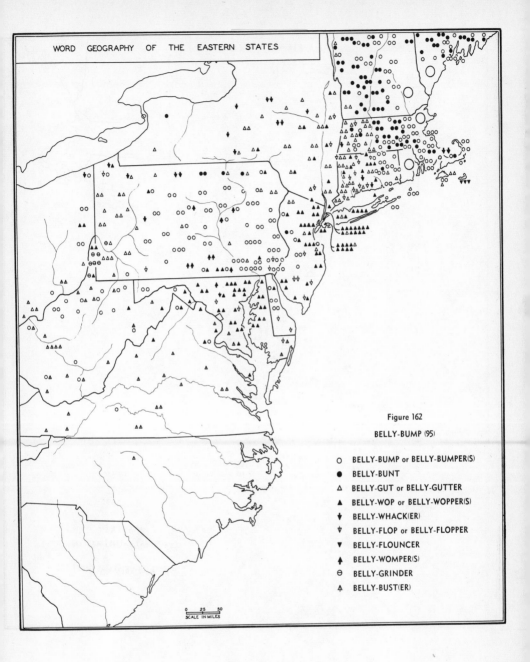

WORD GEOGRAPHY OF THE EASTERN STATES

Figure 162

BELLY-BUMP (95)

O   BELLY-BUMP or BELLY-BUMPER(S)

●   BELLY-BUNT

△   BELLY-GUT or BELLY-GUTTER

▲   BELLY-WOP or BELLY-WOPPER(S)

↓   BELLY-WHACK(ER)

↧   BELLY-FLOP or BELLY-FLOPPER

▼   BELLY-FLOUNCER

↑   BELLY-WOMPER(S)

Θ   BELLY-GRINDER

⚭   BELLY-BUST(ER)

0   25   50
SCALE IN MILES

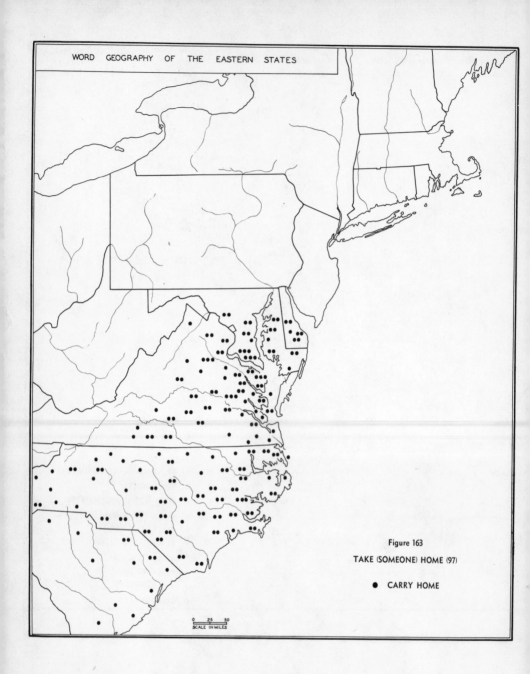

Figure 163

TAKE (SOMEONE) HOME (97)

● CARRY HOME

0   25   50
SCALE IN MILES

Date Due

Demco 38-297